Assault Division

A History of the 3rd Division from the Invasion of Normandy to the Surrender of Germany

To 'Bolo' Whistler

and all who served in the Assault Division

1943–1945

and to the memory of those who died

Tho' much is taken, much abides
Tennyson's *Ulysses*

ASSAULT DIVISION

A HISTORY OF THE 3rd DIVISION FROM THE INVASION OF NORMANDY TO THE SURRENDER OF GERMANY

by

Norman Scarfe

New Foreword

by

Michael Howard

Foreword to the first edition

by

Field Marshal Viscount Montgomery of Alamein KG GCB DSO

SPELLMOUNT
Staplehurst

British Library Cataloguing in Publication Data:
A catalogue record for this book is available
from the British Library

Copyright © Norman Scarfe 1947, 2004

ISBN 1-86227-256-5

First published in the UK in 1947
by
Collins

This edition published in the UK in 2004
by
Spellmount Limited
The Village Centre
Staplehurst
Kent TN12 0BJ

Tel: 01580 893730
Fax: 01580 893731
E-mail: enquiries@spellmount.com
Website: www.spellmount.com

1 3 5 7 9 8 6 4 2

Printed in Great Britain by
T.J. International Ltd
Padstow, Cornwall

Contents

List of Maps

NEW FOREWORD

by

MICHAEL HOWARD

"IN WRITING about a military campaign" Norman Scarfe begins modestly, "it is certainly an advantage to have taken part". It certainly is. Imagine the 'advantage' that would have been enjoyed by an aspiring professional historian who served on board HMS *Victory* at Trafalgar, or fought under Wellington at Waterloo. And that is what, effectively, the young Norman Scarfe did. As a young artillery officer he landed with the first wave of British troops on the Normandy beaches on D-Day, firing his guns while the water swirled round his feet. Thereafter he fought with his division throughout the bitter campaigns of the ensuing autumn and winter, until Germany surrendered and he could get on with his life.

'Getting on with his life' meant returning to Oxford and beginning his serious training as a professional historian. But he had already witnessed too much history to leave it unrecorded. It was on his own initiative that this history was written, and he wrote much of it while still an undergraduate. One might have expected that this initiation would have led him to adopt military history as his speciality, and it is a loss to military history that he did not. As it was, his professional career led him in a very different direction. A medievalist by inclination, while teaching at the University of Leicester he came under the influence of the great historian of landscape, W.G.Hoskins; and this, combined with his own expertise in domestic and ecclesiastical architecture, was to make him the leading 'local' historian of his generation, with an encyclopedic knowledge, in particular, of his own native East Anglia.

For most of his career Norman Scarfe has belonged to that sadly obsolescent breed, the independent scholar, and has thus

vii

perhaps missed the wider réclame he might have enjoyed in a tenured university post. But he has used the time that might otherwise have been spent in teaching and administration by producing a flood of distinguished publications as scholarly as they are readable. The respect they have earned him among his peers is indicated by an honorary doctorate from the University of East Anglia and a recent festschrift, *East Anglia's History*, in honour of his eightieth birthday.

Assault Division is thus not only a skilful record of what actually happened on D-Day and after, as seen through the eyes of a uniquely well-placed observer. It is the 'master-piece' in the literal sense of the word, of a young historian who went on to prove himself a true master of his craft.

Michael Howard
2004

FOREWORD

(to the first edition)

by

FIELD-MARSHAL VISCOUNT MONTGOMERY

I HAD the great honour to command the 3rd Division in the early days of World War II. During those days the Division gained for itself a very fine reputation; it never failed to achieve what was required from it; it always stood firm as a rock in battle.

This reputation was maintained in the campaign in North-West Europe from the assault on the beaches of Normandy until the capture of the City of Bremen; right up to the end of the war.

Now we are at peace.

We must never forget those grim days of desperate struggle and achievement. We are still going through difficult times; we are not yet out of the wood. Let us face up to the problems of the future by drawing strength from the memory of our splendid achievements in the past

Montgomery of Alamein.

FIELD-MARSHAL.

NOTE

SINCE most readers find it irksome to have pages littered with explanatory footnotes and after six years of war are, however involuntarily, fairly well acquainted with army terminology, explanations of any such terms as could not be avoided have been relegated to a glossary on page 277. Wherever feasible, army usage is adhered to, so that, for example, the 2nd Battalion the Royal Warwickshire Regiment becomes in the narrative, as it always did in the Division, the Warwicks; the 3rd Reconnaissance Regiment (N.F.), the 3rd Recce Regiment; and so on.

New Preface and Introduction

In writing about a military campaign it is certainly an advantage to have taken part. At the very least you know what the weather was like, and the terrain, you also know which participants to consult, and what to look for in which war-diaries, remembering (as I very clearly do) that war is not fought with the convenience of military historians in mind. When it was my duty to keep our official war-diary up to date, and we were in action, other duties came first. If we were not in action, there was not much to record. I suppose Sir William Napier's *The History of the War in the Peninsula* is so memorable because he was there, indeed in the thick of it, commanding a famous regiment; also of course because he wrote so vividly. He enables us to feel present, for instance at the opening of the battle of Salamanca in 1812, when Wellington noticed 'with a stern contentment' that his opponent had extended his left wing too much. He 'fixed it with the stroke of a thunderbolt', quietly ordering the commander of the 3rd Division to lead a general attack

The 3rd Infantry Division was a regular division of the British Army, and has a very long history. In this book I cover barely two years, from September 1943 to May 1945, in which time it led one of the greatest, and most general, attacks ever recorded.

A 20-year-old gunner subaltern, I found myself, with rare serendipity, joining one of the 3rd Division's three field-gunner regiments on the very day they received orders to start training for the Allied amphibious assault on Nazi-occupied north-west Europe. Though ours was a regular division, my regiment was one of two territorial exceptions among all the regular components: ours was the 76th (Highland) Field Regiment, Royal Artillery and I found it encamped in the exalted grounds of Drumlanrig Castle, near Dumfries. That day's exciting news of our assignment to the Second Front led to a notable celebration in our mess that evening, and probably in every mess throughout the Division. I at once became aware of the benefits of joining a regiment with interests in Scottish distilleries.

That winter we spent on realistic large-scale amphibious Exercises. I learnt that General Montgomery, about to take charge of all the land forces involved in the assault on Europe, had in the first year of war been the 3rd Division's commander and was still very clearly remembered as a dedicated promoter of large-scale and very testing Exercises. As soon as we got into action we had reason to be deeply glad of such experience.

As gunners, for instance, we had to know how to fit, into a long Tank Landing Craft that was barely the width of two Sherman tanks side-by-side, four of our guns, which were each mounted on the chassis and tracks of a Sherman tank. As if this was not enough, these had to be parked on the landing-craft around a full-scale Sherman Tank from which, once we were ashore, the guns were commanded: (aboard, we used the ship's bridge for Fire Orders). In addition, we had to load, on to our LCT deck, heavy half-tracked vehicles full of ammunition, for our guns fired 105mm shells, weighing about 33lbs. These tracked vehicles all had to be reversed on to the landing-craft so that the guns could he fired over the bows as we ran ashore from something over 10,000 yards out at sea. As we ran in, we lowered our sights to keep the beach-defenders' heads down until the Commandos and the 1st Suffolks went ashore with the FOOs (Forward Observers for the guns) who could observe and correct our fire.

Rehearsing all this in the Moray Firth, we used often to imagine it was the 'real thing'. Early in May 1944 we had moved down to Sussex and Hampshire, and we took part in Exercise *Fabius*: it was so realistic that we sailed far out towards the French coast before turning about and 'performing' our assault landing on the beach at Littlehampton. As we sailed south in Exercise *Fabius*, some of us wondered, briefly, if this could be 'the Day'. It seemed uncanny to be heading for France and not to be challenged by the *Luftwaffe* or by German gunboats: it seemed as if they had been deliberately deflected from us. On 1 June, the blissful weather turned grey and the sea choppy. When we finally set sail on the 5th, we had no doubt it was the real thing: we unsealed our secret orders and discovered where we were really going. 'Poland' turned out to be Caen.

Firing hard for these last miles of the run-in, and then firing most of the morning from the beach, we fortunately had little time for fear. (Another distraction from fear, perhaps fortunately, was the seasickness and general queasiness which seemed to affect almost all of us on those nineteen hours of a fairly uneasy crossing: the arrival on a rather dangerous beach at least offered relief from that endless rolling effect of the sea-swell on a flat-bottom landing-craft.) A gunner is liable to under-estimate the nervous strain put on infantrymen who are for so much of the time closer up against the enemy. It was very salutary for me to read, in a frank history of 2 KSLI, a battalion that contributed not only to D-Day's fighting but to the whole campaign with admirable distinction: 'So began the battle [on D-Day] which we all hope will be the most terrifying we have undergone. Later battles were worse, but none had – to the majority – the horror of the unknown, nor had any started with so great an expectation of heavy casualties'.

I remember our own Brigade Commander, after a final briefing in May, telling his officers that we should be prepared for up to eighty-per-cent casualties as leaders in the Assault brigade. I suppose he had been instructed to say that, and I suppose we were as prepared as possible for such a calamity. But seeing how few of our landing-craft were hit, let alone sunk, and then how comparatively few casualties we sustained as we fired four very prominent self-propelled 105mm guns from the Norman tide-line all morning, from about 08.25 (I remember thinking of breakfast at home). I remained confident, and of course very heavily occupied. The beach seemed to be under sporadic small arms fire from the windows of the increasingly unattractive boarding-houses facing the sea: we very quickly put a stop to that. But there was the more troublesome random fire from long-range guns on our left flank, from the direction of Honfleur and Le Havre. As they were firing straight along a beach full of invaders, our flanks rather exposed, it is surprising how little damage they achieved before they were reduced to silence by the Navy and the RAF. The infantry we were supporting were making their way steadily inland until the Suffolks were held up by an unexpectedly formidable concrete blockhouse called Hillman (see the last page of the plate section).

That involved some difficult Close Targets under the very noses of the undaunted Suffolks. Over the next three days my regiment was also answering desperate calls for fire in defence of 6 Airborne troops holding Pegasus Bridge against attack after attack by German armour and infantry. On 9 June General Gale, the 6 Airborne Commander, wrote to thank the CO of our Regiment for 'most generous and rapid support without which we should have been unable to hold our position'. That would have exposed 3 Div's left flank very dangerously to damage from 21 Panzer Division.

We didn't take Caen on D-Day. Michael Howard in a wise essay on 'The Caen Controversy', 2002, understands, and states for the first time, that 'to allot Caen as the aspirational objective was entirely legitimate . . . But to make its capture on the first day of operations the linch-pin of Allied strategy was quite unrealistic unless far greater resources had been allotted to the task than those of a single (albeit augmented) infantry division; and more resources could not possibly have been funnelled through the bottle-neck of the beach-head in the time available'. Of course, for us, Caen was an absolutely serious objective. We all felt a sense of failure that we were not in and around Caen by the end of D-Day, but we already understood the value of fighting flat-out for an 'aspirational' target. When, that afternoon, we knew that the 21 Panzer Division was already in action in front of us, we found it suddenly much more difficult to imagine ourselves in possession of that already heavily damaged city, vitally important though its possession remained as a main centre of potential communications. How clearly I remember taking part in the massive barrage, with Typhoons rocketing in support, and 9 Brigade reaching the northern approaches to the town as light faded on 8 July. Next day the crumpled rubble of Caen lay in our hands.

Later in the campaign, I think we were particularly proud of our conduct in the battle for Overloon and Venraij (chapter 6) and in the even more intense fighting between the Maas and the Rhine (chapter 8). We knew what we could do, and were extremely indignant if outsiders failed to recognise the triangular Divisional sign we wore on our sleeves. It was a simple upright black triangle divided by an inverted red triangle. I persuaded

Colonel R C Macdonald at the War Office to ask the Field-Marshal how he came to invent it. The reply came back that the sign was to indicate the combination of threes in the 3rd Division with its three brigades, just as we had guessed!

When I was still with 3 Div at the end of 1945 we had moved to Palestine. Divisional HQ was on Mount Carmel, at Haifa. One day I went to see the Divisional Commander, Major-General 'Bolo' Whistler, later General Sir Lashmer Whistler. He was the ideal divisional commander. The photograph on page 6 of the plate section shows him (with the Corps Commander) looking exactly as he was: a big man, with a cheerful grin that endeared him to the whole division, from the brigadiers downwards, and with the priceless gift of inspiring confidence, making the right decision, and seeing it through. You always knew exactly 'where you were' with him. (He made one mistake: he smoked, and died bravely but 'before his time' of lung cancer.) The reason for my seeing him on Mount Carmel was that the Division we had known (I for slightly longer but he so enormously much better) was beginning to break up, and be dispersed. I asked him if I could write a history of the Division we had known and been so proud of. I wrote a draft first chapter: he read it and immediately agreed. I said I'd need to go back to Whitehall, to work in the Cabinet Offices, where the war diaries of all the divisions were stacked underground in the care of Mr C V Owen. He gave me 'an old-fashioned look', again agreed, and I was posted at once. He then asked the various units of the Division if they would do their best to furnish their own recollections of 'their' campaign, and these were sent on to me.

For them, I was especially indebted to Steve Hemingway of the Suffolks, Jack Harrod of the Lincolns, Ken Bradshaw of the Ulster Rifles, R C Macdonald, who commanded in turn the KOSBs and the Warwicks and whose offices with Lord Montgomery secured me his Foreword and his explanation of the triangular divisional sign which he 'invented'. I was also extremely indebted to Humphrey Wilson of the Norfolks, Guy Radcliffe of the KSLI (whose own fine history of 2 KSLI appeared at the same time as *Assault Division*, from Blackwell's at Oxford), and Bob Moberly of the Middlesex. Sapper Stanley

helped with the training period in Scotland, and so did my friend
Peter Lloyd of the KOSBs.   Bill Renison was very generous in
letting me see and quote from his unpublished reminiscences of
his command of the East Yorkshire battalion.   My pride in
serving with the 3rd Division is only matched by my gratitude
to Michael Howard for the generosity of his appreciation of its
History.

Time and Tide first published the lines at the head of
chapter 7.   Unless otherwise acknowledged, photographs were
reproduced by permission of the Controller, Photographic
Division, Central Office of Information.

For further reading I want to commend:

Sir John Smyth, VC, MC, *Bolo Whistler: The Life of General Sir
Lashmer Whistler, GCB, KBE, DSO*, 1967.

Carlo d'Este, *Decision in Normandy*, 1983

Max Hastings, *Overlord: D-Day and the Battle for Normandy*, 1984

Patrick Delaforce, *Monty's Ironsides: From the Normandy Beaches to
Bremen with the 3rd Division*, 1995

Tim Kilvert-Jones, *Sword Beach: 3rd British Infantry Division's Battle
for the Normandy Beachhead, 6–10 June 1944*, 2001.

And, in French, Eddy Florentin's *Guide des plages du Débarquement
et de la Bataille de Normandie: 6 juin–12 septembre 1944*, Perrin, Le
Mémorial de Caen, 2003, describes very usefully not only the
topography of the different D-Day landings, but also that of the
whole Normandy campaign.   It takes the form of seventeen
itineraries, followed by a fully detailed bibliography, a list of the
various War Cemeteries, useful addresses for visitors, local
committees, bus routes, tours, Les Amis du 1st Suffolk in
Colleville Montgomery, etc.

Preface

DURING ALL our military training we used to try to keep in mind " the object of the exercise," though it sometimes seemed very obscure. The object of this exercise is clear and simple. It is to express and record and commemorate achievements of an Infantry Division in the last two years of the Six Years' War against the Axis Powers. These are achievements of which fifty thousand men feel proud (for so many are estimated to have belonged to the Division when postings and casualties and replacements are counted), but of which hardly anyone else has even heard, for the identities of most Divisions—to say nothing of the identities of their members—are in wartime sacrificed to censorship.

But when war ends and censorship relaxes, the identity of a Division, always subject to gradual change, is completely transformed by the demobilisation scheme. When I saw this happening in the 3rd Division, it seemed to me a matter of the keenest regret. Not that I felt that the Division ought to have been kept together : I, too, was an ardent believer in the civilian way of life, and have since adopted it. But I think it meant something to every one of us to belong to the 3rd British Infantry Division. We were always prouder of the Divisional Triangle on our sleeves than of the campaign ribbons we used to wear, and I felt that whatever it was we were so proud of was worth preserving if possible.

Our pride was principally in the steadiness in battle that Field-Marshal Lord Montgomery has remarked in his Foreword : we thought we could be relied on. That other Divisions also thought we could be relied on is testified in such accounts as, for example, Martin Lindsay's *So Few Got Through*. We relied on ourselves, then, and we could be relied on to co-operate. I cannot think of any two qualities that better become men, whether their business is war or peace.

This history of the 3rd Division in the last great campaign in the west is further evidence that in the men of Britain these qualities abound. It has little to do with heroics, though there

17

were more brave actions than could be recorded in a dozen volumes of this size. The Division was not fighting for some ideal, some hare-brained theory of racial supremacy, such as can inspire German Divisions. The British are better at practice than theory, and the Division fought well for no better reason than that the Germans had to be finally defeated at their own game of war : the alternative was to acknowledge them masters of Europe, if not of the world.

In a recent essay, in which he admirably debunks the American journalist Ralph Ingersoll, Mr. Robert Henriques concludes : " Let's go back to the old-fashioned, outmoded, laborious process of studying the records, thus writing real history, thence making true and logical deductions. . . ." Sound advice for Ingersolls, but truth exists in historical imagination as well as in historical documents, and, while historians of strategy must confine themselves largely to the records of the Higher Formations, I doubt if it would be possible to produce anything like an accurate picture of a Division's activities from a study, however close, of all the official records. When it was my duty to compile the official War Diary of my unit, and the unit was in action, other duties always came first : if the unit was out of action, there was nothing much to record. But at the Headquarters of higher formations War Diaries were, doubtless, attended to more carefully, though one has to appreciate continually that the war was not conducted for the benefit of historians !

The delight of writing a Divisional history lies in the *range* of the subject : it is a formation sufficiently compact and intimate for the personalities of the various units to emerge and grow familiar, as they cannot in any higher formation if only because the component units of Corps and Armies are ever changing ; at the same time it is a formation sufficiently large to count among the decisive factors of the success or failure of an Expeditionary Force. At once we observe the intention of a formation commander of the General Staff and the working-out of that abstract intention as fully as is humanly possible by the individuals down through all the ranks of his command. But individuals have no place in a War Diary, which is a record of general activities, such as the start of an attack, the taking of an objective, the arrival of reinforcements, or the withdrawal of a unit for rest and "maintenance." And even then the timings recorded are more often than not those when the messages were received at the battalion, brigade or divisional H.Q., instead of those when the action really took place. So that official War Diaries are not a Divisional historian's main source.

I have constantly used the War Diaries for the verification of events, while I have been entirely dependent on them for the tactical information upon which General Rennie made his plan for the Division's assault on *Queen* Beach on D-day. And I must take this opportunity to thank Mr. C. V. Owen and his staff at the Historical Section of the Cabinet Offices for their ready assistance with the innumerable files. But throughout the narrative my first sources have been the personal accounts produced for me by the various units of the Division. I am particularly indebted to Steve Hemingway of the Suffolks, Jack Harrod of the Lincolns, Ken Bradshaw of the Ulster Rifles, R. C. Macdonald, who commanded in turn the K.O.S.B.s and the Warwicks, Humphrey Wilson of the Norfolks, Guy Radcliffe. of the K.S.L.I., and Bob Moberly of the Middlesex, for their respective battalion stories. As well, I am most grateful to Sapper Stanley for showing me his personal diary of the special training period in Scotland, to Peter Lloyd from whose experiences in command of a platoon of the K.O.S.B.s I have quoted on pages 240-242 and pages 262-265, and to Bill Renison, whose unpublished reminiscences of his command of the East Yorkshire Battalion are as fine reading as the journals of Martin Lindsay, who commanded a battalion of the Gordon Highlanders in a sister Division over an almost identical period of action. For an appreciation of the Naval part of the invasion I am obliged to the Commodore Commanding 15th Cruiser Squadron, who allowed me to see his copy of Admiral Ramsay's Report to the Supreme Commander ; obliged also to Commander Kenneth Edwards' book, *Operation Neptune*. I owe an acknowledgment to the Editor of *Time and Tide*, who first published the lines at the head of Chapter VII. Unless otherwise acknowledged, photographs are reproduced by permission of the Controller, Photographic Division, Central Office of Information.

My deepest obligation is to Major-General L. G. (Bolo) Whistler, C.B., D.S.O., Commander of the Division, for releasing me from other duties and allowing me to get on with the job, and also for his careful reading of the MS. The proofs have been read by my friend, Jack Simmons, and I am most grateful for the benefits of his judgment. I must state that I was a Gunner Officer with one of the Division's Field Regiments throughout the campaign. Readers will therefore be on the look out for Gunner prejudice, and I would not discourage them. But I fear I am less likely to be charged with that than to come in for a " stonking " from the Gunners themselves for not making better use of my opportunity !

My last point. When I returned from Palestine in March, 1946, to start work on the files at the Cabinet Offices, one of the first persons I met was a youthful corporal of the 1st Suffolks, whose name was Catchpole, and who was one of the handful of survivors with the battalion, and indeed with the same company, from the D-day assault right through to the end. He had just arrived back for a course in this country and was warm with indignation : he described to me his shock at meeting a young girl in a pub who had asked him " what that Triangular thing was on his arm," who, furthermore, had never heard of the 3rd Division. Considering all that fellow had gone through I found it hard to explain to him that there were a great many people at home who could not be expected to care very much about Divisions and their actions. At the same time I determined that this history should be made intelligible to the civilian public as well as to those surviving members of the Division to whom it is dedicated, men like Ulysses' companions, like those that inspired the great Lincolnshire poet, Tennyson :

" Souls that have toil'd, and wrought, and thought with me—
That ever with a frolic welcome took
The thunder and the sunshine, and opposed
Free hearts, free foreheads——"

NORMAN SCARFE.

Felixstowe, Suffolk,
New Year's Day, 1947.

Introduction

THE DIVISION

FOR MANY PEOPLE an Infantry Division remains an abstract military term for a collection of arms and men ; and a soldier is just as apt to have an inaccurate idea of a Division as a civilian. The soldier sees a military formation from his own angle and gets a lopsided view, while the civilian sees it as a whole from outside, but how far outside ! It will be easier to watch the 3rd Division in action if we know more of its physical shape and its spirit.

The size and shape, the *strength* of the Infantry Division, are fixed by the Adjutant-General's branch of the War Office. On war establishment it was, at this time, roughly 17,000 strong. Of this number less than half are Infantrymen, and only one-quarter are officers and men of the rifle companies, the cutting-edge of the Division : the remainder support them and serve them with the means to fight. Readily enough the men of that minority spring into mind, and the Division is thought of in terms of its Infantry Battalions. This may seem unfair, but it is right, because the Division wins its reputation on the achievements of the Infantry : and, more important perhaps, from them comes the spirit of the Division.

No need to labour this difference between front and rear : the story of the Division involves all component units. But there was a tendency in the Press to give the impression that because L-of-C troops were doing their job well they might be equated with any other trained troops who simply " did their duty." It must be admitted that upon Lines of Communication major considerations of strategy depend. But the same may be said of those civilians who were not employed in work of national unimportance : they also served, and often under no less dangerous conditions than L-of-C troops : nor were they given campaign medals.

While it is true, then, that the Divisional Services kept the front-line supplied and were invaluable, much of their fine spirit was derived from the thought of the Infantry who depended on them, who lived up against the enemy, and who went forward into one attack after another until it was all over. That was the relationship in which the 17,000 were bound together. There is good reason to believe that the bonds uniting all the 3rd Division were especially close : they were tightened upon the stretch of beach between Lion and Ouistreham and in the savagely-held fields and woods on the ridge that shielded Caen.

Those were days of effort and danger in which no one could fail to feel proud of his job ; there was glory in driving a bull-dozer to clear a beach-exit, in driving a lorry-load of ammunition or petrol down to the Pegasus bridge at Bénouville and over to the ground held by the 6th Airborne Division, who were supplied by the 3rd Division's R.A.S.C. transport until their own could be brought ashore ten days later. " The enthusiasm of the drivers is terrific " is the typical note of one of their officers. If there was gladness in the performance of the individual task, it was increased with the chance to co-operate.

When a carrier or a tank became bogged, a R.E.M.E. recovery team would work with the crew and set the vehicle back upon firm ground. When Sappers were going to lay mines, they guided the R.A.S.C. drivers of the lorry-loads of mines through the darkness to the site of the minefield. When it became necessary to concentrate three Armoured Divisions across the Orne for the drive south of Caen and 750 shells and cartridges had to be dumped beside each gun in the Divisional Artillery—all in the course of two nights—the movement of ammunition over the bridges had to be geared carefully into the armoured traffic : that it was accomplished without stoppage and almost unnoticed is an example of the finest team-work between Provost, the R.A.S.C. drivers, and the Gunners who went down to the Orne bank and guided the lorries up to the guns. When the Infantry are in battle it is well understood that the Artillery and Engineers will be working with them. When they are training together the expression *marrying-up* is used to describe the common efforts of the Gunners with the Infantry, and in action that union is in a sense consummated, strengthened by mutual confidence.

Such understanding is expected of the " supporting arms," the Machine-gun and Mortar Battalion, the Gunner Regiments, the Sapper Companies : in the event it was almost equally realised with units whose job it was not to supply support but the less spectacular commodities—transport, rations, equipment, repairs to vehicles, even signposts for the Divisional axis of advance. The whole system of interdependence is examplified by the existence in each unit of a Regimental Aid Post. No one feels independent of the Royal Army Medical Corps. But the bond is not just one of bloodshed. It may perhaps be best illustrated by the Royal Signals. It was the function of the Signallers to keep a communicating link open throughout the Division. When telephone-line could not be laid, wireless sets were opened up : the traffic of information and orders was incessant. No unit was outside this network. Everyone was kept in touch.

Quickness to co-operate was nothing exclusive, confined within the Division. We shall trace it in Combined Operations with the Navy and the Air Force, as well as with the other land formations. It is not the whole story. If it were, something would have changed the British soldier ; and it would take more than the greatest military operation in history to do that. He *did* all the things that are attributed to him in this book and very much more, but he also said and thought things that may better be imagined than chronicled. If he were living in a muddy slit-trench with death in the air around him, he undoubtedly wished himself elsewhere and thought disparagingly, if anything, of the soldier whose lot was less unhappy. If he was a technical soldier, say a Craftsman in a Brigade Workshop a mile or two back, he undoubtedly thought less than he should have done of the poor beggar who was just creeping forward on a reconnaissance patrol, and got on with his welding job. Whatever his separate feelings, he had a corporate feeling as well. He still excelled in co-operating when there was need. Everyone knows the large part of School and Army training that is devoted to team-work. The results may best be observed on active service : they are heartening to see and inspiring to share in.

The main point that has emerged is that the spirit of a Division appears in action. With the 3rd Division a new spirit was born in the early hours of 6th June, 1944, that was conceived on the shores of Scotland the previous autumn and carried securely through a wild, northern winter. With all infants, we are told, the early period is the most impressionable, when the character is formed. So it was with the Division. The most formative influence was the restricted size of the lodgment-area for the first month in Normandy, which, so far from producing inhibitions, moulded the finest feeling of common endeavour in the presence of a tangible enemy ; it reshaped the Division's character. And no one who was with the Division at that time will deny that a new spirit was abroad. This was no new Division (was there not a 3rd Division in action on the left of Wellington's line for the last great battle with Napoleon ?), but the point is that, as they were our forefathers who fought at Waterloo, so, in a sense, the men who fought with the Division back to Dunkirk in 1940 were the fathers of the aggressive spirit of the Assault Division.

It is true that the 3rd Division has an unbroken tradition from the time of the Haldane Reforms, a tradition hallowed from the outset of the War of 1914-1918 by its valour in the retreat from Mons. Since then the composition by battalions had been completely changed. In the burning summer's heat of 1940 the Division withdrew gallantly from Louvain to Furnes and Dunkirk. They were fighting then under Major-General B. L. Montgomery, D.S.O., who expressed resentment at being forced back across the Channel in the only terms the Germans could understand. His Division were among the last to leave Dunkirk. After four years they led the way back.

So this is a different story. Mr. Arthur Bryant claims for the British Army that " the episodes in its past on which English historians linger most fondly are those when it was most outnumbered, most lacking in might, and therefore, by our reckoning, most glorious and true to itself—Rorke's Drift or *Mons* or *Dunkirk* or the Rifles dying at Calais . . ." But there is a danger in that distinguished legend : to foster it is extravagant in human lives. We must cherish it *only* as history, not as a policy we can afford to cultivate. This is the story of how we fought when given strength to match the might of Germany : it yields a more profitable lesson.

The unit composition had changed again since 1940 : 185 Infantry Brigade, from the 79th Armoured Division, took the place of the 7th Guards Brigade who had fought alongside the

8th and 9th Brigades up till Dunkirk. So that 8, 9 and 185 Brigades are the three points of the Divisional Triangle. The Triangle, or more precisely the geometrical design of one triangle divided off into three black triangles by a red one, appears on the jacket of this book. It was painted proudly upon all the Naval Landing-Craft that took the Division into action, and bravely carried by every vehicle that went into action, on *Queen* Beach : it is worn no less proudly on every sleeve in the Division. It was stencilled on hundreds of small metal discs and used to mark the Division's route from the Norman shore to Bremen. The explanation most usually given, if you ask the meaning of the sign, is that the black triangles represent the three Brigades of Infantry ; the red is blood.[1]

The three points of the Triangle, then, were 8, 9 and 185 Brigades, and each was made up of three battalions. These battalions are not to be lumped together and given a label. A man's pride in his battalion is a main element of success in the fight. That is one of the few principles which has rested unchallenged since the Napoleonic Wars. The famous and redoubtable Rifleman Harris, tracing so vividly the ordinary soldier's life through the Peninsular Campaign, leaves us in no doubt that the finest army in the world was that which Wellington led, that the finest regiment in that army was the 95th, and that the best battalion in that regiment was that his major commanded. Similarly Quartermaster-sergeant James Anton made no secret of the fact that there was no English regiment to equal a Scottish one, and no Scottish one to equal his own, the 42nd (now the Black Watch). And Captain Mercer, writing of Waterloo, held the view no less firmly that G Battery had the finest horses, equipment, men and discipline, not merely in the British Army but in any army in history. These are natural sentiments, and prevailed in all regiments, it will be seen, no less in 1944 than in 1815.

But Eric Linklater has claimed " a curious thing " apropos

---

[1] The explanation given by an adjutant in a harassing moment was that the three brigades are joined by red tape. Field-Marshal Lord Montgomery, who as Div Commander devised the sign with the help of his AQ, meant just " to indicate the combination of threes "—the 3rd Division, the three brigades and the three battalions in each brigade.

of the 51st (Highland) Division : that " their regimental pride was largely replaced by a greater pride in their Division." The same is not quite true of the 3rd Division, where you never failed to detect an Infantryman's pride first and foremost in his particular regiment. If he were talking to someone from outside of the Division, then you would hear about the 3rd Division. But this would not mean that his regimental pride had been replaced by pride in his Division, for the obvious reason that the exploits of his battalion are nearly all part of his own personal experience, while the exploits of the rest of the battalions are incidental, and gratifying to him only inasmuch as he and they all had a place in their Divisional plan.[1]

Perhaps Mr. Linklater was hinting at a supreme pride in the common origins of the Division. It may not be denied that home ties are of the utmost value to territorial units, but it is doubtful whether as much may be claimed for a Division—even a Territorial Division—especially when it has seen action and received reinforcements. The 3rd British Infantry Division had no claim to a birth and upbringing in some exclusive corner of the British Isles, nor had they need of such a claim.

As a result of reforms towards the end of the last century and again after our temporary but long-remembered loss of face in the South African War, the regular battalions of the line became known as the 1st and 2nd Battalions of a Regiment, the 3rd (Militia) Battalion became the Special Reserve, and the 4th and subsequent Battalions were Territorial Battalions. The nine battalions of the 3rd Division were all either 1st or 2nd Battalions of their respective Regiments. But by 1943, at the time when our narrative begins, of the Infantrymen no more than an average 'of one in three were regular soldiers. Nominally a Regular Division, then, the 3rd Division inherited the traditions of the oldest regular County Regiments and proceeded to carry on those traditions with the prowess of regular, volunteer and conscript soldiers together, fighting together in the same platoons, bringing the guns into action together.

[1] Mr. Nigel Nicholson, in a recent admirable article in the *Spectator* on Regimental Traditions, adds an interesting observation : that, supposing the greatest stimulus to military loyalty to be the sharing of recent experiences, then, " if a company or a battalion has a run of ill luck, the men's loyalty will shift temporarily to the next higher group which can claim an over-all success."

It is evident, then, that the battalions are not to be labelled collectively (as is the fashion with Territorial Divisions) according to some ancient political boundary such as Wessex or Northumbria.[1] But this is not for want of such a boundary. The Danelaw—territories of Scandinavian conquest and settlement along the East Coast in the two centuries before William the Conqueror landed from Normandy—conformed almost exactly with six of the counties whose regiments made up the fighting force of the Division. In fact, a convenient way of remembering the Battalion component is to think first of the East Coast from Suffolk right up to Berwick, where the 1st Battalion of the King's Own Scottish Borderers have their depot. The base of the Divisional Armoured Reconnaissance Regiment is Northumberland—they are the 3rd Reconnaissance Regiment, R.A.C. (Royal Northumberland Fusiliers), and one of the two Territorial units in the Division. That North Sea coastline also joins up the 1st Suffolk, 1st Royal Norfolk, 2nd Lincolnshire, and 2nd East Yorkshire Battalions. In the North the Danes came to the West Coast, reaching, if not controlling, that part of Lancashire which is represented by the 1st Battalion of the South Lancashire Regiment. And with Regiments covering the Danelaw area so conveniently, the Division can immediately take pride in the tremendous fighting and seafaring (Combined Ops) qualities, and the spirit of independence that characterised the Norsemen. This seems appropriate enough. But, as we have seen, the futility of trying to identify formations with territory is at least twofold : in battalions the men who actually came from the area were in the minority : in the Division the battalions themselves are in a minority, albeit an important one. The men of the Division came from the length and breadth of Great Britain.

The battalions that had no place in the Viking theory are no disproof of the spread and depth of the Division's roots in the British Isles. The 2nd Battalion of the Royal Ulster Rifles brought to the Division the spirit and stamp of an Irish regiment : but it was an imported English modesty that prompted their battalion historian to state that " the war was over, and the

[1] It is of interest to note the War Office proposal of 1946 to group together Regiments of adjacent counties in order that, where they are unable to recruit from their own counties, Regiments may preserve some territorial character by recruiting from their neighbours.

Battalion felt satisfied with the part it had played in winning it " :
they certainly had valid grounds for satisfaction. So, indeed, had
the 2nd Battalion of the King's Shropshire Light Infantry and
the 2nd Battalion of the Royal Warwickshire Regiment. The
latter may claim to represent the heart of Shakespeare's England,
the former the heart of Housman's. Finally amongst the Infantry
Battalions we are to meet a famous London battalion, the 2nd
of the Middlesex Regiment (Duke of Cambridge's Own), who
with machine-guns and mortars were the Division's Support
Battalion.

It should perhaps be insisted that the three points of the
Triangle represent the Brigade Groups and not just the Brigades.
For in every event it is in the order of things that the Gunners
are " tied up " with the Infantry. And though for administration
the Regiments of Artillery have their own R.A. brigade organisation, it will be seen how the 76th Field Regiment were in support
of 8 Brigade, 33rd Field Regiment of 9 Brigade and 7th Field
Regiment of 185 Brigade, continuously from the first great
assault to the Cease Fire. Furthermore, one battery of each
regiment was virtually in continuous support of " its own "
battalion. The 76th (Highland) Field Regiment and the 3rd
Recce Regiment were the only two major Territorial units in
the Division : the Territorial members of the 76th Field Regiment were from Fife and Angus, with their depot at Dundee.
The batteries of the 20th Anti-Tank Regiment, R.A., were
" Brigaded " in the same way as the Field Regiments : so to a
less extent were the batteries of the 92nd Light Anti-Aircraft
Regiment, R.A. 92nd L.A.A. Regiment had been converted
from the 7th Battalion of The Loyal (North Lancashire) Regiment
to R.A. in November, 1941. Those Gunners who had been
Infantrymen still kept a strong " Loyals " spirit alive in the
Regiment.

The complete Order of Battle of the Division may be seen in
the second part of Appendix A. Its operation will become familiar
in the course of the narrative, and no more need be said by way
of introduction to individual units. The important idea is that
the Division develops its whole personality in battle, when
ordeals are shared, and commanders win confidence.

The 3rd British Infantry Division was styled British when

it was known that the 3rd Canadian Division was chosen as the flanking division in the assault on the Atlantic Wall. The object was to avoid confusion which might have arisen from the proximity of the two 3rd Divisions. (The coincidence was not confined to the numbering of the Divisions : each had a 9th Brigade commanded by a Brigadier Cunningham !) It is naturally accepted as a compliment when the Division is referred to as " the Ironsides " or " the Iron Division." But they are compliments that were earned by quite different groups of units in quite different circumstances, not by the 3rd Division in its Assault form. " Ironsides " is surely another not entirely justifiable reference to East Anglia, where Cromwell did his recruiting ; and Iron, a symbol of the strength and resolution of the 3rd Division in the Four Years' War,[1] can also suggest inflexibility and cruelty, rust and robots. The distinction of being British, on the other hand, is open to only one interpretation. It is the most suitable of all titles. There was only one 3rd British Division fighting in Europe, and from D-day until the Germans were defeated the men of the Division deserved the honour of their name.

[1] Lieutenant-Colonel T. F. Furnell, O.B.E., M.C., Hon. Secretary of the Association of the 3rd (Iron) Division (1916-18), in a very moving speech on behalf of the guests at the first Reunion of the 3rd British Division (1939-45) Officers' Association, said : " You of the 3rd British Division have more than lived up to the tradition of the Iron Division." This was the highest tribute that he could have paid, and was greatly esteemed, but it remains true that the circumstances of the two wars were extremely different.

Chapter One

PREPARATION

IT WAS NOWHERE a festive summer in 1943 : in Galloway, where the 3rd Division had gone to train for the Sicilian landing, the damp moorlands round the Solway Firth and the overcast blue hills above Dumfries conveyed their melancholy. Perhaps they never seemed more depressing than when the news was announced that the Sicilian job had gone to another Division. The Canadians were full of wrath when, after much unavoidable heel-kicking in England, they saw the Americans given the landing-operations in North Africa : indignantly they demanded to know whether we thought they couldn't fight. We remembered Vimy and Dieppe, and had only admiration for their fighting qualities ; so the 1st Canadian Division landed instead of the 3rd British Division in Sicily in July, 1943. In that month the broad plan for the assault on the Atlantic Wall was completed and only awaited formal acceptance at the Quebec Conference. It concerned an American, a Canadian and a British Division. The 3rd Division was picked to represent Britain.

It is notable that no fundamental of that original plan had to be changed, although when Eisenhower arrived in London as Supreme Commander of the Allied Expeditionary Force the scope and range were extended to include two more Divisions, one British, one American. The 3rd Division knew for a short year the task ahead of them. Every man guessed what would be expected of him and had time to prepare himself. Through the autumn and stormy winter, and the spring of 1944, the Division trained as never an Infantry Division trained before. Here was a job worth doing. It was more than that : it was the chance all men had dreamed of.

The establishment of the " Second Front " was longed for by the Russians, who had not succeeded in stopping and repulsing the majority of Hitler's Divisions without sustaining terrible losses, and it was clamoured for by over-anxious and often irresponsible voices of British and American opinion : it was not altogether dismissed from the minds of the Germans as they waited behind the Atlantic Wall, despite the assurances of the seemingly inextinguishable Goebbels. The less these people knew about it, the shriller were their comments. Every member of the 3rd Division knew something, and loved what he knew. He kept his observations to himself.

With new thoughts for company, men turned afresh to an appreciation of the ground on which they would make their first preparations for D-day. (The ciphers H-hour and D-day, which were added to almost everybody's vocabulary on 6 June, 1944, were already current language in the Division.) The massive Lowther Hills recovered from the gloom that had darkened them since the announcement about Sicily, and if you had driven over the Dalveen Pass to Moffat you would have been struck first by the grandeur of the mountain road to Elvanfoot, then by the atmosphere of Moffat, an apparently dull little town. Moffat was the headquarters of the Divisional Battle School, and the dullness was deceptive. By day the sound of gunfire drifted down the valley from beneath the Devil's Beef-Tub, as a troop detached from one of the Field Regiments of the Divisional Artillery pitched high explosive or smoke shells just ahead of the Infantry, and sometimes, with the wind right, the sound of a boy rattling a stick along the palings of a wooden fence came from the machine-guns supporting one of the companies in the Divisional Inter-Company Assault Competition. But back in camp in the late afternoon the guns were rapidly boiled through, dried and greased by practised Gunners, the small arms received their careful maintenance, the ammunition was prepared for the next day, and then Moffat came to life.

It is difficult, when describing any phase of army life, to avoid a constant reference to sports terms for analogy. For instance, the feeling of personal pride which tingled everyone's spine when the great assignment was announced : it was just like being picked for the best side in football, like getting an international trial. Similarly with this whole question of training : an obvious comparison to make is with the boxing team who are coached and massaged individually and come together only in sparring bouts before the contest. One almost irresistible temptation is to refer to the assault on N.W. Europe in terms of entering the ring for the last round. Was " Q " right when he wrote : " The British are incurably given to mistaking war for a form of sport, and might find their tribal emblem of victory in a statue of Picton fighting the Battle of Quatre Bras (as he did) in a tall hat " ? " Q "[1] went on to complain that Kinglake, in his history of the Invasion of the Crimea, could never get out of the habit of regarding a battle as a sort of glorified steeplechase or fox-hunt and in the crisis of the fight usually had to fall back on these noble sports for a criticism or simile.

In Moffat, and equally during any of the periods of Combined Operations training, " Q " would have found full corroboration of his choice of a tribal emblem. Original dress is a form of self-expression understandable in men who on parade every day must be models of uniformity, though perhaps less easily explained in staff officers exempt from the flatness of the square. Battle School, Combined Ops training, and battle itself provided opportunities for " experiments," and of all the weird garbs that were seen, those reported by 3rd Recce Regiment after their dash to Münster with 17 U.S. Airborne Division seem to have been the most extraordinary—but that story comes much later.[2] Preparing . for battle now means an automatic adjustment of the soldier to his natural background, perhaps by daubing his skin with mud, decorating his headgear, breaking the outline of his shoulders. In Combined Ops the additional discomforts at sea and ashore can be partly compensated by easing dress and equipment, adopting sweaters, cap-comforters, waterproofs.

The Lincolns were practising Combined Ops in Kilbride Bay in September, and Lieutenant Bush is recorded as having tried the not-to-be-repeated experiment of wearing a gas-cape next the skin during a wet landing. The most expressive soul in Moffat in September '43 was Johnnie Bywaters of the 2nd Middlesex. Completely regardless of danger on the Battle Course, his latest eccentricities, not merely of dress, would come up for discussion

---

[1] The reference is, of course, to the late Sir Arthur Quiller-Couch : although few readers will attribute this dictum and complaint to a Quartermaster, " Q " in Army parlance does convey that implication. It is expedient to avoid any confusion that might cause discomfort to Quartermasters.

[2] p. 231 below.

in the course of the evening in the Star and the Buccleuch
Arms. An unfortunate shooting accident deprived the Division
of an individual who would have wrought notable havoc amongst
the Germans.

This form of individualism and the apparent confusion of
sport with war are something superficial. The imminence of
grimmer business is to be recognised in the fact that two days
after Quatre Bras—with a great artillery " stonk "—the French
began to advance at Waterloo, and General Picton's Division
volleyed and charged forward against them : Picton was killed.
On the staff of the Divisional Battle School at that time,
September '43, were three officers who were to be killed in
action with the South Lancs, to take only one Battalion : Peter
Beecroft and Ian Bell, who were actually Forward Observing
Officers of 303 Battery which supported that battalion, and
Major Carse commanding a Rifle Company. In Moffat, Peter
Beecroft's ability to direct the fire of a troop of guns, Ian Bell's
hardy example as an instructor on the bleakest days wearing
only a shirt and a battledress with the cuffs turned up, and
(temp.) Lieutenant-Colonel Carse's command of the Battle
School had begun to suggest things far more serious even than
good sport.

Pill-boxes and obstacles of concrete and steel appeared (by
courtesy of the Divisional Field Companies, R.E.—17, 246, 253)
along the valley. Groups of senior officers watched their
demolition with " Bangalore Torpedoes," " Beehive " and
" General Wade " charges, as the Infantry companies assaulted
in turn. Security assumed greater importance daily as more
men saw the remarkable results of increasing output of war
equipment and transport from the factories and of the infernal
machines devised by 79th Armoured Division in their experi-
mental areas on the Suffolk heathlands, and in their secret lake
and cisterns in Norfolk. The campaign against careless talk was
as successful as the subsequent military campaign which careless
talk could conceivably have doomed to disaster. Most people
saw the film *Next of Kin*, which was valuable security propaganda,
apart from its other merits. Probably the greatest secret of
success was that everyone knew enough to feel the sense of
privilege already remarked, and knowing the issues at stake,

A.D.

C

the alternatives of supreme triumph or a tragedy too terrible to comprehend, kept constant guard over the tongue. So far as is known there was not the slightest leakage of information[1] : that was indeed a triumph in itself.

By the autumn of 1943 the Division had come as close to perfection in its battle drills as a Division could or ever will. Every soldier knew what to do on coming to grips with the enemy on the occupied land of Europe. If they had never been in action before, they had had adequate " battle inoculation." At Moffat the " students " on a Young Officers' Course did well to survive as rough a fortnight as was ever inflicted by a real enemy, and at the end they staggered to the top of a hill at three o'clock in the morning and were told to " dig in " in a certain area. Before dark the troop of guns had ranged on this hilltop and they remained laid on their target. Before dawn they opened up with 100 rounds gunfire (i.e. from each gun), first on one side of the trenches, then, while Sappers exploded charges almost upon the trenches to represent the passage of the enemy barrage overhead, the guns laid on a point to the other side of the trenches and went on. In daylight the nearest shell-crater was found eighteen yards from a slit-trench : near enough !

Demonstrations were then required of the Gunners, who carried out a model " crash action " below Wee Queensberry, engaging targets visible from the gun-position and later allowing the Infantry to lay and fire off a round themselves. The Middlesex, at that time organised in three Brigade Support Groups, held a Support Battalion Day at Moffat on November 13th. Spectators

---

[1] In the *Sunday Express* of 31 March, 1946, Captain Harry Butcher, U.S.N.R., Naval Aide to General Eisenhower (1942-45), cites three detected American leaks : they were plugged before they could reach Germany. Captain Butcher's diary has its uses, but certainly as it appeared in the *Sunday Express* it did much mischief. Examples of his judgment are the entries under 19 and 20 July, 1944 : " Around evening Tedder called Ike and said that Monty had, in effect, stopped his armour from going further. Ike was mad. Monty always wants to wait to draw up his administrative tail," and " Tedder phoned Ike and reflecting the disappointment of the air at the slowness on the ground, said that the British Chiefs of Staff would support any recommendation Ike might care to make with respect to Monty for not succeeding in going places. Ike appeared quiet and rested, but blue as indigo over Monty's slowdown." There is no mention of the appalling weather or of General Bradley's failure to start his attack on the 19th, recorded in Eisenhower's own report : " This break in the weather also delayed the First Army attack scheduled for 19 July." (Supreme Commander's Report, p. 46.) For the events of those days see pp. 117-23 below.

from the whole Division witnessed the fire-power and accuracy of their Medium Machine-guns and 4·2-inch Mortars. The Moffat courses were brought to an end. Now the problem to be mastered was how to get ashore and put these lessons into practice.

So far the Division had been through as much Combined Operations Training as anyone but the Commandos: 8 and 9 Brigades especially thought themselves old hands at the game. They had been up at the Combined Training Centre, Inveraray, in the spring and summer of 1942 while the possibility of a landing that summer on the French coast was being considered. The plan was rejected as unsound by General Freyberg and Admiral Ramsay, and replaced by the North Africa and Sicily projects.[1] That early training seemed elementary in the light of what followed, but the canvas-and-plywood craft with outboard motors and the lightly defended beaches at least gave troops an idea of what was in store for them. (It might well have been all the training they were to get before recrossing the perilous Straits of Dover : but General Freyberg perceived the unlikelihood of our being able to maintain a bridgehead while our shipping was restricted by a closed Mediterranean.) In 8 Brigade the Suffolks say they found the training " not particularly popular," but the East Yorks " all entered into it with the zest and high spirits it demanded." It cannot be denied that the change from ordinary field training was welcome. In 9 Brigade the Lincolns claim that their first spell at C.T.C. Inveraray, was the one that will live longest in their memories, and when the time came for them to leave they " waved good-bye to the Wrens in the Signal Tower and watched the height known as the *Airmen's NAAFI* fading into the distance feeling that Combined Ops were a good thing." That was in 1942.

On August 19th, 1942, the Dieppe reconnaissance in force was made and costly but invaluable lessons were learnt. These were applied to the preparations for Sicily. So that when the

[1] There is now a hot and unprofitable controversy in which foolish men are saying that we should never have been bustled into the N. Africa and Sicily operations by an impatient public, but should have remained inactive in 1942 and early '43, building up sufficient landing-craft and troops for a " Second Front " that year. Of course the people who argue thus were the loudest section of that impatient public in 1942.

Division (185 Brigade had just joined 8 and 9) saw C.T.C. in the spring of 1943 there was a remarkable change. Every sort of obstacle bestrewed the shore of Loch Fyne, and the hills were infested with strongpoints. Field artillery and Vickers machine-guns supported the assaults, and day after day men returned to camp tired and mudstained but with heightened confidence and spirits. This was the stage from which the training for the biggest Combined Operation was developed : the training for Operation *Overlord*.[1]

.   .   .   .

All the time the courses, demonstrations, competitions were going on at Moffat the individual Battalions, Gunner Regiments and Sapper Companies were perfecting themselves in their various assault roles. When Moffat closed down, units and Brigades had their last chance to become complete amphibians before the gathering together of the whole Division in the Christmas period for the combined assault exercises. They appreciated and made good use of that time between the first news of the task and the " gathering of the clans " around Inverness and the Moray Firth. It was the time when units were still scattered fairly widely over Scotland, preserving their dearly cherished independence ; when Platoon and Troop Commanders were satisfying themselves that theirs was the best platoon or troop in the company or battery ; when Company and Battery Commanders were satisfying themselves that theirs was the best company or battery in the Regiment ; when Regimental Commanding Officers were satisfying themselves that theirs was the best regiment in the Brigade ; when the Infantry Brigade Com-

[1] Formerly known to the Division as *Exercise* Overlord, the whole topic was at that time avoided by common consent. Now that Commander Kenneth Edwards, R.N., has published his book, *Operation Neptune*, we had better accept the popular usage of *Operation Overlord* and " its naval component " *Neptune*. The confusion originated in the fitting fog of secrecy in which the degrees of security were enveloped. *Neptune* was the security grading given to operational orders and documents that revealed in clear the time and place of the operations, *Overlord* was the code word for the orders and documents in which time and place were in code. *Bigot* indicated the special *procedure* for the handling of *Neptune* documents, to ensure that they were not seen by those not entitled to see them. In the natural absence of a general pronouncement on such delicate matters the " natural " assumption was made that *Neptune* referred to the Navy's part in the total operation Overlord, though it is hard to see why the Army should therefore accept the role of *Bigot* !

manders were each assuring the others that theirs was the best brigade and was the obvious choice when it came to leading the Division in the Assault. The C.R.A., Brigadier G. G. Mears, M.C., R.A., had not so much to lose when this choice of Assault and Follow-up Brigades was made. Gunners would anyway be landing with the first troops ashore, and guns would at all events have to be ashore within about an hour of H-hour.

Units always prefer to be well away from higher formations, Divisional Headquarters in particular, to feel completely independent. At certain stages of training this is good for the unit and serves to create exactly the spirit needed later for integration into the pattern of the Division. Now they were on their own until they had found their sea-legs and got the feel of the Navy. All this experience was on the West Coast of Scotland at Inveraray, Dorlin and Kilbride successively. At C.T.C., Inveraray, men were getting hard and continuous practice in embarking and disembarking themselves, their equipment and vehicles, day and night, first in platoons, finally in brigades. At Dorlin 'there were wilder, harder conditions and thoroughly wet landings on the isles of Eigg and Rhum in emphatically foul weather. There was plenty of wind and rain and mud, too, in Kilbride Bay, and a 200-yards wade ashore only made the troops feel the more satisfied that this was realistic training for the day they began to look forward to, believing now that they were equal to the job for which they had been chosen.

It may be seen that units were much on the move, and these moves in themselves were a valuable break from routine. Not that all moves were made with men enjoying the changing scenery from the comparative comfort of Army transport. For example, when the East Yorkshires left Inveraray the rifle companies marched over a hundred miles carrying full equipment for a further month's hardening on the Ardnamurchan peninsula, scrambling and firing over the hills and practising the Company Landings in Kentra Bay.

The 20th Anti-Tank Regiment, meanwhile, had practised at Inveraray the ways of loading and beaching towed guns and sailing with them on L C T. They were finally equipped with one troop of American self-propelled M. 10's (the Model 10 is a 3-inch gun on the chassis of a Sherman tank, a fine anti-tank weapon, with only slightly less penetrating power than the 17-pounder) and two troops of towed 6-pounders in each of their four batteries. The 20th Anti-Tank Regiment soon discovered that " travelling on a rough or even quite smooth sea in an L C T or L C A was no joke. Land-bound soldiers, unaccustomed in any case to travel by sea, rolled in the agony of seasickness ; and when eventually put ashore, merely requested from their officers permission to lie down and die. This was not good enough. It was not improved by the assertion of the Admiral that sea-sickness was merely a question of morale. It was only slightly improved by the issue of sea-sickness tablets and vomit-bags. It must be said that many soldiers were not helped to have faith in the tablets when at the same time they were issued with vomiting-bags." It might also be remarked that the prescription for taking the Hyoscene Hydrobromide tablets was not helpful : they were originally prescribed to be taken one hour before feelings of sickness were experienced—a difficult time to predict ! Danger was sensed and then it was all too late.

The Field Regiments sailed in turn from Wemyss Bay to Rothesay on the Isle of Bute. All three Batteries of each Regiment had eight American self-propelled M. 7 *Priests*—105 mm. howitzers mounted on Sherman tank chassis—and at Rothesay they passed the days sailing round Bute, through the Kyles, and firing over the bows of the L C T on to Inchmarnock, a smaller island to the south on which Saint Ninian once lived and, more recently, Rothesay dypsomaniacs were cured. Sometimes the guns would anchor for the night off Tighnabruaich preparatory to a dawn-run-in on Inchmarnock. This shooting from the deck was strange at first, but soon senior officers were invited to watch demonstration shoots on to Strone Point. The temperature was steadily dropping as the winter drew on, but severe cold did not prevent the Gunners from enjoying their experiments in this unorthodox gunnery, from being well content with their Combined Operations role. At night there was a cheerful, bright atmosphere ashore as soldiers, sailors and marines got together in that Clydeside holiday resort : the sound of singing on the waterfront, the shouts of the seamen out in the bay, and the twinkling red, yellow and green lights of all the craft at anchor were a gay contrast with the accustomed nightly gloom over the rest of blacked-out Britain.

One of the special tasks for which the Royal Engineers of the Division were training was bridging. It was not long before the planners knew they must prepare for the bridging of the tidal Orne and the Caen Canal. Like another great advance in constructional engineering, the *Mulberry* prefabricated harbour, the Bailey Bridge was a product of the tremendous inventiveness and creativeness inspired by the nation's emergency. This Bailey Bridge over the Orne was the first to be constructed in France. 71 Field Company, who were under command of the 3rd Division in Normandy, did their training for this task on the Humber at Goole, while the Divisional Field Companies trained on the Irvine at Irvine in Ayrshire.

December came, and the 3rd Division was moving up into the north for the full exercises in planned assault on the Atlantic Wall. The roads north of Perth were reported snowbound. Units were split up for the move and parties were detailed to travel, some in lorried road convoys, some by rail, and regiments with heavy armoured equipment had some parties accompanying their armour by rail and some on the R.A.S.C. tank-transporter convoys. These last had the most eventful journey, "staging" four nights and arriving in Inverness in the wintry dusk at the end of their fifth day. They had come by many tales since leaving the Lowlands : how they changed transporters in the dark in the Shieldhall district of Glasgow, how squads of Glasgow police on motor-bikes had escorted them straight through the amazed crowds queueing up for their evening entertainment, who had not expected to see such great monsters charging by night up Sauchiehall Street : how their tanks had to dismount as they approached the Grampians, and tow the transporters over the frozen roads and through passes where the snow had drifted : how they had come on and on, north through Dunkeld, Pitlochry, Kingussie, Strathnairn, getting impressions of pine forests and silent snows that sometimes gleamed and glistened as if Montrose's men still marched over the mountains and their swords reflected the low sun.

The stations round the edge of the Firth were not luxurious : Inverness had never expected to see so many troops and members

of the other fighting forces. But everyone got some sort of accommodation, and those who were fortunate enough to begin this
period in what comfort Fort George offered, the regular home of
the Seaforths (who had never before been " out of residence "),
gave way to people less fortunate and based themselves for the
latter half of the period on a dismal site like the four-times con-
demned Nissen camp out at Muir of Ord. The Headquarters
of the Division were established in Inverness in the Cameron
Barracks, grim as any Scottish baronial hall, its grey granite
dominating the Moray Firth out to the North-east and the town
sprawling below its west wall. The Planning Staff were already
cut off from their fellows and were working in London at Ashley
Gardens.

Under the expert, discerning eye of Major-General W. H. C.
Ramsden, C.B.E., D.S.O., M.C., who had commanded 50th
(Northumbrian) Division with distinction in the desert, the
players had learned their parts in the drama, and were assembling
here for rehearsal, getting together for the first time. It was to
be an Anglo-American production under the supreme direction
of General Dwight D. Eisenhower.

The appointment of General Eisenhower as the Supreme
Allied Commander was not made until January, 1944. But the
plan of COSSAC (Chief of Staff to Supreme Allied Commander)
had been completed the previous July, accepted by Churchill,
Roosevelt and the Staffs at Quebec, and had already begun to
affect, directly or indirectly, the lives of every man, woman and
child in the United Kingdom. Its tremendous material requirements, for example in Landing-Craft, many of which had to be
constructed in the streets outside the workers' houses, so great
was the pressure of work in shipbuilding and other engineering
yards, are material for another book on the social implications of
the D-day preparations, and have in fact already been lightly
treated elsewhere. It is sufficient here to notice that the intensification of activity in the 3rd Division at this time was symptomatic
of the whole country's concentrated striving.

All that most members of the Invasion Division knew was
confined to what they saw : it was enough to widen the eyes of
the most hardened American-film addict. It had been
known to the Planning Staffs since last June that the landings

would take place on the Normandy coast between the Rivers Orne and Vire. That coastline had been selected chiefly because of the shelter afforded by the Cotentin peninsula against prevailing westerly winds, and of the possibility of insulating the wedge of France between the Seine and the Loire by destroying all the bridges over those two rivers. Naturally this was not general knowledge, but its early selection enabled the few who did know to collect the most intimate details of the landscape and enemy defence and reproduce them in such a way as to provide perfect training for all concerned : and it left no one the wiser about the exact location in Europe—though doubtless many protested they were ! This method involved everyone in the use of code words, such as *Queen Red Beach*, and *Morris, Daimler, Hillman* (known enemy strong-points), so that they became familiar to every unit and passed into common speech.

In October, 1943, Admiral Sir Bertram Ramsay, who had been at grips with the formidable complications of the Naval side of Combined Ops since May, 1942, was appointed Allied Naval Commander-in-Chief of the Expeditionary Force and took over the " X Staff " from the Commander-in-Chief Portsmouth. In November, Air-Marshal Sir Trafford Leigh-Mallory was appointed Commander of the British air component. On Christmas Day, General Sir Bernard Montgomery was appointed to command 21 Army Group. At the same time Major-General T. G. Rennie, D.S.O., M.B.E., the Black Watch (R.H.R.), was appointed to command the 3rd Division.

Major-General Tom Rennie had seen all his previous action with the 51st Division. As a major on their Divisional Staff he had been taken prisoner at St. Valéry-en-Caux in June, 1940, and within ten days had made an astounding escape. At El Alamein he commanded a battalion of the Black Watch, and won the D.S.O. He was proud to take command of a Division as keen and fit to fight as the 3rd Division were—to a man—at the close of 1943. To him was entrusted the responsibility of combining all the units and groups of fighting men into the irresistible Force which would break into Normandy on the extreme left of the seaborne invasion.

That Force, the Assault Group of the 3rd British Infantry Division, comprised not only units whose names already begin to be familiar, who properly provide the chief characters in this book, and who were the central figures in the act of invasion as in the ensuing acts. In addition, for the special task of assault, the Division took under command the 27th Armoured Brigade, one unit of which (the 13th/18th Royal Hussars) would take the plunge from Tank Landing-Craft five thousand yards out at sea and strike out for the shore in its Dual-Drive (amphibious) Sherman tanks. Under command also came all the various units administered as 101 Beach Sub-Area. That included the two Beach Groups under the 5th Battalion of the King's Regiment and the 1st (Buckinghamshire) Battalion of the Oxford and Buckinghamshire Light Infantry respectively, with Field Companies of R.E., Stores Sections, Field Dressing Stations, Pioneer Companies, R.A.F. Beach Sections, Forward Supply Units, Beach Recovery Sections, R.E.M.E., and R.N. Commandos. It also included the Port Operating Group, with its companies of specialists, the Field Squadron, R.E., which would clear underwater obstacles, the Beach Sub-Area Signals, and the Heavy and Light Anti-Aircraft Regiments, R.A., in support of the Sub-Area.

Besides all this there were gathered under command of the Division many G.H.Q., Army and Corps troops, and borrowed units, such as 4 Commando from 1 Special Service Brigade, the 53rd Medium Regiment, R.A., 5 (Independent) Royal Marine Armoured Support Battery, two detachments of L.C.O.C.U.s, R.M. (" Frogmen "), 5 Assault Regiment, R.E. (less two squadrons), detachments of 22nd Dragoons (equipped with tanks to " flail " mines), 71 Field Company, R.E. (who worked with 106 Bridging Company, R.A.S.C., and the Divisional Engineers on the Orne Bridges) and 263 Field Company, R.E., from XII Corps Troops, who would assist 629 Field Squadron to clear glider-landing strips for 6 Airborne Division. Finally the main body of 1 SS Brigade and a R.M. Commando of 4 SS Brigade were placed under command until the landing was made, when they would be deployed to either flank, 1 SS Brigade coming under command 6 Airborne Division on crossing a certain report-line (*Mallet*).

The story of these additional units only coincides with that of the Division during the training and opening stages of the campaign, though 101 Beach Sub-Area were to be responsible for the landing of all men, vehicles and stores for the Division (along with those belonging to 6 Airborne Division and a proportion of those for 1 Corps Troops) long after the Assault ; until D plus 55 days in fact. And units like 53 Medium Regiment, R.A., and 71 Field Company, R.E., were, as it turned out, to renew their connection with the Division deeper in Europe. What is most remarkable is that, with all these units under command, a specially incremented but normal-sized Divisional H.Q. Staff were efficiently administering a formation twice the strength of a normal Division, and at the most crucial stage in its history. The permanent members of Divisional Headquarters were devoting most of their time to questions of planning.

The Beach Sub-Area had joined the Division from its training areas at Dundonald and Gullane in November. They began their " wetshod " exercises with the Division in the Moray Firth. The first two large-scale exercises took place in December. It had been decided that a fair reproduction of the actual tides, beach, ridges and lateral roads likely to be encountered on the great D-day could be obtained by substituting Caithness for Kent and Morayshire for Calvados. The course south across the Firth from Lybster was approximately 90 miles, the same length as the final course south across the English Channel. The town of Burghead was subjected to a shadow of the distress awaiting Ouistreham. In its honour these December exercises were called *Burger* 1 and *Burger* 2.

Now, for the first time, the whole process of the invasion was practised. Marshalling camps were established on the Black Isle, in the damp pinewoods and on the moors beside the Munlochy-Rosemarkie road, " hards " were constructed on Chanonry Point to ensure vehicles at least a solid beach from which to embark—it was certain there would be trouble enough driving ashore at the other end—and conditions " at the other end " in Burghead Bay were made to conform as nearly as possible with what was known of the *Todt* fortifications. Now all units met the Naval units with whom they would finally approach the enemy beach, and a great friendship developed between the two Forces. To begin with, of course, a few mistakes and misunderstandings befell. The 20th Anti-Tank Regiment tell the tale of a Battery Captain *G* who asked the rating at the wheel of his

craft on what bearing they were running. " I don't know, sir,"
was the reply : " I'm following the craft ahead." " Where is
the craft ahead ? " " I don't know, sir, I haven't seen it for
about an hour." The end of that was a landing well outside the
battle area, which under conditions of real war would have been
disastrous. But it was precisely to avoid such disasters that
infinite thoroughness was insisted on in all the Combined
Training.

This Naval Force, which would be responsible for " the safe
and timely arrival of the assault forces at their beaches, the cover
of their landings, and subsequently the support and maintenance
of their rapid build-up ashore," was named Force " S," the
initial letter of the sector upon which the 3rd Division was
directed, Sword Sector. Its commander was Rear-Admiral
A. G. Talbot. Every effort was made after the arrival in the
Moray area to embark troops in " their own " craft for each
exercise and for the subsequent operation. All reasons of good
comradeship aside, understanding between soldier and seaman
was important for the Infantry who had to change craft from
large Infantry Landing Ship into cockleshell Assault Landing
Craft at the Lowering Position (a most aptly-named point seven
miles from the hostile shore). It was just as important for tank
crews, whether they had to leave their Tank Landing Craft on
an armed beach or whether (if they were D-D) they proposed
to plunge overboard and " swim " for it. And it was especially
important for the Field Regiments of the Divisional Artillery who
had to fire over the bows of the L C T at a range of 11,000 yards
before H-hour, firing on the run-in to 4,000 yards, when they
ceased firing and prepared to go into action ashore. All three
" arms " of the landing troops wanted perfect co-operation with
the Navy, and they achieved it over this period.

Movement Control and the staffs of the camps in the marshalling area profited by all these exercises, which each, in broad
plan, followed the same course, with only slight modifications in
detail arising out of the previous exercise.

Beginning in the unit, each exercise involved every man in
intensive preparations. One of the most formidable jobs which
confronted drivers of all types of vehicle, from the light James
motor-cycle to the Sherman tank, was waterproofing. True, it

was not proposed to ride motor-cycles ashore from the craft, but they were liable to be submerged even when strapped high behind the turret of a tank. Tanks themselves, and other " A " vehicles, required the most elaborate modifications : special " hardware " in the form of funnels or chutes had to be welded over air inlets and exhaust outlets, and all joints, valves, " breathers," in fact most of the engine itself, had to be sealed over with a special asbestos compound or a plastic substance called *Bostik*. Much of the work had to be undone as soon as possible after the dry land had been gained to allow the engines to breathe and keep cool. But it was imperative that no vehicle should " drown " : they were all too precious.

To see the roof of a jeep and the driver's head moving across the water shorewards was not uncommon, though the shock of diving into cold water from the ramp of a landing-craft often caused the driver to raise his foot from the accelerator : to stall the engine thus was fatal, and the shock had to be withstood. To achieve the highest standard of waterproofing, courses of instruction were attended at Rhyl and other centres, and R.E.M.E. Light Aid Detachments and unit teams often had to work 24 hours a day in shifts in order to be ready for the next exercise and test. There was no point in being *nearly* waterproof : you either drowned your vehicle or drove it ashore.

Units had other equipment problems. For example, wireless sets also had to be waterproof as well as faultlessly maintained for their vital function : there could be no line-communications in an assault. One unit had to net seventy-six out-stations on the regimental group. The most untechnically minded can see the difficulties in devising a procedure for operating such a congested net, and then keeping normal wireless discipline. To anticipate, that particular net was a complete success on D-day.

Lastly, there was the question of personal equipment. The Quartermaster issued every individual with kit according to the special Assault Scale, which applied to all units in the Assault Group and was designed to make each invader self-contained for all his personal needs. A special assault jerkin was designed, with pockets and packs all in one piece, to fasten in front with a toggle that could be released instantaneously. Over all was worn the lifebelt familiarly styled " Mae West " and a new light respirator. A new steel helmet was issued, supposed to give more protection. Each man received two 24-hour ration-packs and an emergency ration. He also received before the last of the exercises a new battledress complete with unit and formation signs. The scale of spare underwear, boots, woollen comforts, anti-gas protectors was prescribed, and after that it was recognised that each man knew best with what to complete his own load, knew what he needed to do his own job and how it was most easily carried.[1]

Besides equipment problems, which were legion, there were the countless special tactical problems for which every unit had to prepare and *brief* every officer and man. (It was a mistake to borrow this legal expression to describe the complicated orders and instructions that are unavoidable for a Combined Operation. It seems unlikely that a barrister's instructions are ever in fact reduced to brevity, but it is certainly true that Admiral Ramsay found it necessary to compile his operation orders in the form of a printed book of foolscap three inches thick, that the Divisional Operation Order covered fifteen pages and several amendments and appendices, and that this application to detail was completely justified.)

With all these problems trial and error was the only way, and there were enough trials to correct the majority of errors. As far as the units were concerned, once the preparations within the unit were complete all they had to do was set off for the marshalling area at a given signal, and the rest was comparatively easy. At this stage in the exercise Movement Control were supreme. Everyone else became a serial number. This had its advantages in that a little of the responsibility of " routeing " and timing was removed from the unit officers and drivers concerned. Indeed, supreme Movement Control was probably the only practicable method of moving such large forces. But the 8th Brigade rightly raised the objection that when the Assault Brigade is marshalling and loading its craft, it is deploying for battle and therefore responsibility must lie with the Brigade. Casualties in marshalling were being reported to Movement Control Headquarters : they were the first concern of the Brigade

---

[1] Originally the basic load per man was 95 lb. This was considered excessive, and reduced to 65 lb. (approx.) by arranging to bring in spare boots, etc., as " stores."

H.Q. With follow-up formations it was a relief to devolve responsibility for movement temporarily on another body.

As it was, Movement Control shepherded everyone along the treacherous roads of Black Isle to concealed vehicle parks where trees grew up to the verges : they conducted the troops in and out of leaky tents : they directed the convoys on down to the hards. Landing Craft were signalled to beach, and units assumed the responsibility for getting aboard. In the case of L C V and L C T an extremely careful process of loading had to be adopted : vehicles and tanks had to be backed on board (otherwise they would have had to back off, a method of joining battle suitable in cock-fighting but undignified in modern assault, even with the menagerie of *Crabs* and *Crocodiles*[1] that accompanies the battle nowadays, turning the average landing-craft into a sort of Noah's Ark). The loading of landing-craft did require infinite care in order not to waste a square inch of priceless shipping space. To that end much time between exercises was devoted to loading trials down at the hards with all the men and vehicles and craft concerned.

Once aboard, the principal cares were Naval and navigational, though a few more personal ones cropped up out in the Firth, confined largely to the troops aboard L C T. In a rough sea tanks had to be shackled to rungs in the metal deck and to one another, to prevent their sliding and damaging or causing the craft to list. One particularly squally day the sight of the L C T astern breaking its back against a wall of water provoked the inevitable dry humour and a little dismay among the watchers in a similar craft.

This period was not without its toll of casualties amongst men : some were fatal. It is fitting to quote from the History of 253 (West Lancashire) Field Company of the Division's Royal Engineers, which sets aside a page in remembrance of one of these men. It reads simply : " Although the title of this book is *D-day to VE-day*, it would be incomplete without a reference to Corporal Harry Worthington, who lost his life in the operational clearance of a beach minefield at Nairn in Scotland on 5 April, 1944.

[1] Since D-day *Kangaroos* and *Buffaloes* have joined the menagerie, which also contained *Weasels* that performed well in mud and *Porpoises* whose performance was pathetic.

" Without such men as Harry Worthington D-day would have been impossible." And underneath is printed the tribute of one of his fellow Sappers :

> " Generous, fearless, respected,
> He had but to ask—we'd obey.
> His memory lives on to guide us
> And strengthen us on our way."

The landing in Burghead would be made, men remembered what they had been told to do at the " briefing," and then, usually after not more than twenty-four hours—of varied but invariably wet and severely cold conditions—ashore in the beach-head area, units dispersed to barracks, arranged hot baths and a hot meal, and prepared for the next exercise.

While valuable experience was thus being gained by the 3rd Division and the flotillas of the Naval Force " S," planning was proceeding at a higher level. *Burger* 1 and 2 were over. Christmas was celebrated in Inverness in the traditional way by the three arms of the Service, who were combined as never before, together and also with their auxiliaries, who were all " in on " the Combined Operation : " Wrens," for example, might have been seen driving 3-ton lorries out of the Cameron Barracks Gates at daybreak, or deciphering *Most Secret* signals, or typing, or tele-printing or operating the Naval exchange. Over Christmas the announcement was received that Montgomery would command 21 Army Group. He arrived in London on January 3rd, and at once examined the COSSAC plan and the available intelligence of German strength in the West. He was in emphatic agreement with Eisenhower, who decided that assault on a three-divisional front " was in insufficient strength, and that to attain success in this critical operation a minimum of five Divisions should assault in the initial wave."[1]

It is not very hard to imagine the effect of this on the Navy and on the two new assault Divisions, the 50th (Northumbrian) Division and the 4th U.S. Infantry Division, who immediately required ships and training areas and a thousand other lesser things that are no less important in terms of success. It affected the 3rd Division in so far as the operation had to be postponed

[1] Supreme Commander's Report, pp. 3 and 4.

a month (it had been tentatively timed for the first days of May) to allow for the provision of more ships and training. Another effect of that additional burden on shipping was that each Division was restricted to 2,500[1] vehicles in place of the 3,200 originally planned. Otherwise exercises went on as usual. *Grab* followed *Smash*, and details of loads and timings were gradually worked out and improved upon. The decision taken by Admiral Talbot and General Rennie on Exercise *Grab* to land the Assault Group at all costs, in weather conditions of sea and temperature far worse than anything encountered on D-day, gave immense confidence to the whole Force when the 6th of June turned out grey and rough. There was still one major change to be made in the 3rd Division's plan.

It was revealed (to the few) that the 3rd Division had been honoured with the task of landing north of *Poland* (code name for Caen) on the extreme left of the seaborne forces, and of linking up with the 6th Airborne Division inland at *Rugger* and *Cricket* (code-names for two bridges : remark the ever-present sporting touch). The landing was to have been effected by two Infantry Brigades, 8 and 185, with the 9th Brigade in reserve. On February 4th Montgomery arrived in the north to inspect and address units of the Division, a member of which he had been, and afterwards to watch an assault exercise. From the bonnet of his jeep he gave his word that there would be no assault until he was satisfied that a lodgment could be guaranteed, that the Germans would have cause to remember the Division they pushed back into the Straits of Dover in 1940. There was a gale warning and Exercise *Crown* was twice postponed 24 hours. Embarkation eventually proceeded on the 8th and D-day was the 9th. Lieutenant-Colonel J. E. Shearer, M.C., who had come to the 3rd Division from the Regular Reserve of Officers as Chief Umpire to the Division, was killed that day umpiring the exercise. It is not a formality to state that the Division lost an officer who had quickly won the deepest respect of everyone who knew him. After Exercise *Crown* it was decided to assault with 8 Brigade on a single brigade front, 185 Brigade coming in two hours later as Intermediate Brigade. This was the last change of plan, and it was given its first try-out on February 22nd

---

[1] In fact 2,603 vehicles landed with the Division on June 6th.

in Exercise *Anchor*. Planning could now be completed to the last detail. This final stage of the planning was referred to as Exercise *Baron*.

Aberlour House was carefully prepared and set apart for the Divisional planning. At this country house on the Spey, near Rothes, the Divisional Planning Staff arrived from London on February 26th. And here in March came the Intelligence Staffs of the three Brigades to " read themselves into " the outline Divisional plan. This took ten days. Then the Commander of 8 Brigade, Brigadier E. E. E. Cass, C.B.E., D.S.O., M.C., came to Aberlour House with his staff, and produced an appreciation of the task of the Assault Brigade. Finally 8 Brigade " Order Group " came and were given full information regarding the operation, down to the newly completed Brigade plan. This *O Group* included Commanding Officers of all units under 8 Brigade for the landing.

Until one has read through the exhaustive details of the Planning Memoranda, the innumerable tables of craft-capacity and the allotment of men and vehicles for each tide, the rival bids for more loading-space, the inevitable succession of amendments, and the Divisional Commander's official correspondence with higher authority, it is impossible to appreciate the accomplishment of the Divisional Planning Staff. Exercise *Baron* was probably the most gruelling exercise of all.

There was one factor that might have upset the whole plan even at this late stage. In February the enemy put into operation his scheme to obstruct beaches with under-water obstacles, starting at high-water mark and working down to low-water mark, thickening them up in depth as the months went by. Apparently Rommel, the German Army Group Commander, was not satisfied that with concrete defence works, coastal batteries, an armoured mobile reserve, we should be sufficiently occupied.[1] Most of the obstacles were known to have *Teller* mines or fused shells fixed on to them, whilst there were *Teller* mines attached to floating rafts. And most of the obstacles would

---

[1] Neither, for that matter, was Rundstedt satisfied. Both he and Rommel were agreed that the Allies must never be allowed to secure a firm foothold on the mainland. Where they disagreed so fatally was in the matter of the armoured reserve. Rommel wanted his tanks right forward : Rundstedt wanted to hold them back in reserve.

be submerged at high tide. The effect on the plan of their last-minute appearance was less than it might have been. Obviously they dictated that the landing must be in daylight and must be made as far as possible below them, if they were to be cleared. We shall see soon how this affected the fixing of H-hour. The fact that a daylight landing had been practised all along was indeed fortunate and cause for satisfaction. At the earliest planning conferences the military representatives had hankered after a night landing to ensure tactical surprise. The Navy, however, preferred daylight for infallibly arriving at the right beach : what was more, daylight would facilitate aimed air and sea bombardment. Daylight prevailed. Though the Sicilian sea-landing had been successfully made in darkness, the best results in the latest Pacific Operations confirmed the decision to land after dawn.

The outline plan, as Brigade staffs were now aware, was, in Army Group language, " to secure a lodgement on the Continent from which further offensive operations could be developed." The intention of the Commander-in-Chief of 21 Army Group was to assault immediately north of the Carentan (Vire) estuary, and between the rivers Vire and Orne, with the object of securing a lodgment area that would include airfield sites and the port of Cherbourg. The Second British Army was to assault on the left and protect the flank of the First United States Army while it captured Cherbourg and the Brittany ports. Second Army was to assault with XXX Corps on the right and I Corps on the left. I Corps was to assault with 3rd Canadian Division on the right and 3rd British Division on the left.

The 3rd British Division, then, was going to land on the left flank. The honour that lay in that commission was not so apparent then as it is now, when we can see in retrospect how the " *further* offensive operations " were planned : how " the build-up for the break-through was to take place on the RIGHT while the enemy was to batter himself against a strongly-held pivot in the Caen area on the LEFT."[1] The pivot in the Caen area on the LEFT *was*, indeed, strongly held by the 3rd Division. But even in March the prospect looked honourable and formidable enough to those who knew the plan.

[1] *Notes on the Operations of 21 Army Group* compiled by G (Ops) Records (Restricted), p. 12.

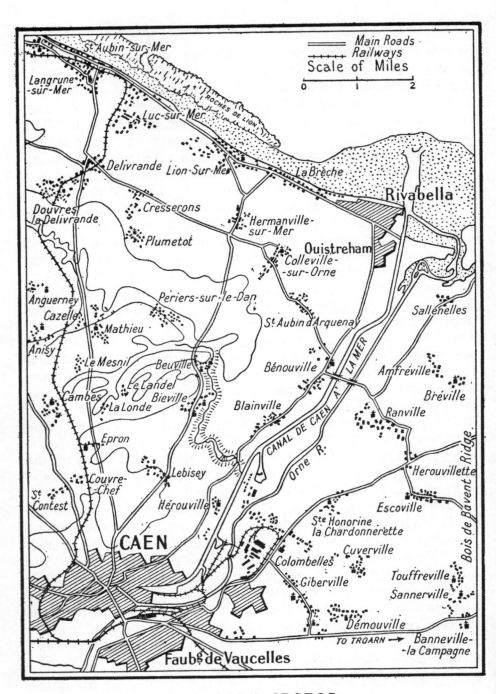

THE CAEN SECTOR

The main enemy strength, which totalled ten Panzer Divisions and forty-nine Infantry Divisions, was known to lie in wait in the Pas de Calais area—on the left flank of the Invasion ! It was common knowledge after the Dieppe raid that all ports, even minor ones, were most heavily defended—that was why it had been decided to rely on maintenance across beaches, and to construct the *Mulberries* : of all the ports in the actual landing areas Caen and Ouistreham were the largest. The Le Havre promontory, with its massive coastal defence works, lay to the *left* rear of the bridgehead, and commanded directly the approaches and beaches across the Seine Bay, the prospective Sword Sector. Finally, waiting in the bridgehead area were five Infantry Divisions along the coast and two Infantry Divisions behind the coastal defences in the Cherbourg Peninsula : immediate reserves for the Normandy area were the 12th SS Panzer Division, away to the *left* at Lisieux, and the 21st Panzer Division, which was prowling round Caen. " Task for 3 Brit Inf Div to secure the high ground NORTH of CAEN and, if possible, CAEN itself ; to relieve 6 Airborne Div on the bridges over the CANAL de CAEN and the R. ORNE at BENOUVILLE and RANVILLE."[1]

The great body of the Division was unaware of the decisions that so closely affected its destiny. It was to be the extreme left flank, they heard. Where though ? Norway ? Holland ? Pas de Calais ? The popular bet was France. Cheerfully, but with an important question-mark persisting in mind, everyone made ready for *Leapyear*, the last of the great exercises in the north.

Leapyear was a success and very encouraging. Unit preparations were completed, and on the night 27-28 March loading was ordered to proceed from the floodlit yards at Chanonry. By morning everyone was aboard. The flotillas formed up and in the late afternoon set sail up the Firth to the north-east for Lybster and Wick. Off Lybster the going was very bad, and waves were breaking over the bows of L C T. The course south for Burghead began on time, but on the morning of the 29th when the time came for the run-in from the Lowering Position, it was decided to sail into Cromarty Firth for shelter. The weather was extremely rough and looked like deteriorating. One exercise

[1] *Notes on the Operations of 21 Army Group*, p. 6.

had already been carried out despite all the elements : it was decided that the best benefit would be derived this time by waiting for better weather. So the day was spent idly at anchor off Invergordon and the Sands of Nigg. In intervals between showers of snow and sleet the sun would burst out from the clouds and silver Sunderlands of Coastal Command would resume their target practice with " flour-bags " in Cromarty Bay.

The night was quieter, and in the early morning the Force sailed proudly out over the swell, past Tarbat Ness, the caves and cliffs of " the Scottish Riviera," deserted save by the gulls, and across to the Lowering Position. The run-in began. The guns thundered and the landing was made. There was more snow and sunshine as the bridgehead was consolidated and units went chasing off on an extended exercise through Darnaway Forest and up the valley of the Findhorn.

Leapyear was a success, and the Division was ordered to the concentration area in the South of England. The move took place immediately. Everyone knew what the move meant and was glad.

As the craft of S Force sailed down the whole length of the east coast to Portsmouth, the Division was migrating the whole length of the land. This mass migration coincided with Easter and warm weather, and while there is nothing likelier than that the holiday-makers out hiking and cycling had earned their holiday that year, their presence on the roads and apparent indifference to the infinite procession of convoys making their way southwards from all over the island strengthened the soldier's suspicion that for the time being he was apart. Normally it is hard to find men to ride motor-bikes in convoy : there were plenty of volunteers on this journey, particularly from north-countrymen ; inevitably the thought came to mind that this would be their last chance to look on their wives and sons, their parents, their countryside. They never failed to rejoin the convoy, which eventually stopped at one of the hundreds of tented camps raised among the trees in the south of England. The whole southern coast was converted, as in the time when we feared invasion, into an armed camp ; this time men felt the very opposite of fear.

It was a pity that invasion could not commence at once. But we have remarked how an additional month was required to provide training and ships for two more Divisions. For the Assault Group of the 3rd British Division this meant a period of waiting comparable with the period before the doors are opened for the first paper of a vital examination (not to take another simile from the sports field). The period was made easier by the embarking, after the first month, on the last of the amphibious exercises, in which three of the five Forces took part. Exercise *Fabius* (its name recalling Quintus Fabius, the General who was styled *Cunctator* after his classic delaying actions fought against Hannibal ; recalling, too, the mood of more modern Fabians, " the inevitability of gradualness ") helped to occupy the minds of the men who were ready to plunge into battle, into what was —despite the most excellent Intelligence service—ultimately unpredictable, unknown.

Fabius took place on May 3rd and 4th. At this time security was so good that most of those on the exercise were not sure that it might not be the operation itself. On the other side the Germans were apprehensive. On all sides the newspapers were getting worked up in anticipation almost to the point of hysteria. The cover and deception achieved with wireless and dummy-craft was remarkably successful. On the night May 3-4 the three Forces sailing before a freshening south-westerly breeze from the Isle of Wight area turned to starboard in a feint towards the coast of France.[1] Apart from one enemy aircraft attack upon a destroyer there was no enemy reaction : tribute chiefly to the Royal Air Force. The Forces turned again and landed on agreeably inoffensive beaches between Littlehampton and Bognor. It was an encouraging experience. But the waiting was resumed and the suspense heightened.

Exercise *Handsup* is the name that was given to the move south and all subsequent administration of the moving into position for embarkation. The Division was divided into four blocks : Main Bodies, which would land on D-day and D-day plus 1 ; First Residues, landing between D plus 2 and D plus 6 ;

---

[1] This particular piece of deception was apparently wasted on the Germans : in February, 1946, Blumentritt, von Rundstedt's Chief of Staff, ruefully admitted in an interview with Major Milton Shulman of the Canadian Army Intelligence Staff, that the sailing of these Forces was never even reported at the Headquarters of the German Western Command.

Main Residues from D-day plus 7 onwards ; and First Reinforcements. As the normal reconnaissance role had to be carried out by various specialist units during the assault phase, the 3rd Recce Regiment suffered the mortification of standing by during the invasion until they could come into action, and make up for lost time, on the 19th June. One hundred of the officers and men of the Regiment were fortunate : they were formed into either Contact Detachments (for the provision of an additional communicating link between the assaulting units), or a Traffic Control Group, both parties landing on D-day. To the remainder of the Regiment went the main task of operating *Handsup* : that is to say, they were given control of both lots of Residues.

It is wrong to suppose that no one had anything to do as the hour approached. Divisional Ordnance were working harder than ever before, supplying last-minute indispensable needs. R.E.M.E. teams and unit drivers worked like Trojans, or rather like Britons, to ensure that waterproofing was 100 per cent sound. R.A.S.C. drivers were at the wheel all day, fetching Ordnance stores, taking men who were not in the Main Body of Assault Group to camps farther inland situated according to whether they were to rejoin their units " over there " on D plus 2, D plus 7, D plus 14, or whatever date they would be needed. Members of units with armoured equipment were fully employed up till the last minute on their maintenance and waterproofing preparations. It was the foot-soldier who had hours on his hands at this time, and he was the man who least wanted to think. His uppermost thought was : " Why can't they get on with it ? "

There were 24-hour passes for a time : that helped the man who lived in London or the south. Perhaps he got two, if he was lucky. The electric trains were crowded. Otherwise the day was filled with routine that was so obviously designed to kill time that it only succeeded in maiming it. After that, there were marquees fitted out as cinemas, canteens and rest-rooms. Fastened to trees all over the camp were loud-speakers that issued sepulchral over-amplified summonses for somebody or other to report to the Camp Commandant's tent, or disturbed the quiet dusk with : "Look to your black-out. Black out now !" —a nightly warning ; if only they would call forward the first craft-load ! Most books were boring and newspapers unreadable.

The beer was restricted and was hardly beer. The weather was flawless ; there had been no such weather since the summer of 1940. It was ideal for a camping holiday : it was tormenting. Hot spring sunshine filled every lane and every wood, and even caught the air as if under a magnifying-glass, so that it seemed to be scorching, on the point of breaking into flame.

After *Fabius* it quickly became clear that—well, now for it ! Wiring round camps was doubled and tents were set aside in each for " briefing " with strong guards posted outside and C.O.s and I.O.s and staffs working long hours at the preparations within.

On May 8th General Eisenhower, Admiral Ramsay, General Montgomery, Air-Marshal Leigh-Mallory and others met to decide the hour and day. The original idea had been to land three or four hours before high tide and about forty minutes after nautical (dawn) twilight. The Navy wanted as many hours as possible of rising tide, and the Army wanted the shortest possible run over the exposed beach. Both wanted adequate daylight for observing shoots and as many hours of daylight as possible for the build-up, in fact a second high water before nightfall. Then the under-water obstacles had been reported, and were the most considerable factor. They varied in depth on the different beaches. It was therefore decided that there should be individual H-hours, according to the depth of the obstacles. The earliest was fixed at 06.30 hours, the latest (Group G J2) at 07.55. Three days in every fortnight produced suitable conditions. The first timing of H-hour depended on which of those days the assault was made. The day was fixed at June 5th. There could be postponement till the 6th, or, if the worst came to the worst, till the 7th. This decision was signalled to Commanders on May 23rd.

Meanwhile, on May 13th General Eisenhower visited and spoke to the Division. His sincerity was impressive. Everyone laughed when he said he knew what some of them thought of the Americans, and that he had the advantage of knowing what some of the Americans thought of them. And everyone knew the truth in his remark about thinking ourselves not Allies, but one indivisible team. " It is good to see you looking so fit and in such good spirits. I had heard so much about you from General Montgomery : and he certainly did not exaggerate." In conclusion he said : " I can promise you a big party in Berlin when it's all over, and that party will be on me ! "   How much was in fact contributed to that party by this great American was perhaps best summed up by the Public Orator in Oxford on St. Crispin's Day, 1945, who described him simply as " leader of 5,000,000 men in a war conducted with a wisdom and concluded with a decisiveness never before surpassed."

" It can't be far off now," was one of the most gratifying conclusions drawn from General Eisenhower's visit, and a further portent was the visit on May 22nd of the King.   As they lined the Hampshire lanes, the King walked slowly past each one of his representatives upon so great an undertaking.   This formality which our Sovereign goes through with men proceeding overseas on active service must have seemed to him more than ever poignant as he, and they, contemplated the imminent event ; very soon, now, it would resolve itself as the most glorious or most disastrous passage of arms ever attempted by the nation or by humanity.

On Friday, May 26th, French francs were issued, and a booklet with a few French phrases and summary generalisations about French habits.   A little more of the terrible secret was out, and one or two were rash enough to say :   " I told you so all along ! "   " Briefing " began, and camps were sealed : no one was allowed to go outside the barbed wire.   This final briefing was carried out down to the last detail and the last man.   Each unit organised the briefing of all sub-units over the next two or three days, and any man could spend as long as he liked studying the contents of the " briefing tent," which held more excitement than any circus-booth or museum exhibition.   Here was the fascination of an exhibition, only whereas a museum usually exhibits the past, this was designed to show men into what was coming.   There was a specially-drawn wall-map of the whole beach-head on the scale of about 21 inches to the mile.   There were larger scale-maps, some with defence overprints.   Then there were models of selected sections of the Divisional Assault Area, ground photographs collected from tourists and special agents, and air photographs high and oblique (wave-top) photographs, with stereoscopes, anaglyphs and an epidiascope to aid realism

Men also heard encouraging details about their combined support ; the programme of Naval and aerial bombardment was unprecedented, almost unlimited and quite unimaginable. There were two security precautions : all maps, models and photographs were specially prepared for the occasion and still bore the familiar code names : and no one who had been in one of those tents was allowed to converse with anyone who was not in the Assault Group. As part of the last precaution all out-going mail was held up at this stage until after the landing had been made.

On Tuesday, May 30th, the heat was sweltering, almost insufferable, and men were doing the only thing they could do in the circumstances—basking in the sun and remarking complacently that it had " turned out nice again." In the course of the day similar groups, gathered all over the Divisional Concentration Area, were approached by their officer or N.C.O. with a quiet familiar order such as : " O.K., get your kits on." It was an order they had longed to hear, and had seemed so long coming. Marshalling had begun.

The immense machine was in motion. Lane after lane of closely-parked vehicles seemed to come alive and move gradually forward. From now on it was up to Fate and Movement Control. Movement Control worked magnificently. Fate was less reliable. The 1st day of June, Thursday, dawned dull and grey : this after two months of unbroken sunshine ! It was no use recriminating. That day Eisenhower, Ramsay and the others met, consulted the meteorological experts, shook their heads and hoped against hope. The same thing happened on Saturday afternoon. The troops went aboard, their eyes on the sky.

Early on Sunday morning, at 4.15, the Commanders again assembled in the operations-room at Southwick Park. After hearing the views of the meteorological team, and then that of his Commanders-in-Chief, General Eisenhower made the heavy decision ; D-day was postponed 24 hours.

It was worst for those who had already sailed out into the pitching Channel, units of " U " Force from Devon and " O " Force from Portland, for example. It was quite bad enough for the men of " S " Force, still at anchor in Portsmouth harbour, who could only skulk on the decks and scowl at the traitor sky.

On Sunday afternoon, when the Invasion fleet might have been on its way, another meeting was being held at Southwick Park. Since the early morning meeting the meteorological experts had predicted the weather for June 6th. " The wind would back to the west and south-west and decrease to force 3 to 4 (7 to 15 knots). The waves in mid-Channel would decrease from a height of 6 feet. The further outlook was unsettled, but some breakdown in the westerly weather conditions could be expected." This was more optimistic, and General Eisenhower said : " We will sail to-morrow " : D-day for Operation *Overlord* was to be June 6th.

Meanwhile, on board their various types of landing-craft, the Division spent a squally night and rose from the deck on Monday morning to find no sign of change for better or worse. The fall of Rome was announced that morning on the eight o'clock news, and only helped to aggravate the feeling that this should have been D-day, the disappointment that the announcement of the Invasion of France had not coincided, as had obviously been intended, with the capture of Rome. But the morning passed and no further postponement order was received. One by one craft slipped away from their moorings, on past the gallant old *Victory*, with its inspiration, and some of the troops saw Mr. Churchill and General Smuts watching them from a destroyer. And as they sailed out of Spithead they saw their Commanders, Rear-Admiral Talbot and Major-General Rennie, standing together on their Headquarters Ship, H.M.S. *Largs*. The Admiral hoisted a signal to wish them Good Luck.

Chapter Two

INVASION

(i)

THE ASSAULT

> O, do but think
> You stand upon the rivage, and behold
> A city on th' inconstant billows dancing ;
> For so appears this fleet majestical,
> Holding due course to *Ouistreham*. Follow, follow !
> Grapple your minds to sternage of this navy,
> And leave your England, as dead midnight still ;
> For who is he whose chin is but enrich'd
> With one appearing hair, that will not follow
> These cull'd and choice-drawn cavaliers to France ?
>   . . . the nimble gunner
> With linstock now the devilish cannon touches,
> And down goes all before them. Still be kind,
> And eke out our performance with your mind.
>   (Prologue to Act III of *King Henry V*)

As soon as they were clear of the sheltering shores all men in the Force had let go all hope of a steady crossing. Unfalteringly the flotillas had moved to their battle-stations at the great forming-up area known as " Piccadilly Circus " to the south-east of the Isle of Wight, and already the unnerving heave and rock, the sensations of a high sea, were recognised. Men began to cast oblique glances at one another, and to perceive that they were not alone in their misgivings : the efficiency of those tablets was already in doubt. At first they were all occupied : the sealed packages were broken open, and operational orders, maps and traces were scanned. At last the names " in clear " ! So *Poland* was Caen, *Portugal* was the Caen Canal, and they'd probably be in Caen this time to-morrow ! Of course they might have expected to land near the inter-section of four 1 : 50,000 maps,

so that all four have to be folded down and accommodated
beneath the talc of a small map-board ! There was by now no
doubt at all about the tablets.

Once in formation, each Force took its bearing and pressed
forward in line ahead—in two apparently endless parallel lines
of widely assorted craft—for its Lowering Position about seven
miles off its selected beach. The Headquarters Ship, H.M.S.
Largs, had done similar service in *Torch* and *Husky*, the landings
in North Africa and Sicily. Now the old veteran was one of five
great nerve-centres in the most vital and intricate operation of
them all, and standing up to the test. The other large craft, the
Infantry Landing Ships, *Dacres*, *Glenearn*, *Cutlass*, *Battleaxe*,
Broadsword, *Astrid*, *Maid of Orleans*, *Goathland* and *Locust* (advancing
in that order) were all as familiar as the *Largs*. Men aboard
them were the fortunate ones : the following sea seemed to roll
them less than smaller craft—particularly L C T—on account of
their size. That is not to say that a number of the men cooped
up below hatches escaped sea-sickness : L S I made only a
comparatively easy crossing. And then there was the Lowering
Position to face, the unhappy transfer, and ninety minutes in a
tossing little L C A.

But these familiar craft actually carrying the Division, about
250 all told, were only occupying the foreground of the greatest
naval review in all history. Around and beyond moved Covering
Forces and Escorts. Ahead the Fleet Minesweeping Flotillas
were steadily cutting channels that the Assault Force might
navigate safely : a most difficult sweep, with considerations of
a turning tide, was made with complete success. The foremost
craft of " S " Force was not conspicuous at the early stage of the
crossing. It was the midget submarine X 23, whose task was to
mark the limit of the assault area for the oncoming armada.
X 23 had taken up her position just off the beach before midnight on June 4th, knowing nothing of the postponement. They
had to remain submerged for nineteen hours on June 5th, with
no air-conditioning plant, lying on the shallow bottom which
they knew to be mined. Three hours before dusk that day the
leading minesweepers were in sight of France !

That the German coastal defence forces failed to engage
these minesweepers is more than surprising. That they took no

warning from their sweeping activities is almost incredible. Yet the fact remains that the invasion followed as a tactical surprise. It can only be assumed that the Germans decided that the minesweeping was another feint, and declined to be drawn.[1] We need not put all our success in achieving this surprise down to German stupidity. We were operating an elaborate cover and deception plan throughout the period of preparation. This included the temporary sinking of the *Mulberry* harbour off Dungeness, the concentration of our bombers upon the Pas de Calais area prior to D-day, and the assembly of our normal shipping in north-eastern ports, due, chiefly, to the occupation of the southern ports by invasion craft (well camouflaged). The illusion that we had designs on Norway was heightened by the intensification of our mining of the Southern Baltic and the Kiel Canal and by a series of air attacks on U-boats off the Norwegian coast shortly before D-day, aimed simply at preventing their joining the U-boat squadrons in Brest and the Biscay. Radio measures, alternate wireless silence and activity, and simulation schemes, added to the German bewilderment. In addition their radar had been dislocated for them by the R.A.F., and we were making deliberate diversions against the Pas de Calais and Cap d'Antifer. Towards the end of May we went to the length of sending off to Gibraltar a British actor closely resembling General Montgomery.

The final element of surprise was the weather. Let it be admitted that the forces taking part (naval as well as military) were themselves slightly surprised to be venturing out across a Channel as rough as that, though it is true that this particular Force had attempted and survived worse in Exercise *Grab*. Weather conditions did make invasion seem unlikely. We now know that the Chief German Meteorologist, Major Lettau, reported to the German Commanders that after June 4th conditions would be unfavourable for several days. He seems to have overlooked completely the " weather front " that was to pass through the Channel early on June 5th with relatively good weather following it, and that gave Eisenhower the opportunity

[1] This is now confirmed by Major Milton Shulman in his remarkably fine book, *Defeat in the West*. German Intelligence Staffs had cried " wolf" too often. " Life was relatively serene amongst the German formations in France on the evening of 5 June, 1944 . . . The invasion seemed weeks away . . ."

he wanted. There is now no question that Eisenhower's most momentous decision was right, though we shall see how it was precisely this condition of the Channel that contributed most to the detriment of the operation of the 3rd Division's plan.

The Division, we see, was not alone as it made its uneasy way south into the grey night. There was comfort in the sight and thought of so much aerial and naval support. And the dreadful plunge and shudder of the craft was bound to come to an end. One after another the great buffeting waves were breasted, and, though in distance it was not a long voyage, the length of time for most of the Division was between seventeen and twenty hours. Those hours grew to resemble eternity, and to the men watching through the night it was like a voyage into another world. In a sense, that is what it was.

In mid-Channel the waves were between five and six feet high, and a force 5 wind (16 to 20 knots) was blowing from the west. Still there was no resistance from the enemy, and it was gradually becoming clear that we had achieved the tactical and strategic surprise that had seemed too much to hope for ; it was still unbelievable. Shortly after midnight six gliders passed overhead on their way to secure the bridges over the Caen Canal and Orne (*Rugger* and *Cricket*). Half an hour later they were followed over by the 3rd and 5th Parachute Brigades of the 6th Airborne Division who were going to land in the close strip of country between the Orne and the Dives to protect the left flank of I Corps. That must have woken the Germans up. Flak was observed ahead. But it was all strangely quiet. Sometimes each landing-craft seemed to be on its own, then suddenly the stern of the preceding craft would appear almost under the bows. A quiet order from the bridge, a change in the engine tempo, and the craft drifted apart again.

Another three hours passed before the desultory discharge of tracer from the enemy coast ahead developed into something like fireworks, with considerable bomb-flashes. In the darkness overhead a steady roar was developing. This was Phase 2 of the Assault. (The " softening-up " of the assault area prior to D-day was Phase 1.) This morning the Allied Air Force estimated that they had 31,000 airmen over France between midnight and breakfast-time. The weight of bombs dropped defies imagining. It was fairly distributed.[1]

At last the day broke beneath low clouds. The Naval bombardment forces joined in the good work of the Air Forces with calibres varying from the 15-inch guns of battleships and monitors to the 4-inch guns of *Hunt* class destroyers. This was no indiscriminate blasting, but a concerted attack on known enemy batteries and strong-points. It was the beginning. The elements themselves had failed to deflect these relentless forces. The Navy were showing the Division what they could do with odds against them, and the Division, no less stricken by the elements, waited undaunted to show the Navy what they could do. What the elements could not achieve it was perhaps unreasonable to expect of the Germans. Reports from Germany go to show that they shared our relief, and welcomed the end of the agony of waiting. In Berlin that day there were excited cries of : " Sie kommen, sie kommen ! " But altogether there was little indication that our arrival was welcomed. And though the enemy manning the coastal defences must have spent a night of extreme discomfort, and while it is unlikely that their apprehensions of the night equalled in unpleasantness the amazing revelations of daylight, they were not dismayed into inaction.

Bombarding Force " D " was on the flank to port of " S " Force, preparing to engage enemy batteries between Ouistreham and Villerville, and screened by smoke from the observation of Le Havre gunners. At 5.15 a.m. the enemy made a half-hearted attack upon this Bombarding Force. Three torpedo boats suddenly emerged from the smoke-screen, fired a number of torpedoes and hurried back into the cover of the smoke. One torpedo could just be seen approaching H.M.S. *Largs*. The Divisional Commander's ship was saved by putting her engines to Full Astern, and the torpedo passed a few feet ahead of her. A second torpedo hit the destroyer *Svenner* of the Royal Norwegian Navy ; the *Svenner*, sailing but two hundred yards astern of the *Largs*, sank almost immediately.

Seven miles from the shore the first Infantry Landing Ships,

[1] " Without the intervention of Bomber Command," writes Marshal of the R.A.F. Sir Arthur Harris, " the invasion of Europe would certainly have gone down as the bloodiest campaign in history, unless, indeed, it had failed outright—as it would undoubtedly have done."

A.D.   E were arriving at the Lowering Position, heaving-to and anchoring. A and B Companies of the East Yorks and A and C Companies of the South Lancs moved to their loading positions by five of the L C A in the davits of each Battalion L S I, and were quickly hoisted overboard. Round them the other craft deployed swiftly for the assault. Forming up and timings were extremely complicated, in accordance with the detailed plan : they were well rehearsed, and so far it had all been like an exercise. No one expected this similarity to last much longer.

The information regarding the enemy was that the coast between Courseulles and the Orne was held by the right-hand regiment of 716 Division. In the German Army all the battalions of the same regiment were kept together, and the infantry division, when up to strength, was composed of three regiments, roughly equivalent to our brigades. The Right Regiment confronting the Assault Brigade was thought to be 736, and it was reported that the Division had as many as 40 per cent non-Germans, mostly disaffected or conscript Russians and Poles. It was appreciated that " as a centre of communications and Army, Air Force and Civil H.Q.s, Caen is likely to be stubbornly defended by the Germans within the limits of the forces at their disposal."[1] Among reserve formations 21 Panzer Division was known to have been stationed at Mantes, though " one very recent report as yet unconfirmed, but supported by train movements, suggests this Division may now be stationed in an area between ten and thirty miles south of Caen. It could therefore intervene against us on D-day and we must be prepared for it."[2]

The information regarding the topography of the assault was admirably detailed, and had, in conjunction with the maps available and air photographs, provided everyone with a familiar landscape. Of *Queen* Beach it said : " 3 Br Inf Div beaches are good assault beaches. The sand is smooth and firm, except for a possible soft strip above high water." That " possible soft strip " ought to have been underlined. The width of the beach was expected to be as follows : " From the back of the beach to low water—average 400 yards ; from the back of the beach

[1] Divisional Intelligence Summary issued with the final Operation Order dated 14 May, 1944.
[2] Ibid.

to high water—average 30 yards." But those were the figures given for normal conditions. " In the event," wrote Admiral Ramsay to General Eisenhower, " the weather had built up the tide in the bay, and on no beaches, except Utah, was obstacle clearance satisfactory before the obstacles were immersed." But that was not all. At high tide the width of *Queen* Beach should have been sufficient for vehicles to manœuvre laterally along it —" average 30 yards." " The weather had built up the tide in the bay " : it left barely 30 feet.

The latest beach obstacles were described with accuracy. The assaulting troops would first meet two groups of ramp type (" knife-rest ") obstacles starting 300 yards down from the back of the beach. Then they would come to a double row of stakes running continuously across the beaches, 30 to 60 yards between stakes, 230 yards down from the back of the beach. The last of the under-water obstacles began 180 yards from the back of the beach and consisted in overlapping rows of " hedgehogs " twenty feet apart and fourteen to seventeen in a row. Hedgehogs were constructed of angle-iron after the pattern of the caltrop used in the Hundred Years War, but standing about six feet high. Obstacles were still under construction, and the possibility of mines below high water *was* anticipated. The beach was backed by a narrow strip of sand-dunes rising as high as fifteen feet, its face sloping at forty-five degrees. Between the coast and Caen numerous German strong-points were suspected or known.

Upon the basis of such information Major-General Rennie had been able to make his appreciation, and, with his staff, at Aberlour House, formulate the plan that was now being put into tactical operation at the Lowering Position.[1] In conformity with an ambitious Corps plan, in which 3rd Canadian Division on the right would secure a covering position on the general line of the Caen-Bayeux road from Putot-en-Bessin to Carpiquet aerodrome, and on the left 6th Airborne Division would deny the enemy the use of the area between the Rivers Orne and Dives north of the road Troarn-Banneville-Colombelles, it was the intention of the 3rd British Infantry Division to land on the beach at La Brèche, capture Caen and establish a bridgehead south of the River Orne at that place. To this end 8 Brigade

[1] Alternative plans were prepared to allow for faulty landings or initial repulse.

Group were about to run in from the Lowering Position, " assault on *Queen Red* and *White* beaches and secure the beach-head to include the high ground about Periers-sur-le-Dan and St. Aubin d'Arquenay."[1] Under command 8 Brigade were the 13th/18th Royal Hussars, 5 Assault Regiment, R.E., and 4 and 41 Commandos, as well as the Machine-Gunners, Gunners, Sappers and Field Ambulance " habitually affiliated " to that Brigade.

Wireless silence had already been broken by the Gunners of the three Field Regiments. All the sets had been netted before sailing, and now came the anxious moment of test, when sets were switched on and the net checked. The great fear was not so much that out-stations might have drifted off net, but that the Germans might be jamming them effectively. Gunner communications are indispensable in battle ; without them they are powerless to provide artillery support, but that is not all ; Gunner representatives with the forward Infantry are much better equipped than the Infantry themselves with the means of communication, and their signals are correspondingly more dependable channels of information from the front. Afloat, with parties distributed over so many craft, here was the supreme need for wireless perfection. No less than that was achieved.[2]

Closely linked, then, and synchronised, the Gunners joined in the naval " free for all " which was in full fling. They " touched off the devilish cannon " a mile outside the Lowering Position, loosing over two hundred shells a minute as steadily they closed in on the target and dropped the range accordingly.

The remainder of the East Yorks. and South Lancs cheered their Assault Companies as they sailed away from the Lowering Position, then themselves stood by to be loaded. As Battalion H.Q. of the East Yorkshires moved off in their L C A past the *Largs*, one of the East Yorkshiremen sounded the General Salute

[1] Op. cit.

[2] Royal Signals (and the R.A. signallers) won gratitude all round on D-day. The distinction of fitting seventy-six out-stations into a workable group was achieved by Lieutenant Whiteman of the Royal Signals, though he was appropriated by 9 Brigade H.Q. before he could see the practical success of his efforts. It has already been remarked that, as an additional stand-by for the first fortnight of this operation, the 3rd Recce Regiment supplied twelve wireless Contact Detachments to aid Infantry communications. The Assault Brigade Signal Instructions drawn up by Captain Macbay, R. Signals, and issued with the Operation Order, occupied, with appendixes, thirty-nine pages of foolscap !

on his bugle. The Admiral and General acknowledged it ; it was a stirring gesture.

Meanwhile the Assault Companies were making hard for their beaches. Shells were noticed to be falling among the waves and the craft, and there was no point in hanging back now where one hit meant writing off a whole crowded craft. It was a tense journey, that first bold approach to the shore. The general feeling, one that marked everything to do with D-day, was that nothing was impossible for a force that could be mounted in the might that was evident all around.[1] But though this seemed to bode well for a successful battle it did not go so far towards removing the purely personal sense of mortality. However, most minds were occupied by the scene ahead, where, apart from drifts of smoke and flashes and great clouds of dirt as the full weight of our shells and rockets landed, the Calvados coast was clear.

From the sea there was nothing much to be seen except a dreary row of boarding-houses along the featureless flat front, thickening up on the left into Riva Bella and the little port of Ouistreham with its church-tower and lighthouse, at the mouth of the Orne, and on the right into the small seaside resorts of Lion and Luc-sur-Mer. (Was it Burghead lighthouse after all, or the Sussex shore, and the whole thing a bad joke—just a stage nearer the actual invasion ? The situation was so familiar that this thought must have crossed every mind, to be quickly rejected.) The houses joining Riva Bella and Lion-sur-Mer were marked on the map as La Brèche. It was appropriate that *Queen Red* and *White* Beaches should have been opposite La Brèche ; in French it means the breach ! Those houses were built along two lateral roads, the first narrow and backing the beach, the second broad, two hundred yards inland. They were connected all along the front by a series of narrow roads, which, once cleared, would serve as beach exits.

Queen White was on the right, the first objective of the South Lancs. There ! That looked like the house with the turret shown on the photograph just to the right of *White* Beach, between exits 10 and 11. And that was surely the flat-roofed " sun-trap "

---

[1] The common expression of this in plain English was : " This'll shake the bastards ! " It was spoken with a cheerful note of confidence.

of a modern house at the end of *Red* Beach. Then *that* must be the strong-point Cod !

In one of the craft making for *Red* Beach was " A " Company Commander of the East Yorks, Major C. K. King, known widely in the Division as " Banger." He held the attention of the men who were lucky enough to be in his craft by reading them the famous passages from *King Henry V*. Minds that would otherwise have been uneasy with natural apprehensions were filled with the encouragement of King Harry :

> " On, on, you noble English !
> Whose blood is fet from fathers of war-proof,
> Fathers that, like so many Alexanders,
> Have in these parts from morn till even fought,
> And sheath'd their swords for lack of argument :
> Be copy now to men of grosser blood
> And teach them how to war !
>   The game's afoot :
> Follow your spirit. . . ."

Major King's action was akin to Wolfe's at Quebec almost 200 years before, and worthy to be remembered with it.[1]

Advancing in front of the four Infantry Companies, the crews of the D-D Shermans, A and B Squadrons of the 13th/18th Hussars, had reached a position 5,000 yards off-shore where they thought their tanks stood a chance of swimming for it. (In less heavy seas they would have been launched 7,000 yards out.) All fifteen tanks of A Squadron and nine tanks of B Squadron struck out for the shore. Rear-Admiral Talbot has paid a just tribute to " the determination of these gallant men to use their amphibious tanks in the manner for which they had been designed."

Forward with this group was an F.O.O. from each of the Field Regiments. The job of these F.O.O.s was to observe the fire of their regiments upon the selected part of the beach strong-point *Cod* on the East Yorks' beach, and make any necessary

[1] That " Banger " had in mind the image of Wolfe reading Gray's *Elegy* seems certain, since Quebec is first among the battle honours of the East Yorkshire Regiment, and September 13th is always celebrated by its members.

corrections. The L C Ps of 33rd and 76th Field Regiments were sunk, but the F.O.O. of 33rd Field Regiment was picked up by the L C P of the 7th Field Regiment, and the fire of the Divisional Artillery was observed from that craft.[1] The other F.O.O., Captain "Jo" Daniel, R.A., was killed.

Close behind the swimming tanks were the assaulting infantry and also L C Ts containing the flails, bulldozers and armoured vehicles, R.E., of the eight gapping teams and four obstacle-clearing teams. Behind them were the Rocket Craft and then the Divisional Artillery. It was now past seven o'clock and H-hour was 7.25. Steadily they drove on together.

Captain Lyon, of A Squadron, records : "The seaworthy quality of the Sherman D-D astonished me, but it was necessary to adopt a zigzag course to avoid getting beam on to the tide. The Squadron appeared to me to be keeping excellent station." Nevertheless they were retarded some five minutes by the rough sea. This may have been the reason for the A.V.R.E. flotilla's attempt to overtake, driving right across the port bows of A Squadron. The beach was now obscured by bombing and artillery concentrations, and about ten per cent of the drenching rocket-fire from the L C T (R)—whose decks grew red-hot—was observed to fall short. It caused the A.V.R.E. flotilla to go full astern together, and, when they overtook the Shermans a second time, led to the ramming of two A Squadron D-Ds. One of the victims, Captain Denny, reported : "At about 800 yards I was rammed by an L C T, and we sank immediately, the tank going over on its beam and sinking for about 25 feet, ending upside down. Although the crews were wearing A.T.E.A. and Mae Wests, they never appeared again, as I did not see them during the 30 minutes I was in the water." This same officer, describing the short range of some of the unmistakable rocket concentrations which fell among them, says : " The Squadron kept good station in spite of these intrusions." The moment the squadrons beached the enemy opened fire, and four tanks were disabled. Five more were swamped in the breakers. Thus there were only five effective Shermans on the East Yorks' beach and eight on *White* Beach,

[1] The one " eye " left open to spot for the Artillery worked admirably considering that " cramped conditions are aggravated by the fact that nearly everyone, including the Marines and myself, is being violently sick," according to the log kept by Captain H. W. Bruce, M.C., R.A.

though the latter were joined forty minutes later by the five that had been unable to launch at sea.

The idea was that the D-D Shermans should land just ahead of the Assault Infantry Companies and R.E. gapping teams and keep the enemy's heads down, while the Infantry went in at H-hour to finish off the enemy, enabling the gapping teams to work undisturbed at least by enemy small-arms fire. But the D-Ds had been slowed down by the heavy sea, and they all landed roughly together at 7.30. Already the front line of obstacles was awash. The tide was rising fast, flowing up over the sand at a visible pace. And those armoured vehicles, R.E., that landed ahead of the D-D tanks and Infantry were some minutes without the close support planned. They were not likely to give that a second thought. This was the time for calm thinking and swift action. To clear the beach of those obstructions, both the inanimate and the very animate, was the job ; to make haste, for the next wave of men would break and flood up across the sand in a few minutes, and succeeding waves would develop the regularity of Atlantic rollers advancing over the shore.

These R.E. gapping and obstacle-clearing teams all succeeded in disembarking with the exception of one L C T carrying a gapping team for *White* Beach. After the first flail was discharged from this craft a close enemy anti-tank gun hit the second flail, which jammed on the ramp door, while a second hit caused an explosion aboard and killed Lieutenant-Colonel A. D. B. Cocks, Commander of 5 Assault Regiment, R.E., the man who was in command of all beach clearance and gapping teams.

Our terrific barrage and bombardment " lifted " on ahead as our Infantry assaulted the beach defences : and just as the East Yorks and the South Lancs felt the relief of the solid sands under their feet, the Germans were emerging from the solid and comfortably furnished underground shelters, which seem to have given them good protection from everything but shock. Within a few minutes the enemy was applying the fire of rifle, machine-gun, mortar and field gun to *Queen* Beach, particularly to *Red*, opposite the *Cod* strong-point. The South Lancs on the right had severe casualties in A Company, Major Harward, the

Company Commander, being mortally wounded,[1] and one of his subalterns, Allen, killed breaching the beach wire. They sent C Company left to assist the East Yorks in the reduction of *Cod*, while Lieutenant R. W. Pearce, M.C., took command of A Company and directed it right towards Lion-sur-Mer. On this beach the gapping teams had opened four exits at the end of an hour, despite heavy casualties in men and tanks.

On *Red* Beach C Company of the South Lancs were engaging the active *Cod*, when the H.Q. and remaining companies of the South Lancs landed almost on the strong-point. B Company went in to help them, and Major Harrison, their Commander, was killed immediately. So was Bell-Walker, who assumed command and led an attack on a pillbox. Battalion H.Q. moved up towards the sand-dunes near an 88-mm. position, and the Battalion Commander, Lieutenant-Colonel R. P. H. Burbury, was killed by a sniper's bullet as he directed this assault.

The *Red* Beach gapping teams suffered crippling enemy fire, lost most of their tanks and were nearly all reduced to clearance by hand. Their first two exits became blocked by damaged tanks. They managed to open one gap with lateral communications after an hour and a half, and two more within the next quarter of an hour. No mines were found on the beach itself, though the exits and strips behind the dunes and beside the streets were thickly inlaid with them.

The obstacle-clearing teams fared worse. Their work was more formidable even than they had expected ; their first discovery was that every ramp-type obstacle and a number of the stakes, steel hedgehogs and concrete tetrahedra were armed with a Tellermine or Anti-Aircraft shell with push-igniter to operate against the first craft that fouled them. The situation was aggravated by the high tide and swell. By the time the un-armoured element of the obstacle-clearing teams got ashore the seaward ramps stood in six to eight feet of water and were about to be submerged. Enemy small arms were still active and mortar-fire was coming down. Men on *Red* Beach were swimming in an effort to remove the mines and shells, and a number were dis-

---

[1] Each battalion, landed with its M.O. and a section from its Brigade Field Ambulance. The light sections of the two Beach Group F.D.S.s set up two Beach Dressing Stations on each beach, where they passed 24 very harassing hours.

lodged and dropped to the bottom. Then, as more L C T ran ashore, it became impossible to work at the deep obstacles. Fortunately it had become evident that the obstacles were not preventing the discharge of craft and that some of the mines were failing to detonate.

During these early tasks on the beach the casualties to the flails, A.Vs., R.E., and bulldozers amounted to 50 per cent of the machines. 5 Assault Regiment, R.E., suffered heavy casualties amongst their officers, and 629 Field Squadron lost nearly 20 per cent of their men, some of whom were drowned. From among the Division's own engineers, 246 Field Company, affiliated as usual to 8 Brigade, landed one assault demolition team with each of the assault companies of Infantry and a mine-clearance team with each of the four reserve companies of those two battalions. It was one of the platoons of 246 Field Company, landing at five minutes past eight, that made the first exit off *White* Beach with a borrowed armoured bulldozer, before proceeding, according to plan, to search and clear and mark a forward route to Hermanville. The East Yorks, supported by the surviving tanks of B Squadron of 13th/18th Hussars, and the South Lancs supported by the survivors of A Squadron, both accompanied by their affiliated F.O.O.s of the 76th Field Regiment and with one F.O.O. of the 33rd Field Regiment, had begun the advance inland.

The hinterland was not hard to defend. It is quite easy to visualise, especially easy for those who saw it then : the wind was very fresh, and, blowing the clouds fast across the sky, it uncovered the sun at intervals throughout the day. The effect was that the prepared, sensitive minds of the men were exposed to a series of flashlight photographs that were developed on the spot and printed indelibly.

Behind *Red* and *White* Beaches and the houses scattered all along the front lay a strip of marshland impassable to vehicles. This extended back some 500 yards and then gave way to an area covered with orchards, where the green cornfields were hedged and the hedges were buttressed by poplars and elms. These and the apple-trees almost hid Hermanville, a straggling little village about a mile from the sea. The one road connecting it with the coast ran back from the extreme right of *White* Beach.[1]

[1] See front end-papers and p. 52.

It may be seen, therefore, why every vehicle coming ashore had to move to the right at the first lateral and then keep to this main Hermanville road until it was over the marsh-strip. It was possible to deploy into the orchards and farmyards on either side of the road once this strip was crossed. Through Hermanville passed a main lateral road running parallel with the beach. Following it out to the left from Hermanville, it bent slightly right into Colleville[1] and then sloped gradually down through St. Aubin-d'Arquenay to the Orne bridges at Bénouville. Behind this lateral road was the Periers-sur-le-Dan feature, which was rather a rise than a ridge, although *Morris* and *Hillman*, the 10·5 cm. battery and Battalion H.Q. strong-points set into it, dominated the beaches. This feature was quite bare, so that *Morris* and *Hillman* relied for concealment on the lie of the land, which nowhere exceeded 61 metres above sea-level. This " Periers feature " was the furthest objective of 8 Brigade.

Beyond lay Caen and the objectives of 185 Brigade. Over the Periers ridge the road descended into a gully containing a small brook that ran into the Caen Canal at Beauregard. The road crossed the brook, followed it through the adjacent villages of Beuville and Biéville, rising steeply into Lebisey Wood. We need trace it no further : it crossed to " Hill 64 " and fell down into Caen, which was not more than about nine miles inland. From the sea the Caen Canal and the Orne gradually cut in across the Division's front diagonally from the left. A secondary road ran along the near bank of the canal from Ouistreham into Caen. Across the Orne valley high ground rose on all sides, the Bois de Bavent overlooking the airborne landing area, and to the south the hills of Normandy.

On the beaches organised German opposition had been overcome. There was still promiscuous sniping and often heavy shelling along the foreshore. But 8 Brigade's advance inland had begun, and all the time the landing-craft of " S " Force were beaching hard. It was inspiring to watch those skippers navigating, avoiding the mined obstacles if they could, but anyway driving " full ahead together " for the shore-line ; they spared

---

[1] Originally Colleville-sur-Orne, this fair village has, in July, 1946, honoured us by rechristening itself Colleville-de-Montgomery. Its former title was not particularly appropriate, since it stands two or three kilometres from the bank of the river Orne.

no effort to give " their " troops a " dry " landing.   German
gunners knew the range and hit several of those craft before
they were able to unload and sail back to England, their crews
supremely proud of the triangular sign their craft bore.

The whole of the 1st Battalion of the Suffolks (8 Brigade's
Reserve Battalion) landed in one flight from twenty-five L C A,
and quickly formed up.   By nine o'clock the South Lancs had
taken Hermanville from the Germans and established their
Battalion H.Q. there.   (Their A Company had continued
their advance along the coast into Lion, and it was not until
late in the day that they were extricated from street fighting !)
By 9.30 the Suffolks had assembled near Hermanville, and were
advancing left into Colleville.

Meanwhile the 76th Field Regiment, R.A., and Commandos
of 1 SS Brigade had landed on the tail of the Suffolks ; 4 Commando moved east along the sea-front to destroy an enemy
coastal defence battery in Ouistreham and rid the town of the
enemy, while the rest of the SS Brigade, under Brigadier Lord
Lovat, M.C., made off for the bridges at Bénouville to join the
6th Airborne Division.   The signal that those bridges were taken
intact had already been intercepted and set everyone's spirits
soaring.

On completion of the " run-in " shoot by the Divisional
Artillery, their flotillas had to cruise off-shore until the guns
could be landed.   The 76th Field Regiment were first ashore and
immediately went into action on *Red* Beach.   One of their craft
was hit five times, struck two mines and caught fire while still
loaded.[1]   But the rest of the regiment got on to the beach,
where they were in action five hours before moving to a gun-
position inland.   Their quick response to calls for fire were to the
credit of the Gunners in a position that was not designed for
easy gun control ; yet they only complained that there weren't
enough calls for fire !   Craft continued to deposit men and
vehicles amongst the guns as they fired.   Loud-speaker wires
would have been cut into small pieces, and as fire-orders came

[1] The craft was out of control and the skipper was obliged to order " Abandon ship."
Three of the troop's guns were still serviceable, however, and Lieutenant Morrall
was unable to abandon them. The gunners remained with the guns and luckily the
craft ran ashore. They succeeded in running off not merely the undamaged guns,
but a goodly prize of naval rum.

down from the F.O.O.s now advancing inland they were relayed to each gun by wireless, though owing to the general din and confusion all round, runners from each detachment were being used. At the same time the tide was running in swiftly over the flat sand and the guns were soon standing in some feet of surf. Craft were still beaching all round, and one, with fires aboard and steering-gear knocked out, was swept along the beach, hitting two guns and destroying their water-proofing shutes. They continued firing, but the engines were "drowned." All the time the F.O.O.s were reporting good progress.

This was the position when the Mayor of Colleville himself arrived on the beach to welcome the invaders. He judged it a suitable occasion to wear a gleaming fireman's helmet, not unlike an inverted brass coal-scuttle. In such circumstances (as in a nightmare) nothing seemed incongruous.

The 76th Field Regiment landed primarily in support of 8 Brigade. Until they landed the Infantry depended for support upon the Navy and 5 (Independent) R.M. Armoured Support Battery, whose 16 Centaurs with 95-mm. guns would have been available at H plus five minutes, but only 50 per cent managed to get ashore and they could not get in touch with the F.O.O.s. They and the 33rd Field Regiment were grouped under command of Lieutenant-Colonel Mervyn Foster, R.A., the Commanding Officer of the 76th Field Regiment. 33rd Field Regiment normally supported 9 Brigade, the Reserve Brigade. They were therefore able to join first 76th Field Regiment, then, for 185 Brigade's advance, the 7th Field Regiment, until finally 9 Brigade landed. At that time one battery of the 76th Field Regiment would be in direct support of the 6th Airborne Division, with the remainder of the regiment "on call" to protect the Orne bridges against enemy counter-attack. The 33rd Field Regiment landed half an hour after the 76th and joined them in action on the beach. Then 185 Brigade came ashore.

(ii)

THE FOLLOW-THROUGH

Three large landing-craft of 185, the Intermediate Brigade, were hit before disembarkation, and there were casualties between the beach and the Brigade Assembly Area north of Hermanville. The laden men struggled ashore in four feet of water, clinging to ropes run out to the beach by the Navy. But by 11 o'clock the three infantry battalions were assembled inland and ready, and Brigade H.Q. was established in Hermanville. The King's Shropshire Light Infantry were in the middle, with the Royal Norfolks on the left and the Royal Warwicks on the right. The K.S.L.I. were to mount the tanks of the Staffordshire Yeomanry, from 27 Armoured Brigade, and advance along the main axis to secure Caen as quickly as possible. The Norfolks on the left and Warwicks on the right were to mop up and secure objectives captured by the mobile column. But there was no sign of the Staffordshire Yeomanry, who were caught on the beach, which, so far from being cleared, was becoming more tightly congested as the tide came in. And in the Assembly Area the two most westerly companies of the Warwicks came under accurate machine-gun fire from German positions towards Lion and Cresserons. Lieutenant-Colonel H. O. S. Herdon, their Commander, prepared a plan for attacking these positions, subject to the approval of the Brigade Commander, Brigadier K. P. Smith, O.B.E.

The Brigadier was in an unhappy dilemma : whether to launch the assault on foot or wait for the tanks. The General's order was that " this advance will be carried out with speed and boldness so that the enemy's local reserves can be overcome quickly and the Brigade established on its objective ready to meet counter-attacks by reserve formations which may develop towards evening on D-day." The question was whether more speed might not be attained by waiting for the tanks than by committing the troops to an attack on foot. Available intelligence was that on the left the East Yorks were still moving across the open marshy ground under observation and mortar-fire, in their advance on the enemy position *Sole* behind Riva Bella, that the Suffolks had cleared Colleville without much trouble, as the Commandos had just done some of the work on their way through to the bridges. But the Suffolks had still to attack *Morris* and *Hillman,* which stood right in the way of the Norfolk advance.

At midday Lieutenant-Colonel F. J. Maurice, commanding the K.S.L.I., reported to Brigadier Smith that only about one and a half squadrons of the Stafford Yeomanry were clear of the beaches, and that a large minefield apparently covered the right flank of Hermanville across the axis of advance originally planned for the tanks. They could not leave the road on account of the bog and were consequently nose to tail and all stationary whenever there was a hold-up ahead. Brigadier Smith therefore ordered the K.S.L.I. to advance on foot along the main axis, Hermanville-Beuville-Caen, immediately, the Stafford Yeomanry to " marry-up " as soon as possible. The Norfolks were to wait in Colleville, to pass through the Suffolks as soon as *Morris* and *Hillman* were clear.

Lieutenant-Colonel N. P. H. Tapp, R.A., was at this " Order Group." He had been watching his regiment, the 7th Field Regiment, as, shortly after beaching, they roared past Hermanville cross-roads to deploy just to the south in the open fields, and just in front of the South Lancs, the southernmost infantry in the area. The infantry, feeling the strain and reaction from their first attacks on the beach positions, were surprised, relieved, and greatly cheered at this spectacle. In the Colonel's words : " I do not know if the Gunners knew they were the foremost troops at that time. They were probably better disposed to enjoy the honour in retrospect ! I grew more and more cheerful as I counted the guns and vehicles going past,[1] and by 12 o'clock was able to say to the Brigadier : ' The 7th Field Regiment is in action with all its assault vehicles and ready to support its affiliated tanks and infantry.' "

At 12.15 Brigadier Smith received intelligence of enemy

[1] Explaining how " with one or two very helpful Military Policemen and an increasingly hoarse voice " the congestion difficulties had been overcome, the Second-in-Command of the Regiment said : " There was a natural and very correct reluctance to leave the track because of the danger of mines. But from my previous observations, I was able to direct the guns in Infantry tracks through the corn. Although this caused words with a Sapper officer, none of the guns was blown up and they got through much more quickly."

tanks in front of Caen, of heavy enemy fire from Periers-sur-le-
Dan, and of stiff enemy opposition to the Canadians on the
right flank. He ordered the Warwicks to disengage the enemy
in their original Assembly Area and occupy the area left by the
Norfolks. The K.S.L.I. moved off up the Periers ridge. In them,
they knew, was centred the whole hope of the Division : theirs
was the central thrust of the assault, and aimed at Caen. They
soon dealt with the machine-guns and mortars that opposed
them on either side of the cross-roads just forward of the crest.
But before we can follow them further we had better be clear
about the beach situation and the extent of the beach-head
secured by 8 Brigade.

The clearing of the beach-exits proved to be about the
hardest and most heart-breaking job of the invasion. No sooner
had one crisis been overcome than another arose. The tide came
up quickly, and the beach was eventually reduced to a width of
10 yards instead of the 30 yards anticipated. This meant that
vehicles had to land immediately facing one of the exits if they
were to get off the beach ; there was not much scope for lateral
movement. The exits were no longer marked, however, by the
coloured windsocks that the Navy knew and made for. During
one period of heavy enemy shelling, from inland and from the
coastal batteries along the left flank, it was obvious that the
Germans were ranging both on the windsocks and on the sixty
barrage balloons brought over for beach anti-aircraft defence,
some of which had already been cut adrift. The Divisional
Commander ordered the immediate loosing of the remainder.

The problems were innumerable, but a main one was the
soft strip of sand at the top of the beach over which bridging
vehicles and many others had to be towed by Beach Section
recovery teams ; this amongst all the welter of transport edging
towards the exits, stranded landing-craft, derelict D-D tanks
and Armoured Vehicles, R.E., and, not least, over fifty self-
propelled guns (including the eight of the 5th R.M. Battery) all
firing from the water's edge, and having to advance up the
beach at one point when they looked like getting out of their
depth. Finally, blockages were frequently caused *beyond* the
exits by tracked vehicles losing their tracks on mines between
the exits and first lateral, and later on, when there was a hold-up

on the road across the marsh, a continuous column extended nose to tail right back into the exits and was itself the cause of obstruction to tanks not yet clear of the beach.

If more were needed to aggravate a critical situation, the Commander of 5 Assault Regiment, R.E., had been killed at H-hour, and the Commander of 5 Beach Group was killed some hours later, as he was carrying out a reconnaissance of the westerly beaches. Major Carse, who had commanded the Battle School in quiet Moffat, took over command of 5 Beach Group. For the first four and a half hours of the assault craft had been beaching to time, and the majority had been able to discharge immediately. Then it was decided to hold up all beaching for half an hour to clear the beach. This action was justified. When beaching was resumed, the tide was ebbing and the exits were clear.

8 Brigade were still attacking strongly defended positions. The East Yorks found resistance at *Sole* much fiercer than had been anticipated. Incidentally, they were not the first to reach it. The chronicler of the 2nd Middlesex, relating the action of their A (machine-gun) Company, writes : " No. 4 Platoon, under Lieutenant Milne, were reorganised and went off via Colleville to strong-point *Sole*, expecting to find the East Yorks Battalion H.Q. Instead, the leading carrier came under fire from a light anti-tank gun." However, the East Yorks had cleared *Sole* by 1 o'clock and the F.O.O. with C Company, Captain Featherstone, established his party in an O.P. on the enemy position. They were " slightly embarrassed by the appearance of eighty Germans surrendering from a dug-out. A wide burst of Sten-gun fire at the leading German, before it was clear what their intentions were, hastened the process. A section of the East Yorks were asked to take the Germans in charge." The East Yorks now made preparations for the attack on the gun position at *Daimler*. Their Commander, Lieutenant-Colonel C. F. Hutchinson, was caught by enemy mortar fire in a sunken lane, wounded, and had to be evacuated.

By 1 o'clock the 10·5 cm. battery *Morris* had fallen to the Suffolks. It had been " softened-up " by the six-inch guns of the cruiser H.M.S. *Dragon*, and the R.A.F. had attended to it. As soon as the F.O.O. of 76th Field Regiment started ranging to register it, a white flag was hoisted and the sixty-seven German gunners emerged with their hands up. The advance began on *Hillman*. Captain Ryley, commanding the company which was to attack *Hillman*, received an unpleasant shock as he crawled forward on his reconnaissance. It had not been clear from air photographs that there were deep concrete shelters on the position, although the pillboxes, steel cupolas and emplacements were easily recognisable. Fire from a cruiser was never brought down, as the F.O.B. had been knocked out earlier. Nor was there any sign that the position had ever been attacked from the air.

The breaching platoon, under Mike Russell of D Company, and Lieutenant Heal, R.E., crawled forward through the corn under cover of H.E. and smoke from the Artillery, breached the two belts of wire and cleared a track through the enemy mine-field, " working just as if they were on training and yet within 50 yards of the enemy," wrote their commanding officer, Lieutenant-Colonel R. E. Goodwin. One section crossed the gap and immediately came under heavy machine-gun fire from one of the cupolas. The section commander, Corporal Jones, was killed as he tried to work his section forward. The Platoon Commander, Lieutenant Powell, came forward with a PIAT team to deal with the cupola. A message was sent back to inform Captain Ryley that they were pinned down, but the first runner was killed on the way. Another Artillery concentration was brought down, and Ryley led the rest of the Company in attack, but only he, Lieutenants Tooley and Powell and Corporal Stares got through the gap. They took a few prisoners, but most of the enemy had withdrawn into the concrete shelters. Sergeant Lankester went forward to join Powell and found Tooley and Corporal Stares mortally wounded. Moving back to report the situation, Captain Ryley was killed, and Powell took command of the Company.

The Divisional Commander came to see what progress had been made.[1] " I explained the situation," wrote Colonel

[1] General Rennie was ashore by 10.30 a.m. ; unlike the situation at Suvla with Mahon, Stopford and Hammersley, the difficulty lay in restraining him from risking the dangers of the front-line. Later in the morning the Corps Commander was seen walking in Hermanville. Neither wore a steel helmet. At 5 o'clock that afternoon General Rennie was able to inform Brigadier Smith that he supposed St. Aubin to be clear since he had just driven through it in his jeep !

Goodwin, " and he said we must capture the strong-point before dark, so that we should be dug-in on our consolidation positions before the enemy armour, that was reported to be in the neighbourhood, could attack at first light." 185 Brigade had encountered the 2nd Battalion of 192 Panzer Grenadier Regiment supported by self-propelled guns on the Periers ridge. Already the Division was face to face with the 21st Panzer Division, thought to have been from 10 to 30 miles south of Caen.[1]

An additional squadron from the Stafford Yeomanry were now going in with the Suffolks to clean up *Hillman*. The minefield gap was widened and safely crossed after another five minutes' artillery bombardment. Fifty prisoners were taken, though there was a grisly business in the deep shelters and galleries ; some Germans fought on to the bitter end, and had to be blown out of their emplacements by heavy explosive charges laid by the battalion pioneers. Gradually resistance decreased and the success signal was given at a quarter-past eight in the evening. It was not till 6.45 the next morning that the commander of 736 Coastal Defence Regiment, a full colonel, emerged with three of his officers and seventy other ranks from a concealed shelter that had been overlooked the previous night ! [2]

The East Yorks, supported by B Squadron of the 13th/18th Hussars, the 76th Field Regiment and the Self-Propelled troop of 67 Anti-Tank Battery, R.A. (which had been ashore since 8.15 that morning), had captured the 75-mm. battery *Daimler* by 6 p.m. Seventy prisoners from the coastal artillery battalion were taken, with several 40-mm. anti-aircraft guns. This com-

[1] This battalion had moved into Buron three weeks before the assault, and, merely in accordance with Rommel's general policy, came right forward to the Periers ridge on the evening of 5 June. Lieutenant-General Edgar Feuchtinger, the Commander of 21 Panzer Div, came directly under Von Rundstedt's command. Though Rundstedt passed the buck to the defunct Führer in his interview with Major Shulman in October, 1945, it remains true that Feuchtinger got not a word from him till 7 a.m. on D-day, and no operational order till 10 a.m. : Rundstedt needed no higher authority to commit 21 Panzer Div. It was the one Division in immediate reserve capable of affecting the battle, having about 170 armoured fighting vehicles. At 10 a.m. Feuchtinger had decided to wait no longer, and attack the airborne troops immediately, but at 10 a.m. " I was ordered to stop the move of my tanks against the Allied Airborne troops, and to turn west and aid the forces protecting Caen "—i.e. against the 3rd Division.

[2] With that, 716 Infantry Division, of which 736 was the right-hand Regiment, practically dissolved as a fighting unit.

pletes the 8 Brigade background to the advance of 185 Brigade that afternoon.

The K.S.L.I. had begun their thrust for Caen, advancing over the Periers ridge in order of Companies X, W, Y, Z, and with C Squadron of the Stafford Yeomanry and F.O.O.s of both the 7th and 33rd Field Regiments in support. The Battery Commander with Colonel Maurice was Major Ian Rae, who was with the battalion throughout the campaign, earning their tribute : " of the greatest ability, courage and cheerfulness, he was to be a tower of strength to each successive Commanding Officer." The first crest was reached despite heavy enemy shelling, mortaring and sniping from Germans concealed in the corn. An officer of the K.S.L.I. described how at one point they were driven to take cover, and how, looking round and extremely frightened, he saw Colonel Maurice walking up the middle of the road, " playing with the chin-strap of his helmet as he always did . . . I got up. The example spread, and in a few minutes the men were moving forward steadily."

The route now led down into the gully across the brook at Pont du Ponchel and along to the hamlet Le Homme, past Beuville village on the left to Biéville on the green slope to the right, then on up to Lebisey. On the Periers crest you had a fine view of the country up to Lebisey, and you knew that Caen lay only a couple of miles beyond in the Orne dip. But the descent from the Periers crest was not unopposed. The rear slope was commanded by a battery of six Russian 12·2 cm. howitzers, well sited on that same reverse slope over on the right just north of Periers. It was hoped that the heavy bombers before H-hour and the fighter bombers shortly after H-hour would have dealt with this known battery : " but it was not only alive, it was kicking hard." Tanks and Support Company vehicles were held up at the ridge. Already one of the F.O.O.s, Captain Gower, with the Stafford Yeomanry, had been killed when his Sherman was knocked out. Immediately (it was 2.25 p.m.) Colonel Maurice ordered Major Wheelock with Z Company to attack this battery over on the right flank. And the advancing force was further depleted at this point when Lieutenant-Colonel J. A. Eadie, commanding the Stafford Yeomanry, had to divert A Squadron to aid the Suffolks in the reduction of *Hillman*. But

B Squadron and also B (Self-Propelled) Troop of 41 Anti-Tank Battery, caught up with C Squadron and the remaining companies of K.S.L.I. Colonel Eadie then ordered B Squadron to take up battle positions here in readiness for an outflanking attack by enemy armour. The rest pushed on swiftly as Z Company closed on the howitzers ; the German battery was encircled by wire.

Major Wheelock's company managed to drive the German gunners from their emplacements, but they went to ground and covered the wire with dense machine-gun fire. The Yeomanry Colonel directed a Regimental Shoot of the 7th Field Regiment on to them, but several times the Germans got back to their guns and continued to shell the road until stopped again by the small-arms fire of Z Company. Eventually a Pole was captured who knew the way through the wire at the back of the battery. The gunners fled into the woods, harried for some hundreds of yards by the Company. The guns were then blown up by an unnamed N.C.O. of the Divisional R.E.s, who, though badly wounded, succeeded in " spiking " them all. It was late that evening when Major Wheelock consolidated the Company. He was awarded the M.C. for his great courage during this action. Lieutenant Dixon of the Middlesex, whose machine-gun platoon was protecting Major Wheelock's exposed right flank, was mortally wounded, and his platoon was taken over by Sergeant Rawling, who on the morrow won the D.C.M.

Progress for the main body had become easier, though there were casualties from sniping in Beuville and Biéville ; the latter village was reached by 4 p.m. Y Company, under Major Steel, with a troop of tanks, was immediately sent on into Lebisey Wood, but one tank was bogged in a natural anti-tank obstacle known as *Port*, and only three tanks reached the wood. Y Company reached the front edge of the wood without loss.

The Reconnaissance Troop of the Stafford Yeomanry now reported that a squadron of about twenty-four German tanks was advancing north from Caen, moving very fast. The Yeomanry Colonel immediately asked for the release of A Squadron from *Hillman*, who arrived just in time to take up battle positions to the west of Biéville. He had left B Squadron on the Periers ridge to meet such a threat as this. There were also in position the

6-pounder anti-tank guns of the K.S.L.I. and the S-P Troop of
41 Anti-Tank Battery, R.A.

The German tanks came straight on and were engaged when
they reached the western edge of the *Port* obstacle. There were
about forty of them. Two were knocked out by the Yeomanry
and two more by the K.S.L.I. 6-pounders. The remainder
moved west over towards the thickly hedged fields round Le
Landel, followed over to our right flank by two troops of
A Squadron. As soon as they emerged, No. 1 Troop engaged and
destroyed four, and No. 4 gun of the Self-Propelled Troop of
41 Battery knocked out two, though one of their own S-Ps was
hit and a sergeant and gunner killed. Other enemy tanks swung
still more to the west and made for the high ground above
Periers, where B Squadron were waiting patiently. Three more
German tanks were destroyed and the rest quickly withdrew.
No more left the cover of the trees and hedges. They had lost
thirteen Mark IV (Special) tanks in the encounter.[1] In return
they had hit one M.10 S-P Anti-Tank gun and two Shermans,
none of which was put out of action, though there were nine
fatal casualties.[2]

Men who were wounded near-by were carried to the house
in Biéville, where Mme. Barrett and her invalid daughter lived.
The house was under heavy shellfire, but Mme Barrett was
utterly fearless and tireless in her efforts to tend our men, and,
being a trained nurse, she undoubtedly saved the lives of the
more serious casualties.

During the German counter-attack on the right, Major Steel's
men had reached the northern outskirts of Lebisey. Here they
were held up by machine-guns firing from the houses, and a party
of about forty Germans was seen making its way round the right
flank. Major Steel was killed by a machine-gun bullet ; at this

[1] 3 Br Inf Div Int Summary No. 1 : Period to 2359 hrs 7 June.
[2] This was the main outcome of the orders received by General Feuchtinger at 10 a.m.
Feuchtinger afterwards stated to Major Shulman : " Once over the River Orne I
drove north to the coast. By this time the enemy, consisting of 3 British and 3
Canadian Infantry Divisions had made astonishing progress and had occupied a
strip of high ground about ten kilometres from the sea. From here the excellent
anti-tank gunfire of the Allies knocked out eleven of my tanks before I had hardly
started. However, one battle group did manage to by-pass these guns and actually
reached the coast at Lion-sur-Mer at about seven in the evening . . . I retired to
take up a line just north of Caen. By the end of that first day my division had lost
almost 25 per cent of its tanks."

critical moment his Company lost " a man of more than normal intelligence and culture, a fine swimmer and athlete, a commander they greatly respected."

Meanwhile the Norfolks, who had been assembled near Colleville, saw that *Hillman* was an altogether more formidable obstacle than had been expected, and Lieutenant-Colonel R. H. Bellamy planned to slip his battalion past it to the left. They could not, however, go too far over to the left in case they became involved with the possible enemy-defended locality of St. Aubin d'Arquenay. Brigadier Smith arrived with the news that the K.S.L.I. had identified a unit of 21 Panzer Division in Biéville, and that the General's order was that the Norfolks would reach *Rover* before last light. *Rover* stood between Beuville and the Orne bridge, a wooded area on the top of a gentle rise, with the ground falling away more sharply beyond. There the Norfolks were firmly established by 7 p.m., though that thorn-in-the-side *Hillman* cost them about 150 casualties on the way. A single house stood on *Rover*, thereafter to be known as Norfolk House ; one would never have mistaken it for the Norfolk House in the corner of St. James's Square where Eisenhower's early planning took place.

The evening was warm and there was sunshine to cheer things up ; at about 9 p.m., while the Norfolks were preparing to withstand the impact of a probable enemy tank attack, the most heartening, splendid spectacle of that great day slowly came across the sky for all to see. Our men looked over their shoulders and gasped as their eyes brightened : for a minute the eyes of the Germans narrowed with fear. The gliders of the 6th Airlanding Brigade were towed on gracefully, majestically. At a certain point the big aircraft released them, turned, and flew back to England, disdainful of the flak the Germans were pelting up at them. It was a superb manifestation of power, precision and planning.

The Warwicks had the most reason to be delighted at this latest landing. So that they should not get mixed up in a tank battle that seemed likely to develop on the right flank, they had been directed down to the left and along the canal road, St. Aubin d'Arquenay, Bénouville, Blainville. Although several parties had by now passed along on their way down to

the bridge—the Commandos of 1 SS Brigade, " Fox " Troop of
the 92nd Light Ack-Ack Regiment, Sappers of 17 and 71 Field
Companies who were at work on the bridges, and five tanks from
B Squadron of 13th/18th Hussars—there were still numbers of
enemy, chiefly snipers, in the area of Le Port just outside of
Bénouville to the north, and they hotly engaged the Warwicks.
At the very moment the Warwicks were going in to clean up
this area the gliders descended upon it.[1] Jeeps and airborne
troops were seen in the target area. They were able to push
straight through into Bénouville and along the canal road. Major
T. G. Bundock's Company were left behind in Bénouville to
relieve the 6th Airborne Division of the defence of the Canal
Bridge, which ceased to be called *Rugger* and took the name
Pegasus Bridge.[2] The rest of the Warwicks continued to advance,
with Captain Barrett's Company leading. There was opposition
all the way from a mobile delaying force of infantry with 88-mm.
The F.O.O., Gregory, was knocked out in his tank, and so our
guns were no longer replying to these 88s. The Battalion halted
at midnight in the outskirts of Blainville and dug in.

It was not 9 Brigade's day. They landed as Reserve Brigade,
and were to have concentrated in the area of Plumetot, ready
to move rapidly down through Cazelle and Cambes to St. Contest,
to hold the ground between 185 Brigade and 9 Canadian Infantry
Brigade. Brigade H.Q. landed together at 1 p.m. and were
almost immediately struck down by a mortar bomb. Brigadier
J. C. Cunningham, M.C.,[3] with his G.III, Intelligence Officer
and a Liaison Officer, were seriously wounded, and the Intelligence
Sergeant was killed. The rest of the Brigade got ashore through
deep water and reached the Assembly Area with few casualties.
Lieutenant-Colonel I. C. Harris of the Ulster Rifles assumed
command of the Brigade until Lieutenant-Colonel A. D. G. Orr,

[1] Poles and stakes erected by the Germans to prevent just such an occurrence were
snapped like matches by the gliders. It is as well that our similar means of protection in England were not similarly tested !

[2] The French Government has agreed to perpetuate the name in tribute to the men
who first seized it and held it against several determined attacks throughout that day.

[3] The loss of a Brigade Staff and two Battalion Commanders in the first hours of the
landing cannot have been without consequence, but though there were soon further
casualties among senior officers, this crippling in no way approached that in the
disastrous landing on *V* Beach at Gallipoli, when the 29th Division lost all the
brigadiers, two brigade majors, and more than half the battalion commanders.

D.S.O., returned from liaison duty with 6th Airborne Division. Colonel Orr had been Second-in-Command of the Brigade and was now promoted Brigadier.

Over on this right flank it was early apparent that the enemy was far stronger and more active than he was expected to be. 41 (R.M.) Commando had fought their way along to the right through Lion and Luc-sur-Mer, but they were unable to overcome all resistance. As soon as one locality was mopped up, fierce fighting broke out elsewhere, if it had not been going on simultaneously. A strong-point in Lion was held by eighty Germans for two days. The Lincolns were in contact with the enemy holding Cresserons. In front it was known that one Panzer Division was holding Caen. (Another arrived on the right of the Divisional front next day.) And over the Orne the Germans were reacting violently, particularly in the Bas de Ranville, where tanks and S-P guns attacked again and again. At 1 p.m. a critical situation was saved there by diverting to Ranville the leading Commando of 1 SS Brigade, whose own operations at Franceville Plage were thus delayed.

In these circumstances the 9 Brigade plan was changed and they moved to consolidate the left of the bridgehead, covering the bridges. The Lincolns, therefore, remained where they were, the K.O.S.B.s relieved the East Yorks in St. Aubin d'Arquenay, on the main road down to the bridges, and the Ulster Rifles took up a position near Point 61 on the road over the Periers ridge.

During the evening a squadron of 5 Assault Regiment, R.E., undertook an independent operation to capture the lock-gates at Ouistreham. The Squadron Commander with ten A.V.R.E.s destroyed the concrete defences near the gates, forestalling the demolition of one of the bridges. They captured the garrison of five officers and fifty-one other ranks. Meanwhile, down on the bridges at Bénouville, the Divisional Sappers had sustained " a series of casualties that went far towards upsetting the carefully prepared rafting and bridging plans for Class 40 relief Bailey Bridges." By midnight 17 Field Company had lost their O.C. and both reconnaissance officers concerned with getting the bridging material forward. The C.R.E. was blown up on a Tellermine that night, but escaped with minor wounds and shock. The O.C. 15 Field Park Company was landed 24 hours late.

Finally, the first of the sixty-five vehicles, due to be landed
with bridging equipment that evening, arrived the next day,
16 hours late. The command of the units concerned with this
work devolved on Major Upton, who must have felt very thankful
that night that at least the original bridges were still held intact.

Forward with the K.S.L.I., Colonel Maurice had to decide
whether to reinforce Y Company up in Lebisey Wood, or whether
to consolidate in Biéville village, which in any case had not yet
been thoroughly cleared. In view of the fact that enemy tanks
were likely to attack across the open country to the right, and
our own tanks, disposed to meet them, were unable to give any
further close support, and since reserve Infantry was all employed
in consolidation, the Colonel reluctantly ordered Y Company to
withdraw to the Biéville position after dark. During this period
Captain Dane, who took over command of Y Company when
Steel was killed, was directing most effectively the fire of the
7th Field Regiment on to the enemy troops in front of his company.
They returned after dark without further loss.

The adventures of the Division that long day in the early
summer of 1944, and the achievements of so many individuals,
would, but for one consideration, prolong this chapter till it
occupied the rest of the book ;[1] the close of D-day was not like
the close of a book that could be snapped shut, its story put from
mind. When the light in the sky went out that night, the men
who had survived could not jump into bed, turn over, and go to
sleep. They had only completed Chapter Two : there would be
no relaxation, no easy oblivion, until the war ended and the
Germans surrendered. Drake knew before he sailed against the
galleons " that it is not the beginning, but the continuing of any
great matter, until it be thoroughly finished, which yieldeth the
true glory." The significance of this only dawned on the Division
in the dusk of D-day. For a year now all their thoughts and
energies had been directed to this day, and now the day was
done.

The landing, the object of so much training, yesterday the
source of so much agonising personal speculation, was to-day an
accomplished fact. By now the world would know. To have

[1] If, as it is, it seems long and complicated, D-day seemed *very* long, and the mounting
of the assault *most* complicated.

come through history's greatest amphibious assault alive was slightly unexpected. There is a revealing remark in the account of the landing by the Second-in-Command of the 7th Field Regiment, who wrote at the time : " In Hermanville, I was extremely relieved to meet my C.O. I suppose, in my fancy, I had never expected to see him again."

But though the worst was over, the breathtaking moment of landing and crossing the beach, and though men now knew where they stood, the prospects were no less grim for being more apparent. " Assaults were far from easy being and unopposed, an impression which has not perhaps been fully dispelled," wrote Admiral Ramsay to General Eisenhower, going on to express " the greatest admiration of both Navies for the magnificent bearing of the assaulting troops they put ashore. In short," he concluded, " the assaults proceeded according to plan because every single individual taking part had confidence in it." Men fight best who have confidence in their leaders. This obviously still applied to the Germans, as well as to our own men, the difference being the degree of fanaticism with which so many young Germans were determined to subordinate themselves and die. That our battalions did not exult in the number of casualties they sustained is nothing to be ashamed of. " Not that casualties were slight as the journalists gave the public to believe."[1] This day the 2nd Battalion of the K.S.L.I. lost a hundred and thirteen officers and men killed and wounded, and one of the two assaulting battalions, the South Lancs, lost a hundred and seven ; the other assault battalion, the East Yorks, lost five officers and sixty men killed, and four officers and a hundred and thirty-seven wounded. This was on the first day.

The Battalion history of the 2nd Middlesex has the point : " 2 Platoon, in support of the Suffolks, had their first casualties in Colleville, when a mortar bomb killed one and wounded six. In the life of every platoon it is a crucial moment when they get their first casualties. Most of the men had not seen active service before and had been caught up in the excitement of the landing. It was at moments like these that the calmness and experience of the platoon sergeants (in this case Sergeant Robinson) made all the difference." Going into action is the crucial test of a man's faith

[1] Admiral Ramsay, in the course of his report to General Eisenhower.

in himself and his fellows. Unless he is naturally bloodthirsty
(and how many civilian, or for that matter military, Britons are ?)
the Infantryman's personal acceptance of the terms of " action "
is probably the greatest call that will be made on his character
in the whole course of his life. And on D-day it was not only
the Infantryman who found himself in action, but the whole
Divisional Assault Group, every man. That so many thousands
of ordinary men should in our time have performed this supreme
act of faith is the most encouraging basis for the immediate
future, when a common strength of character may succeed in
averting fresh economic crises and wars.

The 3rd Division had done more than all that was expected
of them once details of enemy dispositions were known. General
Rennie wrote after he had been wounded : " Tell them how
magnificent they were . . . They exceeded my highest expectations." From an idyllic life in sunlit woods and warm Hampshire
lanes they were carried overnight across the Channel with half a
gale blowing, and proceeded in one day to disprove the Teutonic
theory of the Atlantic Wall and to form a bridgehead from which,
by nightfall, they were in no immediate danger of being dis-
lodged.[1] That was the achievement. No wonder " morale was
high " that night, and as men dug themselves a hole in the French
earth, or lit the fuse of a tin of self-heating soup and took some
biscuits from the 24-hour pack—the first acceptable meal for
most since that early breakfast on board—they chuckled together
at the thought of the look on Jerry's face as they gave him the
surprise of his life that morning.

[1] There was still the danger that the weather might prevent the naval plan for the
build-up from being carried out. Without the continuous arrival of enormous
quantities of ammunition, supplies, and the reserve formations, the bridgehead
might conceivably have been lost. It was not till 24 hours later that Admiral Ramsay
felt sure that the necessary build-up could be accomplished, as he wrote to General
Eisenhower.

Chapter Three

DEVELOPMENT: THE CAPTURE OF CAEN

IT HAD always been impossible to imagine D plus 1. Try as you would during the days of preparation, you could never project your mind beyond the great assault. The Warwicks were probably the first to succeed in doing so. They were warned in the night that after mopping up Blainville they would have to attack through Lebisey Wood (it was half orchard, half wood) and take and hold Lebisey village. So they knew what to expect of D plus 1. For everybody sleeping was rationed and fitful : through the night there were odd German bombers overhead. Few bombs fell on the Division, but there was incessant gunfire, and the Navy and Beach Ack-Ack kept the sky alight, their tracer draping itself across like strings of coloured beads, hanging a moment, vanishing. Then more hullabaloo.

It was a cold dawn, but welcome as the signal to scramble out of the grave-like hole, stamp the feet to get rid of the stiffness and the earth that had crept down between the shirt and the back. The Warwicks moved into Blainville, which gave little trouble.

There Brigadier Smith, Colonel Tapp of the 7th Field Regiment, and Colonel Herdon of the Warwicks met and prepared a simple fire-plan for the attack. By getting on to Lebisey ridge the Warwicks would greatly advance the Corps plan, which read : " Should the enemy forestall us in Caen, 3rd British Division will contain the enemy in Caen and retain the bulk of its own forces disposed for mobile ops inside the covering position." The Warwicks would attack at 8.45 a.m. A ghastly succession of misfortunes attended their gallant effort and looked like reducing this to a chapter of accidents.

The leading companies set off for the Start Line at 8 o'clock, but first A Company was delayed by snipers, then the battalion carriers and anti-tank guns were completely held up at the brook and marshy ground in the gully. H-hour for the attack was 8.45, when all three Field Regiments would be firing on targets in the wood to the left of the road, while a cruiser engaged the wood and village right of the road. Colonel Herdon decided to postpone H-hour till 9.45 and just got the message through to H.Q.R.A. in time to stop the guns. It was then discovered that B and C Companies on the Start Line were out of communication, unable to receive the message.

Adhering to the original plan, they moved forward at 8.45. With not a shell fired in support, they advanced a thousand yards up over the convex slope, their only cover the corn through which they strode. Colonel Herdon, seeing their unopposed advance, decided to dispense with the fire-plan, and commit the other two companies. 125th Panzer Grenadiers, waiting in the woods, held their fire until the forward companies were within two hundred yards, then they opened up with all their rifles and spandaus. Lieutenant Docherty's platoon managed to get to close quarters with the Germans. Later his body, with several others, was found no more than ten yards from the enemy position he had charged. The rest of the battalion were pinned down in depressions in the ground and a sunken lane. Lieutenant-Colonel Herdon, attempting to move along the front, was shot through the head and killed instantaneously.

So far the enemy had maintained a wedge of defences between the Division and the Canadians on the right, the tip still touching the coast. It was left to 8 Brigade to blunt the tip of this wedge and also clean up the bridgehead area, kicking out those Germans that remained in isolated posts, while 9 Brigade was ordered to march against the thick end of the wedge.

During the morning 8 Brigade despatched two companies from the South Lancs to secure Plumetot and Cresserons, which were duly taken soon after midday. The battalion consolidated round these two villages and one company was established in La Délivrande.[1] This company was later sent to assist 41 R.M. Commando in clearing Luc-sur-Mer, and when this had been successfully completed, the same company was sent to mop up the remaining strong-point in Lion-sur-Mer.

The Ulster Rifles, leading 9 Brigade's advance, reported the village of Periers clear, and the K.O.S.B.s formed up for the advance on Cazelle. They entered Cazelle without opposition,

---

[1] Loosely translated by the least pious members of the Division as " She who delivers the goods."

and at about 12.30 they pushed on down the road to form a firm base in Le Mesnil wood. The wood was occupied without difficulty, but there they were heavily shelled and mortared.

The chief pleasure that morning was when Spitfires of the Royal Air Force dived out of the clouds upon four Junkers 88s and destroyed the lot—to the accompaniment of encouraging epithets from the watching troops. A gunner of one of the Field Regiments fired his Browning as one of the bombers passed low overhead, and who shall dispute his spirited declaration that he had bagged the thing? It fell with the others in flames.

" Fox " Troop of the 92nd L.A.A. Regiment reached the bridge at Bénouville the previous evening, and for five days they defended it alone against air attacks. They beat off eight determined enemy formations as well as single fighter-bomber attacks. Their claim of 17 German planes shot down in that period is confirmed and must be unrivalled. Reid, the Troop Commander, was awarded the M.C. for the magnificent example he set his Troop in five days of great strain and great opportunity. The day before they were relieved, the Commanding Officer, Lieutenant-Colonel H. C. Bazeley, D.S.O., arrived with news that the remainder of their battery, which should have joined them, were aboard the Liberty Ship *Sambut* at midday on D-day, some three miles off Dover, and as the troops were lining up for dinner they were struck by what were thought to be two 16-inch shells from the Calais batteries. Before the ship was abandoned it burned fiercely and there were four large explosions, but losses to the Regiment were less than might have been : eight dead and fourteen wounded.

On D plus 1 the 76th Field Regiment were engaged almost continuously in direct support of the 6th Airborne Division, who were parrying and repelling blow after blow from the German armour.[1] In the afternoon it was reported that Tiger tanks and

[1] On June 9. Colonel Foster, commanding 76th Field Regiment, received a message from General Gale, commanding 6th Airborne Division, thanking the Regiment for support " without which we should have been unable to hold our position." The Official Report on the operations of the 6th Airborne Division in Normandy states that the R.A. link with I Corps " worked excellently while we were sharing 3 Division Artillery, and calls for fire were answered most generously and rapidly. There is no doubt whatsoever that the fire-power available within 6 Airborne Division resources was insufficient to break up a really well supported attack by tanks and infantry. It was in fact the Artillery of I Corps and 3 British Division that enabled the Division to carry out its task. . . ."

a battalion of infantry had broken through and were approaching the Orne bridge. Two Squadrons of the 13th/18th Hussars were immediately sent to reinforce the Airborne Division, and the S-P troop of 67 Anti-Tank Battery, after supporting the South Lancs to Plumetot and Cresserons, also moved down to cover the bridges. The Lincolns, whose place in 9 Brigade was temporarily taken by the Suffolks, moved to St. Aubin d'Arquenay as " long-stop." Progress on the rafts and bridges was subject to these periodic alarms, that called the Sappers off their primary tasks to man defences and provide patrols.

Major Robin Kreyer, the Second-in-Command, took command of the Warwicks when his Colonel was killed. He had a further disaster to face. The carriers and anti-tank guns of the battalion, unable to get over the obstacle from Blainville, had been sent round by road through Beuville and Biéville : as they were late, they thought the battalion would be on its objective and drove straight up the road into the wood. There they were ambushed and fired on from all sides. It was impossible to turn round, as there were walls and houses where the banks ended. Some vehicles managed to get through into the open country, where they were knocked out by anti-tank guns. Quite a number of men who got through the village took to the cornfields and managed to filter back during the night. But all the officers were killed or captured. With his vehicle party was the F.O.B. observing for the cruiser, whose support was now unobtainable. At 4 o'clock three companies of the Warwicks were reported to be surrounded, at 5 o'clock they were being attacked by tanks, and at ten past seven under heavy fire and almost out of ammunition.

The conclusion of this melancholy episode for 185 Brigade is best told by the battalion historian of the Royal Norfolks : it has the authentic reserve of the Norfolk man. " Unfortunately the Warwick attack went off at half-cock," he comments, " and they found themselves in a very difficult position, being unable to move." He goes on : " There was nothing for it, and we had to go and restore the situation. 4 p.m. was our H-hour and up we went, through the sniped village, across the anti-tank obstacle and up through the corn to the wood. It was not easy going, but we managed to get out anti-tank guns and mortars to a position

A wet landing: men of the Intermediate Brigade wade ashore from an Infantry Landing Craft.

Within the photograph:

Ch. at 088772
(Ste. Aubin d'Arquenay)

Rd. junc.
(091791)

23

22

RED

QUEEN

FACING   SOUTH

3023   R.71. 268 16AUG43

An aerial photograph issued to assaulting troops during " briefing."
Taken on a sortie of 16 August, 1943, it therefore shows none of the
beach and underwater obstacles that were erected after February, 1944.
QUEEN RED Beach is the code name for the left hand of the Division's
two assault beaches. The sea-side villas of La Brèche are clearly identifiable.
The six-figure groups are map references ; the numbers 22 and 23 refer
to possible beach-exits. The factory chimneys of Colombelles may be seen
in the middle distance. Immediately to the right of them, but out of
sight, Caen lies in the valley of the Orne.

Major-General Tom Rennie, D.S.O., O.B.E., Commander of the Assault Division on June 6th, commanded the 51st (Highland) Division in the Rhine Crossing. He was killed in the bridgehead. He was just as relaxed on Sword Beach as he appears here across the Rhine.

The crossing on a Tank Landing Craft.

The assault at Le Bréche. 1st Special Service (SS) Brigade, with Piper
Bill Millin, landed with 3rd Division, later coming under command 6th
Airborne Division.

A Tank Landing Craft hit by a shell as her ramp is lowered.

The evening of D-Day. Guns of 76 Field Regiment (self-propelled on Sherman chassis) on the first position inland, south of Colleville. Note the empty ammunition sledges (Porpoises) which were dragged over the landing-craft ramps. Gliders of the 6th Airborne Division descend beside the Orne.

A Gunner Forward Observation Officer's Party works its way inland on D-day.

6th Airborne men in position on road down to Bénouville bridges. 46 sign points to one of 3rd Division's Anti-Tank Batteries.

Left: Major-General L. G. ('Bolo') Whistler, D.S.O., arrived to command the
Division soon after Major-General Rennie was wounded in June.
Right: The Corps Commander, Lieutenant-General J. T. Crocker, C. B.,
C.B.E., D.S.O., M.C.

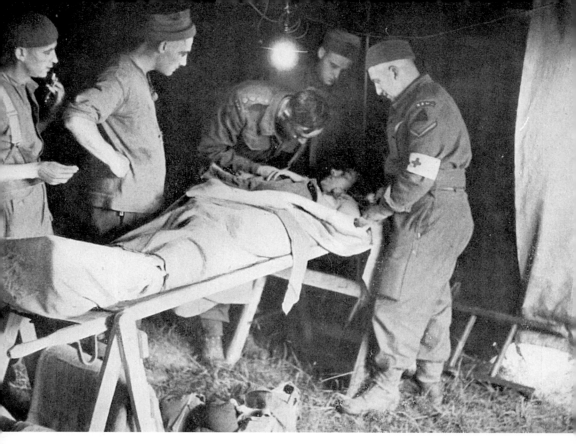

A Divisional M.O. in action.

The Divisional Concert Party entertaining troops about a mile back from the line.

The Suffolks' padre taking a voluntary service at the Divisional Club, Luc-sur-Mer.

A 6-pounder detachment of the K.O.S.B.s in Caen.

K.O.S.B.s firing a captured Hotchkiss in the area of the Caen barracks.

An historic meeting : officers of 9 Brigade and leaders of the Resistance in Caen.

At the Div Training School : camouflage for snipers.

Infantry of 185 Brigade mounted and ready for Operation *Goodwood*.

A section of Infantry advances through the *bocage*.

Joined with the Americans on the Vire-Tinchebray road.

The Commander-in-Chief decorates Sergeant Sharkey for gallantry in Operation
Goodwood.

A First Eight goes forward to the assault over the Meuse-Escaut Canal.

Sappers secure the bridge on the far bank of the Escaut Canal.

A platoon of the Warwicks resting beside the road into Holland.

An Infantryman of the Division.

A mortar crew goes into action near the bank of the Maas.

A patrol out in the river line.

A Divisional Memorial: the Overloon War Museum. From this modest museum of the grim 1944 battle seen through by the 3rd Division, the present Netherlands War and Resistance Museum has grown here.

1946 : Overloon completely resurrected. The trees and the rubble in the foreground bear witness to the battle.

Photographs by Major R. C. Baglin, M.B.E., R.A.

[*Photograph by Major R. G. Tooth, M.C., R.A.*

Across the Rhine at Rees.

A Street in Lingen.

April, 1945 : two Commanders of the 3rd Division.

The last attack.

Colleville Montgomery Hillman, rue du Suffolk Regiment.

Hillman taken! The author at Colleville Montgomery, of which he is a Citoyen d'Honneur.

from which we could give some sort of support. The forward companies were having a bad time and we suffered quite a number of casualties ; enemy tanks were also reported and altogether it was most unhealthy. At this point a big decision had to be made and the unfortunate C.O. had been authorised by the General to make it. Were we to withdraw at last light to the other side of the anti-tank obstacle, or were we to hang on where we were and hope for help at first light ? To judge from future events this decision could not have been otherwise. We pulled out, and with us what was left of the Warwicks. The time chosen was just before last light, and this choice made all the Difference, for as soon as the last troops left the area the enemy shelled it and mortared it severely, fortunately hitting the air where we had been." Just before midnight the 3rd Recce Contact detachment informed Division that the " Norfolks and family " had got back to Norfolk House.

On the right that same day what was intended to be the great German counter-attack was scarcely noticed. It had been co-ordinated soon after midnight by Feuchtinger and Kurt Meyer, Commander of Panzer Grenadier Regiment 25, the right regiment of 12 SS Panzer Division. Meyer looked at the map and said to Feuchtinger : " Little fish ! We'll throw them back into the sea in the morning." But first they had to catch their fish. And when they tried, they found them not so undersized after all. " We decided to drive towards Douvres," stated Feuchtinger, " and 12 SS was to take up assembly positions during the night. Artillery fire was so great that a proper co-ordination of this attack was impossible. Meyer did make a short spurt with some 50 tanks but was driven back. He never reached the start line from which our combined attack was to begin."

In the late afternoon the K.O.S.B.s were suffering heavy shell and mortar fire in Le Mesnil wood when the Ulster Rifles passed through them to attack Cambes, a small, thickly wooded village on the right of the Divisional front. D Company, commanded by John Aldworth, were the vanguard of the battalion, and a squadron of the East Riding Yeomanry were in support. Nothing was known of the enemy's dispositions as the Cambes wood and park were surrounded by stone walls some ten feet high. The approach was costly on account of mortaring and sniping from the woods. Aldworth led two platoons into the left side of the woods and Captain Montgomery took the other two platoons into the right. They immediately encountered cross-fire from machine-guns. " When his Company was forced to withdraw, John did not return with them. When the battalion took the wood two days later, he was found lying at the head of his men, having penetrated deeper into the wood than anyone else. Within a yard or two of him were a number of SS Stormtroopers lying dead." Owing to the high walls and thickness of the wood, the tanks were unable to give any effective support, and the Battalion was ordered to withdraw to Le Mesnil until its attack could be supported by a much greater weight of artillery.

The next day the 2nd Battalion of the Royal Ulster Rifles and the 1st Battalion of Panzer Grenadier Regiment 25 sent fighting patrols into each other's positions, while Colonel Harris of the Ulsters, with Colonel Hussey of the 33rd Field Regiment, carried out a reconnaissance for the attack on the morrow. 25 P.G.R. were the right battalion of 12 SS Panzer Division which had been escorted from the Seine by the Allied Air Force on D-day, but which was nevertheless a formidable division, with officers and senior N.C.O.s all recruited from the Hitler Youth reserves : their dead were found to be wearing an acorn sign and the name Adolf Hitler on their sleeves.

In the attack on June 9th the Ulster Rifles conducted themselves with great gallantry. The intention of the Commanding Officer was simple and direct : " 2nd Bn. The Royal Ulster Rifles will capture and consolidate Cambes." This time the attack was to be launched from Anisy, a village further over to the right, about 1,500 yards north-west of Cambes, with which it was connected by a dusty borderless track over completely exposed ground. At 3.15 p.m., preceded by a series of concentrations from the Divisional Artillery and a Cruiser of the Royal Navy, A and B Companies crossed the Start-line, with the Battalion O Group behind A Company. The men were well spaced out and advanced in good order, direction being steadied by the Colonel from the left. " As the Companies reached the ridge some 1,100 yards from the objective, whence they could be permanently observed by the enemy, they came under a heavy barrage of mortar and shell-fire accompanied by machine-gun fire. The Commanding Officer of the East Riding Yeomanry, who had fought with the Guards, observing the advance from the Start-line, said to himself : ' This is where they get to ground, and the attack is held up.' To his astonishment, the Battalion continued to advance in open order, keeping perfect distance. " Certainly the companies advanced through what appeared to be an impassable barrage showing about as much concern as they did on a field-firing exercise."

Men were falling all round, but the advance continued. A Company under Major Tighe-Wood were particularly hard hit, losing all three platoon commanders and a platoon sergeant. But Tighe-Wood succeeded in establishing his company on their objective and inspired everybody with his cool determination. Corporal O'Reilly, finding himself the senior person in his platoon, took command in the difficult period that followed. In the same company, Rifleman Miller, finding his section leaderless, led them with great initiative. Examples of the admirable temper of these men are countless. Lance-Sergeant McCann, though badly wounded in the face, refused to drop out until his platoon were on their objective. When B Company under Major Hyde came under heavy fire from the flank, Sergeant Kavanagh engaged the enemy machine-guns, and effectively drew the attention of one of our tanks to them. In such assaults, bravery seems to have been unbounded.

B Company quickly reached their final objective, which included the once fine Norman church in the village, and D Company, depleted in the attack two days earlier, went through under Captain Montgomery. Lennox was severely wounded leading his platoon, though not before he had earned the Military Cross. Montgomery, wounded twice, carried on with the one other officer remaining and secured his objective, which had it remained in enemy hands would have been a salient most useful to them for launching a counter-attack. C Company, under Major de Longueuil, fought through the wood on to their objective with great dash, and Bobby Diserens, a young officer known throughout the Battalion for his enthusiasm, was mortally wounded as he ran about, regardless of the enemy's fire, putting his platoon in position. Under Command of C Company were

five Armoured Vehicles R.E. : they came to grips with the
enemy and fought until they were all finally knocked out by
88 mm.s firing from La Bijude. As the Battalion consolidated,
the Germans subjected the position to five hours of a most vicious
mortaring and shelling. During this time Major Brooke, commander of the Battery of the 33rd Field Regiment that had
supported the Battalion through all the period of training
together, was killed. The day was a black one for the 33rd Field
Regiment. Their Colonel, Tom Hussey, was killed by an
88 mm. firing over open sights, and one of their F.O.O.s, Captain
Roose, was killed as he entered the village in his tank. Captain
Cobley's O.P. party were all wounded. The Colonel of the
Suffolks, Dick Goodwin, was also wounded while on a reconnaissance in Cambes, and had to be evacuated.

While all the fire in hell seemed to be coming down in Cambes
wood, and in particular on to the orchard at the approach to
the wood, it was just as exciting running the gauntlet down the
open road into the wood under " cover " of which at least you
no longer presented a personal target to the enemy. The intensity
of enemy fire in the wood from about four o'clock till dusk was
as withering as anything experienced during the whole campaign. Major Passy and Captain McDowell and C.S.M. Bell of
the Middlesex died there. Sergeant Davis continually tended
the wounded and ran with messages up and down the wood.
Captain Neve sat out in the open directing fire on to the
enemy. The Germans failed to mount a counter-attack, and as
the evening turned to dusk the K.O.S.B.s came to reinforce the
Ulster Rifles.

There was little doubt after this that the Germans would hold
Caen at all costs, that they had sited their tanks and Panzer
Grenadiers accordingly. A general reflection may be made now
that in those days savoured of " sour grapes " : it is simply that,
had Caen and all the other objectives been swiftly overcome on
D-day, Hitler might possibly have been dissuaded from issuing
the fatal order that Rommel must contain the Allies in the bridgehead until he saw an opportunity to dislodge them and push them
back into the sea.[1] That order was to cost him at the very least

[1] As it was, (we are told on page 31 of General Eisenhower's Report) " Seventh
Army decided by the evening of D-day that the landings near the Orne constituted

fifteen divisions : had he lured us on to the Seine those divisions would have served him better. Even when the jaws of the Falaise Gap were about to close, when Rommel himself realised the defeat that his mistakes were bringing down on him, Hitler ordered that not a single man should be withdrawn without personal reference to him. That Montgomery sensed the German predicament and exploited it has been somehow overlooked by critics of the Ralph Ingersoll type, who in this first year after the war speak of England's anxiety to conserve the lives of her men—rash from an American in view of the respective proportions of Americans and Britons who lost their lives. But this, as General Whistler points out, is to " flog a dead horse." Eisenhower is not the man to withhold praise where it is due, and simply says : " F.-M. Montgomery's tactical handling of this situation was masterly."

What we have to bear in mind from now until the end of Chapter Four is the gradual operation of the Commander-in-Chief's plan that " the enemy should batter himself against a strongly held pivot in the Caen area on the left " while the rest of the Allied Expeditionary Force broke out, if possible bagging those Germans who were intent on " battering themselves " (it was *their* plan really !) against the pivot. Though the port facilities in Caen might have been useful, it mattered not a German mark whether the actual pivot was Biéville just north of Caen or the faubourg de Vaucelles, the southern part of Caen across the river : and if the operation seemed *too* gradual it was wonderfully fruitful in the end, despite the weather that, in the mid-June gale, came near to marring the crop. The worst *collaborateur* was the weather throughout the campaign.

Now that Eisenhower has presented his full report to the Combined Chiefs of Staff, and so to the world, there is no need to waste time refuting the imputations of an Ingersoll : Caen was one of the world's great battles and everyone knows it. It was won to a very large extent on the will-power and steadfast-

the chief danger in the area so far invaded, and took steps to commit its strongest and most readily available reserves in that sector. Little was known of the strength or objectives of the American landings, and the operations in the Cotentin continued to be regarded simply as a diversionary effort which could easily be dealt with. *This estimate of the situation dominated the enemy's policy, with fatal results, during the ensuing days.*"

ness of the characters in this narrative. The 3rd Division were
holding this line in front of Caen between Cambes wood on the
right and the Canal on the left, till Caen fell on the 9th July ;
and then there was no relief. Standing at either side, like
Herminius and Spurius Lartius in the lay, were the 3rd Canadians
and the 6th Airborne (supported now by the 51st (Highland)
Division), and together they faced the enemy's best tank divisions.
(The figures in Montgomery's Despatch show an estimated
enemy strength in the Caumont-Caen sector of 725 tanks and
64 infantry battalions at the end of June, against 140 tanks
and 63 Infantry battalions in the Caumont-Cotentin sector)
So far from budging during the next few weeks, they put in
limited attacks and gained ground from the Germans.

Entrenched, and nursing an aggressive resentment at having
been prevented in Caen, the men of the Division glowered across
the fields and got to know their bit of the line very well. Summer
had brought the green countryside to full bloom despite the
German occupation, and much of it reminded them of their own
part of England. You often heard the comment, " I still sometimes fancy it's just another exercise," and that was a tribute to
those responsible for the training during the hard months
before the invasion : it certainly did not imply that things
were easy.

Our line and the enemy's were extraordinarily close. On
the right 9 Brigade held Cambes and the part of le Mesnil
wood that lay to the right of the main road. After the evacuation
of four old ladies by the Ulster Rifles on June 12th, Cambes
village was deserted. Villages, peaceful by nature, try to preserve
a dignified neutrality as battle passes through the street, and after
they have been knocked about their ruins convey how deeply
they have been shocked. Sometimes the shock is too much and
they die. And however unimaginative, most men are struck with
the strange spectacle of a village in decay, changed by a week as
by a century. In his description of *The Old Front Line*, Masefield
sees the grass growing in the street of Hébuterne, the bells silent ;
" The beasts are gone from the byre and the ghosts from the
church. Stealing about among the ruins and the gardens are the
cats of the village, who have eaten too much man to fear him,
but are now too wild to come to him. They creep about and eye

him from cover, looking like evil spirits." The horror grows with the strain of static warfare, and a month is quite long enough to produce it. Near Cambes the cottages were too far gone to provide shelter and the companies were dug into the gardens, which yielded a welcome fresh vegetable supplement to the Compo ration. Two houses in the village provided suitable O.P.s and a third was established in the *grenier* of the white chateau. From them it was possible to observe the whole system of enemy entrenchments running round Cambes to Galmanche. The avenue, running from the back of the chateau, straight into la Bijude, was cut by a level-crossing, where our forward sections were lying up, keeping a watchful eye on the German locality 200 yards farther down the avenue. In this part the Germans were never separated from our troops by more than 250 yards ; here and there it was 150.

If the enemy exposed himself it was soon found that he was doing it to distract attention from his main positions, which could sometimes be spotted by the most careful observers where foliage, cut for camouflage, had died, or where some new, suspicious shape appeared. But the only way to estimate the strength of these positions was by patrols. Listening-posts would be put out each night in no-man's-land and patrols would roam abroad on reconnaissance. These would often be undertaken by the same bands of men, usually volunteers, who became expert and revelled in their exploits. But the strain told, and it was a mistake to depend always upon the same men : it was too much to expect of them. The Ulster Rifles relate how easily events on patrol can take a wrong turn. Lieutenant Purcell had patrolled with a section to the outskirts of Galmanche village when an enemy sentry was bumped who shouted " Halt." Purcell pressed the trigger of his Sten. It jammed. Simultaneously the man on either side of him attempted to fire. Both their Stens jammed. Without more ceremony they made one of the swiftest with-drawals on record, " pursued by the shots and shouts of the Boches." The Battle patrols of this battalion were trained and operated by Major Charles Sweeny M.C., who later became one of the Field-Marshal's team of Liaison Officers, and was killed escorting a German admiral to Kiel—the more tragically in that the Germans had just signed the surrender. His chief

patrol leaders were Sergeants Murphy and Martin ; the latter
was killed on patrol.

Soon or late every fighting soldier goes out on a patrol. The
Lincolns claim that every one of their men had his patrol
experience during that first month. One gallant fighting patrol
of the Lincolns went out, like the one described above, from
Cambes to Galmanche. There was a fierce fight, hand to hand,
in which Lieutenant Pacey, one of the leaders, was wounded in
the thigh, and the other, Sergeant Ward, finding himself surrounded, fought his way out with bayonet and grenades, and
contrived to bring two wounded men away with him. In another
raid on Galmanche on 4th July, this time by the K.O.S.B.s, one
of the patrol commanders, Lieutenant Raines, was killed as they
overran the enemy position, whereupon the patrol rallied and
was brought back under the very able command of Corporal
Cameron.

Johnnie Beck, with the 3rd Recce's Contact Detachment in
Cambes, describes in his log his visit with one of the K.O.S.B.
patrols to a forward Gunner O.P. : " Twenty-seven enemy
tanks were seen dug-in in the la Bijude area, but artillery cannot
shift them. Infantry of 12 SS seen digging in front of la Bijude.
It seems shovels and picks well to the fore on both sides. O.P.
receives direct hit and F.O.O. slightly wounded. Rest of us O.K.
Enemy artillery and mortaring now stepped up." That was D
plus 5. D plus 6 was " rather a stay-at-home day. Plenty of hate,
including M.G. fire. Ricochets off trees make a journey to the
latrines perilous." On D plus 7 he records : " General Rennie
arrives into Cambes from the hostile end, and his jeep blows up
on a mine. Short cuts suggested by Officers Commanding Field
Ambulances are definitely *out*."

The Commander was much harder hit than he thought at
the time.[1] On the 14th he went aboard the *Largs* to recuperate
and on the 18th he was flown to England for two weeks' complete
rest. It was with deep, sincere regret that the Division heard of his

[1] On the same day, Major-General Fritz Witt, commanding the opposing 12 SS
Panzer Division, was killed. He was succeeded by the man who had planned with
Feuchtinger a week earlier to " throw the little fish back into the water." At
thirty-three, Kurt Meyer became the youngest divisional commander in the German
Army. Tall and handsome, with searching blue eyes, he is described by Major
Shulman as " the perfect product of Nazi fanaticism." He now serves a life sentence
for inciting his troops to murder Canadian prisoners-of-war.

ill luck. They wanted him back quickly. In the meantime Brigadier Cass took command of the Division, and Colonel Foster of the 76th Field Regiment commanded 8 Brigade.

Down on the left from Biéville to the canal the front was held by 185 Brigade. Here, as all along the front, men were confident and eager to press forward, but compelled to sit and hold. Here again it was a period in which patrolling was the only variation from the cramped life under acute shell-fire. The Norfolks had a curious disposition with the main part of the Battalion at Norfolk House, and three platoons and a carrier section strung out in a line two thousand yards forward, acting as a sort of screen from the canal bank westwards. This was " Duffers' Drift," and thence the Norfolk patrols set out. " On the second day of Duffers' Drift," chirps the Norfolk chronicler, " the enemy, who obviously did not understand, motored down the road and so fell nicely into the trap prepared by B Company. Within a week the bag was one marine officer, thirty-five other ranks, five vehicles and two motor-cyclists. Then someone in the enemy lines must have put up a notice to the effect that no one came back from that particular road."

In the middle, the line was held by 8 Brigade. They were well forward of Periers and held all of Le Mesnil wood to the left of the main road. But here the enemy held a salient, consisting of two farms—Le Landel and La Londe—and the chateau de la Londe. On the night of June 10th D Company of the South Lancs established itself in Le Landel : the absence of enemy opposition was uncanny. The next evening enemy tanks and infantry were forming up at La Bijude for a counter-attack. The weight of our artillery effectively discouraged them. On the 12th, the day after Montgomery had visited Divisional H.Q. to congratulate the Division and presumably to discuss future ops with General Rennie (it was the day before the Divisional Commander was blown up), General Rennie told the H.Q. Staff and the Heads of Services of the probability of counter-attack up through Periers. If so, tanks might break through. Provided that everyone stood firm, the situation could be coped with. All troops were to be informed so that nobody should be surprised. Heavy minefields were sown across the Divisional front by the Sappers in conjunction with the Infantry. They were covered by the

Middlesex machine-guns and by guns of the 20th Anti-Tank Regiment. These preparations give the lie to anyone who still thinks we should have been advancing gaily. We would gladly have done so.

One of our greatest bugbears was that all along the front the enemy were still desperately holding out in fortified strong-points behind our lines. General Eisenhower mentions that " although German claims to the effect of these strong-points in delaying the development of our operations were greatly exaggerated, it was undeniably difficult to eliminate the suicide squads by whom they were held." He goes on to describe the radar station at Douvres that only surrendered on the 17th June as being " the biggest of these points, in the Canadian sector." But it was a team from the 3rd British Division that forced its surrender. There was a legend current in the Division that the German Colonel Commanding this garrison was in the habit of emerging by night to visit his mistress in La Délivrande, and the compiler of the Divisional Intelligence Summary went so far as to suggest respectfully that the lady should be located and suitably booby-trapped.

There is no doubt that enforced inactivity of this kind was harder on morale than any bloody thrust into fresh country would have been : but it was necessary. Inactivity only describes life at the front. This was a period of tremendous activity for the Division's Gunners, who were firing constantly in support of the 6th Airborne and 51st Division in attack and counter-attack over the Orne, besides supporting their own troops with Counter-Battery, Harassing, Defensive, and every other kind of Fire known to the Royal Artillery. Their regular daily expenditure was up to a hundred rounds per gun, and during an attack as much as three or even four hundred rounds. Victor Targets usually brought a few kind words of approval from the lips of the Infantry, who were naturally delighted to see the Germans paid back in their own coin and with interest. One infantryman commented that our gunnery made German gunnery look silly : however silly, it was still extremely inconvenient.

But the supply of shells was only one—albeit a major one— of the questions that exercised the Divisional Services. It was extraordinary how they kept everybody fed and equipped and at the same time built up great dumps of reserves. They had to do it over beaches with no proper port, though by D plus 2 a " Gooseberry " breakwater was formed by sinking various old warships and merchant ships. This made a great difference to the speed of turn round of DUKWs. Anchorage, beaches, and dump-areas were under observation, and shell-fire from D-day until the enemy were cleared from the coast east of the Orne in the second week of August. The performance of the amphibian DUKWs companies and Port Operating troops through all weathers, day and night, and with spells of shelling each 24 hours for six weeks, was truly " of the highest order."

For the first three days the Division (and 6th Airborne Division) had to be supplied from four beach Sector Stores Dumps, as the ground intended for the Beach Maintenance Area was still partly in enemy hands. On D plus 2 an enemy plane dropped a stick of bombs over the area, two bombs hitting the Sector Stores Dump that contained half the ammunition and all the reserve of petrol, oil, lubricant and supplies for the force. An enormous fire started, in which 60,000 gallons of petrol were lost and 400 tons of ammunition. With high courage the troops got the fire under control in just under three hours and saved some of the ammunition. There was further bombing, and small fires were started in the area on the 9th and 10th, but after that maintenance continued smoothly until the Channel was lashed by a gale that lasted from the 19th to 22nd June. (" Thank the Gods of War we sailed when we did," said Eisenhower. After the 7th June the next possible date for Invasion was the 19th.) The final tribute to these supply troops is that the average tonnage per day landed by the two Beach Groups was as high as, and during the storm period higher than, the tonnage landed on less turbulent beaches.[1]

In an early part of the book we saw the state of interdependence, spiritual as well as physical, of the several " arms "— Infantry, Gunners, Sappers, Services. We can now see in some details how the spirits (morale if you like) of the Division were and how they were affected. It is possible to generalise without probing too far into the feelings of the men who, at " Stand-

[1] By the end of the month 274,000 tons of stores had been landed for 2nd Army, much of it through the *Mulberry* at Arromanches ; 3rd Division's contribution at La Bréche was 53,143 tons.

down," dropped into their slit-trenches and pulled out a photograph or a fag. Major " Bob " Moberly, the Middlesex historian,
notes the tendency for a man to become " more and more like
a vegetable " if he is planted for long periods in a one- or two-
man slit-trench. This vegetable mentality was best uprooted in
the Infantry by vigorous patrolling ; paradoxically, enemy
shelling, the other major *event* in Infantry life, encouraged its
growth.   For the Field Gunners and the Middlesex, " crash-
actions " and harassing shoots in a forward area (and subsequent
speedy withdrawals) helped to dispel the feeling that they were
" held " by the enemy. The people who were least affected were
the Services who drove lorry- and DUKW-loads of supplies all
over the place ; Major Cuthbertson, R.A.S.C., for example,
regularly leading convoys over into the Airborne area, and
winning an M.C. And the Services always had another job as
soon as one was finished, though it is said that whenever they
had a break they were quite prepared to dig or die ! But seriously,
they *were* treated to some heavy shelling and bombing, and in
any case it was inevitable that they should reflect more than a
little the mood of the Infantry.
     In turn, the humour of the Infantry depended upon the
Services, who supplied most of the things that made life tolerable.
After the first month the Mobile Bath-Unit and Laundry arrived,
the Div Club set up bravely in Luc-sur-Mer, and there were
cinema shows in the schoolroom in Plumetot. But until then the
regimental Quartermasters had to make what bathing arrangements they could in their echelons, and most troops managed to
get at least one bath in the month. They were supplemented by
the R.A.M.C. Hygiene Section that landed early and found
little to do : it founded some showers in Colleville not far from
Divisional H.Q. The Divisional gun-area (in the line of the
Periers gully from Mathieu round to Bieville) was just far enough
back for the gunners to be able to bath on the spot—though
occasionally they were caught by importunate shelling and driven
to earth naked. With perhaps a couple of tar-barrels and an old
petrol-pump, Battery Fitters improvised baths that would have
done credit to Mr. Heath Robinson as well as to the Swiss Family
Robinson and to Robinson Crusoe in a similar state of nature.
     The important supplies of food and mail were wonderfully

regular. Nobody went hungry, except the forward Infantry in certain stages of later battles, and they knew that could not be helped. Mail was received nearly every day, though the Channel gales held it up. Its importance may be indicated by the fact that well-tried friendships could be temporarily broken by a friend's failure for a mere five minutes to inform you that mail was " up ". and that there was " one for you." The time-lag in homeward mail was incomprehensible. No mail posted in Normandy was delivered at home until over a fortnight after the assault. The food, the mail and the condition of the weather in the Straits were made much of by the journalists in English papers that also began to arrive regularly. One of the most serious factors affecting the morale of the Division was the failure of both the B.B.C. and press to mention it. They would have hated glowing passages of journalese : that was not what they wanted. It was just that they felt a keen injustice in the fact that the Canadians and 6th Airborne and 50th (Northumbrian) Division were almost immediately named and given credit for the operation in which the 3rd Division had played such a proud part. On the 11th June the Divisional Intelligence Summary read : " Disappointment has naturally been felt over the BBC's failure to mention this division as being in the forefront of the assault. The policy is thought to be that divisions are not announced until the Germans have identified and mentioned them in their communiqués." The position must have been put to Montgomery, who visited Div. H.Q. that day, for, two days later, certain papers, including the *Telegraph*, allotted a paragraph to an interview in which Montgomery revealed the Division's presence among the British troops in Normandy. But it must be said that the account of the interview was so unfortunately phrased that it made those members of the Division who saw it furious and rather depressed. In *The Good Soldier*, Viscount Wavell writes : " An entirely exaggerated idea of security has too often been allowed to prevent individual units being named and their exploits told when they occur." That puts it quite plainly.

There was no deep depression of spirits within the Division until 8 Brigade's battles for the chateau de la Londe, of sombre memory. That deadly, desperate fighting imbued the whole

Division with the feeling that any slight advance in future would only be made at a high price in lives. This feeling was thrown off, because brooding did no good, and because, with preparations for the next operations across the Orne from which there were great expectations, the Division saw how highly its spirit and experience were rated, and were soon laughing again.

The terrible irony of the chateau de la Londe was that it was taken quite easily on the night of June 22nd. As part of a limited I Corps Operation " to hold the enemy in strength while VIII Corps break out in a right pincer movement on 3 Canadian Division's front," the South Lancs put in a silent attack on the chateau and walked in. But something seems to have gone wrong with their anti-tank defence, for at 4.40 next morning, as dawn broke, the Germans counter-attacked with tanks and drove them out. Then the Germans set about tightening up the defence, and we know that 5 Company of 192 Panzer Grenadiers were severely reprimanded for the " disgraceful " loss of the chateau on the first occasion, and told that they would now " fight to the death " for it. They were reinforced by between 30 and 40 tanks, a platoon of Sappers and the H.Q. Company of 22 Panzer Regiment, both fighting as infantry.

That day Major-General L. G. Whistler, D.S.O., arrived to command the Division.[1] As Commander of 131 Brigade, the Infantry Brigade of the 7th Armoured Division, in the desert and up to the Volturno in Italy, he had won Montgomery's public tribute of " probably the finest fighting Brigadier in the British Army to-day," and since then he has only increased his reputation. His jeep was quickly recognised by the Division, and so was the cheery grin or wave that invariably answered a salute. One remembers the British Commander before Agincourt, who visited his men " with cheerful semblance

> That every wretch, pining and pale before,
> Beholding him plucks comfort from his looks . . ."

The next day or two saw good advances on XXX and VIII

---

[1] Major-General Rennie's condition was worse than was at first diagnosed. When he was fit once more he was given command of 51st (Highland) Division—his old Division.

Corps fronts, though by June 29th reactions to the VIII Corps thrust became most violent. Along the front from Juvigny to Caen eight Panzer Divisions were concentrated. The weather was as bad as could be. On the night of the 26th, after 15th (Scottish) Division's big drive across the Odon, for the height south of Caen, the guns were in tune with a thunderstorm. It was impossible to secure good aerial reconnaissance of the chateau, and our patrols never succeeded in getting close enough to ascertain the true enemy situation there. Our intelligence was therefore faulty, and this in part accounts for the grimness of Operation *Mitten*, the 8 Brigade assault upon the chateau on June 27th.

Supported by the Divisional Artillery, the South Lancs led in the attack in the evening. There was great carnage. In the end they were beaten off from the chateau, but clung to the wood at La Londe. The Suffolks and East Yorks would have to do it. Rations were brought round to them between 1 and 2 o'clock in the morning and they were ready to move by 4. At seven minutes past the barrage came down as arranged, and eight minutes later in they went. It was still fairly dark. Dense clouds thrown up by the bursting shells added to the already terrifying atmosphere. The memory must accompany those who were present to the grave. It cannot be described. The one incident of light relief that occurred towards the end of the engagement is evidence of the confusion of the struggle. C Company commander of the Suffolks, trying to arrange consolidation, was harassed by a spandau that kept interrupting him. " Suddenly seeing two tanks, he crossed to one of them to ask for fire support on to the intruder. A head rose from the turret and each stared at the other in silence. The gun began to swing round, the British officer bolted, and though chased back on to the position, managed to reach a slit-trench before being fired at. Lieutenant Woodward with a PIAT disabled one of the Mark IVs and the other was knocked out by Private Crick, who was killed almost immediately by shell-fire." The position was consolidated by four that afternoon.

Casualties to that one battalion on 28th June were 7 officers and 154 other ranks killed, wounded and missing. By the end of June battle casualties sustained by 2nd Army were :

	Killed	Wounded	Missing	Total
British	2,960	14,299	4,450	21,709
Canadian	396	1,516	1,177	3,089
Totals	3,356	15,815	5,627	24,798
3rd British Infantry Division sustained over that same period	417	2,280	811	3,508

(These last figures refer to casualties among the 17,000 who formed the Division proper, and do not include those among the many units under command).

It may be seen from the above official figures that the Third Division bore *one-seventh* of the total number of British and Canadian casualties over the period 6th-30th June, at the end of which period there were *fifteen* British and Canadian divisions and *seven* independent brigades in the bridgehead, apart from all the L-of-C troops. The figures need no comment.

Had *Mitten* gone more easily, 9 Brigade with 9 Canadian Brigade would have gone ahead with Operation *Aberlour*, the ambitious attack upon the enemy-defended villages of la Bijude, Epron, Galmanche, St. Contest, Authie and Cussy. When the Corps Commander saw how the fighting at the chateau had gone he called *Aberlour* off. The position remained tense until the 7th July : so tense that the battered 21 Panzer Division were taken back out of the line and replaced by 16 GAF Division fresh from Holland. Then, as resistance stiffened to General Bradley's drive south, after the fall of Cherbourg, Montgomery said it was time to put the wind up the enemy by seizing Caen.

Late in the evening of the 7th, while 9 and 185 Brigades stood briefed and ready, 450 heavy bombers swarmed like black dragons over the sky, unloaded their bombs on the old Norman city, and as they returned the Division was for a time in total darkness beneath a great vaulting cloud of ashes. The men emerged from their trenches and for the first time for weeks breathed freely. The full support of the Air Force gave them full hearts : but the French understood and the men were encouraged. At dawn next morning, with a great rumbling barrage, with Typhoons rocketing in support, 185 Brigade, commanded now by Brigadier Eric Bols, went up and took Lebisey. In the afternoon they went on and took Hill 64. All the time they were under intense shelling and mortaring : the Germans had undisputed observation from the tall factory chimneys of Colombelles across the river. As the light began to fail, 9 Brigade got into position in the northern approaches to the town. At dawn on the 9th the Ulster Rifles sent two strong patrols in through the rubble and ruin : at 9.30 the main body and the K.O.S.B.s advanced on their left. By midday they had reached the Boulevard des Alliés. The Canadians entered from Carpiquet in the late afternoon. Isolated resistance was overcome. Caen lay in our hands.[1]

[1] That is to say, all Caen north of the Orne—the greater part of the city. The *faubourgs* lying across the river were still in enemy hands. The whole situation is amazingly similar to the much earlier capture of Caen by the English under Edward III and his young son, the Black Prince. It was almost exactly six hundred years ago, on 26 July, 1346, that Edward's soldiers entered Caen from the north and found the fortified enclosures of the two great abbeys of William the Conqueror and his queen " undefended and desolate." Caen was not a walled city, and so the defenders retired to hold the *Ile Saint-Jean* across a branch of the Orne. There was a sharp fight at the bridge, but " the English archers prepared the way, and the men-at-arms completed the work." They rested five days in Caen, during which Edward found a copy of a Franco-Norman pact to invade England eight years earlier. He sent it to the Archbishop to read to the Londoners, to show that his campaign was not unwarranted. Meanwhile the English fleet had devastated the coast from Cherbourg to Ouistreham. It looks as if the *Overlord* planners knew their medieval history.

Chapter Four

BREAKING OUT OF THE BRIDGEHEAD

" Well have we done, thrice-valiant countrymen :
But all's not done. . . ."
Henry V, during Agincourt

THE DIVISION had two leading roles in the operations that routed the German Army in Normandy. The first, in Operation *Goodwood*, across the Orne on the extreme left flank of the bridgehead, was no fun at all. The second, in step with an American division on the extreme right flank of the British 2nd Army, was as near great fun as men can expect to get in battle ; going down the Vire-Tinchebray-Flers road at fairly full tilt was exhilarating. The loss of lives takes the fun out of fighting ; though for some more than for others.

The fall of Caen meant much more to the Division than was really warranted by the tactical gain. And when, on July 11th, the Infantry were brought back out of the line in the transport of the Divisional R.A.S.C. Companies, there was a general feeling of relaxation. Even the Gunners felt it, though the guns had to remain in action. The amenities of the Div Club at Luc-sur-Mer were in great demand ; so were such footballs, darts, or any other sports gear as could be obtained from Army Welfare Services. The supreme pleasure was to have a bath and a long, undisturbed sleep. So far there had only been biscuits to eat with the tinned food in the compo packs. On the 13th of July the Biscuit-Eaters were given their first half-slice of bread. It was only half a slice, but it was eaten with greater relish than can be imagined even by those who, two years later, feel the rationing of bread most keenly. Then, on the 14th, after only three days of rest and reorganisation, the Division suddenly learnt that a move into action across the Orne was imminent, that though Caen had been taken, the plan for July was still that " Second Army would continue to contain the main enemy force between Villers Bocage and Caen, and draw to itself its main strength." (The American First Army, working its way down to a position in the area of Le Mans-Alençon, would " seriously threaten the enemy's concentration in the Caen area, or, since the Seine bridges were down, his retreat.")

The possibilities of *Goodwood* were breath-taking. VIII Corps, consisting of the Guards, the 7th and the 11th Armoured Divisions, were to pass through the Orne bridgehead, break through the enemy defences, " advance down the general axis Ranville-Démouville and seize the high ground on the general line Bourguebus-Argences."[1] II Canadian Corps were operating to clear the Colombelles factory area and cover the right flank, while I Corps had the task of " protecting the left flank of VIII Corps, using the 3rd Division." If VIII Corps succeeded in breaking right through, the German rout would be complete. If they were held, if *Goodwood* proved an inappropriate code-word, they would still realise the main intention, and continue to attract the mass of German armour eastward away from the American forces, who after the end of June were building up at a much greater rate than we were (until then we had been level).

The broad prospect, then, was exciting. On that account the Division accepted the abrupt curtailment of its hard-won rest in the best possible spirit. Digging parties were sent across the bridges forthwith to prepare harbour areas, and the main body of the Division was across and in harbour within a couple of days. The main movement had to be made by night over the canal and river, where there was always a great deal of anti-aircraft commotion, especially about midnight, and a number of Junkers were brought down. The lanes and tracks into the " hides " had been carefully reconnoitred by unit guides, but once in the bridgehead troops were never more than a couple of thousand yards from the nearest enemy, and the journey was accomplished in an atmosphere of great suspense. The natural tendency was to speak in a whisper, for fear lest the Germans should hear and detect such a great concentration of forces in a confined space, and act accordingly.

The area in which the Division found itself had nothing at all

[1] 3 Div. Operation Order for Operation *Goodwood*.

to recommend it.[1] There was a wedge of fairly open country typical of the *campagne*, running up from the south past Caen and alongside the river, but to the east this strip was dominated by the Bois de Bavent ridge. This began at the foot with small fields more typical of the *bocage* of central Normandy, completely boxed in by thick hedges and great leafy trees, and was crowned by the denser woods of Bavent and Bures, which the Germans held. Just over the ridge, it descended into the swamps through which the River Dives meandered north into the sea. These swamps must have been the breeding-ground of the swarms of mosquitoes that pounced on the Division the moment it entered the bridgehead, and left off only when it recrossed the bridges, displaying all the time a warm inhospitality, indeed an open hostility, as active as that of the German gunners and mortar-men. They were insatiable, and made life in a slit-trench almost intolerable. Every night they were reinforced by single German bombers who circled overhead and dropped scores of " anti-personnel " bombs. These could hardly miss in such a cramped area, yet the number of casualties they caused was surprisingly small, owing to good camouflage and still more to good digging. Most members of the Division had by now learnt to roof their slit-trenches for protection against splinters from shells bursting above, either in the trees or Airburst, and against anti-personnel bombs.

Goodwood began on the morning of the 18th. The Division's task was " to attack and hold the area of Touffreville, Sannerville, Banneville la Campagne, Manneville, Cuillerville, Le Quai and Troarn," villages that formed a rough triangle, with the town of Troarn as the eastern tip. It was six weeks—to the day—since the assault on the beach and the airborne landings, and this had always been the most sensitive front, over here on the left. Facing east, it is true, they were only confronting 346 and 711 Infantry Divisions, both of a fairly placid disposition : holding the ridge and backed by the Dives inundations, they could afford to be. But facing south the front was hypersensitive. We know now that, owing to the continued success of our deception plan,

---

[1] To a few men in the Division there was nothing new in the area ; for example, 45th Anti-Tank Battery (less I Troop) had fought with 6th Airborne Division through most of June, K Troop playing a brave part in the defence of Le Mariquet on June 10th and 11th against heavy counter-attacks.

the German High Command still feared another landing in the Pas de Calais and were determined that the present bridgehead should never spread left and link up. This accounted for the devotion of 21 Panzer Division to the Caen front; they had been relieved at the end of June by the fresh and equally vigorous 16 G.A.F. Division, and now waited in reserve just in rear of that formation. 1 SS Division and the remains of 12 SS Division were also in the line, alongside 16 G.A.F. Division. It was decided that *Goodwood* should begin with the dropping of a good 8,000 tons of bombs upon these formations.

It was a pleasant sunny morning, and difficult to grasp the meaning of the roaring and vibration that grew in the sky. As usual on such excursions, the bombers flew in a mass rather than a formation, in a pack, like so many omnivorous condors, and as they turned again for England it was possible to feel the warm blast from the enemy's positions and his gun-areas distant three thousand yards or more. During this heaviest bombing of forward positions ever attempted, our artillery and the naval guns fired anti-flak Counter-Battery, and later a full Counter-Battery programme; fifteen Field Regiments, thirteen Medium Regiments, three Heavy Regiments and two Heavy Ack-Ack Regiments joined in. Together with the Divisional R.A.S.C., the three Field Regiments of the 3rd Division had collected and dumped 750 shells and cartridges for each gun, a fair indication of the scale of the shooting. The Canadians on the right, the tanks of the 11th Armoured Division in the middle, and the Infantry of the 3rd British Division on the left, were off to a good start.

The whole of the 3rd Division was committed. The fighting lasted thirty-six hours. It was succeeded by a few days of the most acute enemy shelling and mortaring ever experienced, and by torrents of rain. In outline, the action was as follows :

8 Brigade, supported by 13th/18th Hussars and their habitual Gunner, Sapper and Middlesex teams, were first off the mark. The South Lancs, advancing upon Le Pré Baron, a cluster of farm buildings in the close country already described, were held up at some sandpits defended by the enemy. These were cleared early in the afternoon, and by 8 p.m. the South Lancs had consolidated their objective. The East Yorks had some trouble with

enemy-manned weapon-pits and with anti-personnel mines on
the way, but by 11 a.m. were fighting in Touffreville, their
objective.   Touffreville had missed some of the bombs intended
for it, and the Germans determined to hold it.   The East Yorks
had a great deal of mortaring and sniping to put up with before
opposition was finally· overcome at 6 that evening, and there
was much mortaring to follow.   Touffreville was still being contested when the Suffolks had set out for Sannerville at 10.15 a.m.
But theirs was a different experience.   They took Sannerville at
20 minutes past 12 and Banneville la Campagne at 4 o'clock,
villages that were .battered beyond description.   Those Germans
left conscious were far too dazed to offer any resistance.

185 Brigade's objectives were farther south.   At 9.30 on the
same morning the K.S.L.I. mounted the Shermans of the Stafford
Yeomanry and drove down, through considerable hostile fire,
upon Lirose.   At 10 o'clock there was heavy mortaring at the
railway line, but Lirose was taken after a sharp fight.   The
Battalion pushed on against heavy opposition north of Manneville.   At 8 p.m. the Brigade attacked Manneville with the
Warwicks right and the Norfolks left.   At last light they were
still 200 yards short of the village. ·   •

Meanwhile 9 Brigade, with the K.O.S.B.s right and Ulster
Rifles left and the East Riding Yeomanry in support, advanced
eastwards on Troarn.   On the left a "scissors " bridge was erected
over the Cours de Janville, and crossed soon after 3 p.m. by the
Ulster Rifles.   They were heavily shelled, but gained their brickworks objective, and pushed on to the T-junction a mile from
Troarn, consolidating there after three-quarters of an hour's stiff
fighting.   The K.O.S.B.s had trouble bridging the stream on the
main Banneville-Troarn road, and eventually at 7 p.m. crossed
by the Ulsters' bridge to attack La Croix de Pierre, which they
took at last light, consolidating in an orchard.   Shelling that
night was at random and as indiscriminating as ever, but seemed
to fall particularly heavily on 9 Brigade.

Early the next morning 9 Brigade renewed the attack on
Troarn, while 8 Brigade consolidated, and 185 Brigade, continuing, found both Manneville and Cuillerville abandoned,
occupied them, and beat off a counter-attack by two companies
of infantry and six tanks launched from Emieville at 4 p.m.

Closing up to Troarn, the K.O.S.B.s on the right were hard pressed. The Ulster Rifles were being bled from a church that was held by the Germans on the left flank. At 10 a.m. the K.O.S.B.s and East Riding Yeomanry attacked along the road to the railway station and were violently repulsed. A German counter-attack on La Croix de Pierre was beaten off, and at 10.45 the Ulster Rifles attacked the church from which their left flank was harassed. By midday they had taken the church, but saw fit to consolidate 300 yards to the west,[1] whereupon the Germans re-entered the church and two further attacks failed to dislodge them. At 6 p.m., while the Lincolns, unsupported, executed a very courageous diversion south of Troarn, the Ulster Rifles attacked from the north, but they were still 800 yards from the town when darkness came.

When the Ulster Rifles dug their positions that night, they imagined they would be going forward again at first light. But the Division had done all that was required of it, even though Troarn had not been taken. The eastern wall of the corridor for the armoured drive had been held, and the armour itself, though checked by the enemy's anti-tank screen, and, the next day, immobilised by mud, had achieved " a decisive effect. The 2nd Panzer Division and 9 and 10 SS Panzer Divisions were brought eastwards across the Orne."[2] This was a fatal move. And now it was up to the United States 1st Army, who had been due to attack the day after *Goodwood*, but who were held in suspense till the 25th July by the miserable weather.

Though there was no call for further advance eastwards for the time being, the Division was left holding a nasty position on the corner of this most sensitive front. The Germans made good their heavy losses in troops with heavy shelling and mortaring, and casualties in the Division mounted daily in proportion. The first day in static positions saw the descent of a deluge. Rain poured all over everything, and trenches were flooded out. The

[1] The immediate vicinity of the church was anyway untenable to begin with, owing to fierce heat engendered by a blazing barn. It was here that, aged nineteen, Lieutenant Brian Burges was killed while trying to rescue a wounded officer of the E. Riding Yeomanry who was stranded in the open. Brian Burges it was who led that first fighting patrol of the Ulster Rifles into Caen only ten days earlier ; he had been wounded then in the shoulder, but insisted on carrying on.

[2] *Notes on the Operations of 21st Army Group*, p. 14.

previous two days of fighting had been in tiring intense heat, dust
and mosquitoes, fantastic wreckage where the earth was so
densely cratered that it looked " more like the landscape of the
moon," as several people remarked.   And though the Divisional
Intelligence Summary has it that " through the bulk of the
opposing 16 G.A.F. and 21 Panzer Division (less 192 Panzer
Grenadier Regiment) the air and artillery bombardment made
a rough path that was quickly trodden down by our assaulting
troops," the fact is that the craters were so close together in
places that it was hard to thread a way through them and quite
impossible to get carriers or even jeeps forward.   While there is
no doubt that the bombardment did greatly simplify 8 Brigade's
attack and save them many lives, there is an important qualifica-
tion concerning the advance of the other two Brigades.

By July the Germans were sufficiently conversant with our
tactics to know that our attacks were invariably preceded by a
drenching bombardment of one sort or another.   Nobody can
accuse the Germans in general of failing to grasp the obvious in
military tactics ; it is in the realm of strategy (as well as of the
peaceful pursuits, of course) that they make such hopeless
blunders.   In this case they had been quick to form a conclusion,
and further along the front the Commander of the Panzer Lehr
Division, reporting on June 22nd to 1 SS Corps, recommended
as his first point that " (a) The main line of resistance is to be
occupied only thinly (with O.P.s at the most important vantage
points).   Losses through enemy artillery bombardment are
thereby minimised. (b) Behind every sector a local reserve must
be held close at hand and must be supported by tanks. These
reserves advance the moment the enemy bombardment lifts from
the main line of resistance."

This is precisely what happened at Troarn and Manneville
on the 9 and 185 Brigade fronts, and on our armoured front at
Bourguebus, where by nightfall on the 18th small groups of
enemy tanks, chiefly Panthers, but also Tigers, were reported
all round our thrust. It has to be remembered that both these
tanks were more heavily armoured than ours, and mounted a
gun which, in the case of Panthers, equalled our 17-pounder,
with the added advantage that it could fire H.E. as well as A.P.,
and in the case of the Tiger, was superior to any tank or anti-

tank gun we possessed. But it must also be remembered that, although the German armour was just what was wanted in Normandy, their lack of speed and lower technical reliability told against them in the great advance.

Starting on the afternoon of the 18th from ground that had just been taken with comparative ease by 8 Brigade, 9 Brigade found themselves up against stiff opposition almost immediately. The Ulster Rifles sustained 4 Officer and 98 Other Rank casualties between the 18th and 20th July. On the first afternoon their B Company came under direct fire from two 75-mm. guns. Lieutenant Lyttle gathered some men and together they successfully attacked each gun, killing some of the gunners, giving chase to the remainder, and capturing both guns intact ; Lyttle won the M.C. One of the most notable individual deeds was performed the next day by Sergeant Sharkey when the Ulster Rifles were dealing with the pestering church on their left flank. Sharkey, using what cover he could, dashed to within 20 yards of an active machine-gun, and, darting into the open, personally killed the crew with his Sten. Nearby enemy, demoralised, withdrew. Later, when his depleted platoon pushed on, Sharkey was again prominent, dashing from trench to trench, killing those who failed to give themselves up. But Troarn, like Caen before, was no ordinary objective. It was not only a focal point, a key junction in the enemy supply route for troops west of the Dives, but also a very defensible bulwark. Later on the 18th, the 3rd Battalion of 731 Grenadier Regiment, arrived on bicycles to reinforce the defenders. Tigers moved back into the town, and those of their guns they could not get back the Gunners of 16 G.A.F. Division destroyed.

Even so, there were far too many German guns and mortars firing all along the Divisional front at this time.[1] Men walked about with one eye on the nearest slit-trench or crater (there was no scarcity of the latter), or were unable to walk about at all for long periods. The Nebelwerfer, multi-barrelled mortars, or *Moaning Minnies*, were a special nuisance. In their favour it should be said that they gave plenty of warning of their approach.

[1] It must be recorded that in this particular period, a remarkable number of the German shells were duds and failed to explode ; probably the response of the slave munition-workers to D-day.

The moment of discharge was signalled by a loud noise that has
been likened to the sudden rending of six strips of canvas (one
for each barrel), then followed the familiar moan, swelling as it
grew nearer. It did not take a man long to decide whether or
not to go to earth.[1]

The Lincolns in their brave feint to the south of Troarn, to
the position—in the middle of the German Defensive Fire tasks
—known to them as Black Orchard, lost the most heavily to
German guns and mortars. In the course of Wednesday and
Thursday, the 19th and 20th July, alone they lost 210 officers
and men killed and wounded. Their Commanding Officer,
Lieutenant-Colonel C. E. Welby-Everard, was wounded in the
shelling and had to be evacuated. Their Second-in-Command,
Major D. R. Wilson, found himself commanding a battalion
that was 19 officers and nearly 400 men below strength. Lieut-
ant-Colonel C. G. Renny of the K.O.S.B.s was wounded, and
they were commanded by their Second-in-Command until
Lieutenant-Colonel J. F. M. Macdonald arrived on the 26th.

In 185 Brigade, the K.S.L.I. were now commanded by Lieut.-
Colonel C. G. Millett, O.B.E. ; Colonel Maurice, their distinguished commander on D-day, had been killed by a stray
German shell two nights before Lebisey wood was finally taken
and Caen entered. They now lost two other D-day leaders in
Major Dane, killed, and Major Wheelock, who died of his
wounds. The position of the K.S.L.I. in the chateau grounds
at Manneville was cramped by stone walls, houses and trees,
and made more nerve-racking by wounded horses charging in
all directions at intervals all through the day and night. The
Norfolks were also haunted by the sight of lacerated horses
from the Le Quai racing establishment. " Here we had to stay
nine days, subject to shells, mortars, and, most of all, Nebelwerfer. Towards the end they had us fairly well pin-pointed,
and there was a steady flow through the R.A.P. At this time
the weather was frightful, water poured into the Command Post,
and things got so uncomfortable that there was nothing for it
but to laugh." Here the Norfolks had their first case of exhaustion.

---

[1] The Germans had a taste of their own medicine when the Middlesex found a
Panzerwerfer, had it repaired by R.E.M.E., and fired it into Troarn. It provoked
immediate fierce retaliation on the Ulster Rifles, who rang up to say how much
they admired it, but would they please, please stop firing it at once.

" It was the red light, and immediately everyone set himself to find a solution. The best answer was to keep men's minds fully occupied, so the Slit-trench Quiz was started. This proved most popular, and with the occasional firm word from leaders, what might have been an epidemic was stopped. Everyone had a narrow shave here, and the orchard was reduced to a collection of broken trees."

It was on the evening of the 20th, as the front stabilised and the rain fell, that the Germans put in a local counter-attack at Cuillerville, with infantry supported by two Tigers. They had forced a decimated B Company to withdraw from its position, when Major Bundock, commanding D Company, went forward himself with a PIAT and drove off the enemy. B Company reoccupied the position. Major Bundock was awarded the D.S.O. During this period east of the Orne, the Warwicks lost 8 officers and 239 men killed and wounded.

The position was once more one of frustration and stalemate. There was some satisfaction to be got from reading the captured files of 14 Nebelwerfer Regiment ; or those of the equivalent of our H.Q.R.A. of 16 G.A.F. Division which had been overrun in Manneville, and from contemplating all the enemy armour lying derelict among the bomb-craters ; there were four Tigers (one of them upside down), one Panther, twelve Mark IVs, three Mark IIIs, seven 20-mm. Ack-Ack S-Ps, and four anti-tank guns counted in the woods round Cuillerville. But it was a melancholy sort of satisfaction, and chiefly pleased our Counter-Battery staff. For the rest, the only condition that would have made their losses bearable and cheered their troglodyte existence in wet holes in the earth would have been a break-through. After all the high hopes of *Goodwood*, this still seemed no more likely on the Division's front than it had done six weeks ago, and battalions were now at half-strength. But the casualties were not in vain ; though in one sense the losses were irreparable, their effect on the survivors was to strengthen them to see the business through and give such sacrifice some meaning. And certainly the Germans paid heavily in proportion : the 700 prisoners taken by the Division in *Goodwood* may by normal estimates be said to have represented a good 2,000 casualties all told.

The obvious symptom of increased rot in the state of Germany
was the attempt by the Generals to kill Hitler : it was made on
20th July, the day the rains descended, stuck our troops in the
mud, and grounded our aircraft, and so perhaps it is understandable that the younger fanatics opposing us should have
regarded the miscarriage of the attempt as just another demonstration that Providence was with the divine Führer. Not that they
heard much about it, with no wireless or newspapers. One
prisoner interrogated at Divisional H.Q. had been told con-
fidentially and in a whisper on July 22nd that Hitler had been
wounded and that the circumstances were not known.

It was clear that the Division was in need of a change of air
and scenery. On the Headquarters staff the " G boys " had been
manning the Command Post continuously through the whole
period of tense operations. In addition they had sustained
casualties, and, on the Q staff, the DAQMG, Major Roger
Brennan, had been killed on D plus 3. After *Goodwood* the G II,
two G IIIs, and the L.O.s were changed and given a well-
deserved rest. And now good news came from the American
front. General Bradley had started his advance on the 25th and
by the 28th had sealed off the enemy's escape route from the
north of the peninsula by capturing Coutances. At this point
the Canadian 1st Army and United States 3rd Army were
formed. The first was to take over those Corps engaged
in the slogging match down the Falaise road, while the latter
was to drive south from Coutances and break through Avranches
into Brittany. British 2nd Army, meanwhile, was to concentrate
on a central thrust in the Caumont area, side by side with that
of the American 1st Army on Vire. The Division was destined
to operate at the adjunction of these two armies.

The unexpected good news of the move was received on
July 31st. All ranks, from the sanitary orderly up to the General,
must have been cheered to hear that the Division was to be used
as Monty's mobile strategic reserve. Perhaps General Whistler
was particularly pleased : coming to the Division from 7th
Armoured Division, he had been used to " getting a move on,"
but so far the Division had been checked at every step (indeed,
so had the 7th Armoured since they came to Normandy on the
Villers Bocage sector). Anyway, the next fortnight suited everyone

excepting the Germans. For them it was probably the most disastrous fortnight of their lives.

The move back across the Orne to the old familiar area took place immediately. It was August 1st, roses were obtained for " the Minden Boys," and the Suffolks and K.O.S.B.s were able to commemorate that earlier summer's day (when " a single line of infantry broke through three lines of cavalry and tumbled them to ruin ! ") modestly but better than they had hoped. That day the Division was placed at the disposal of the British 2nd Army and came under command of VIII Corps. The next day the move began away over to the right of the British line. No one was anything but relieved to leave behind the mosquitoes, the stench, and the pervading sense of peril that characterised Troarn, but when it came to travelling westwards along the Periers ridge and men looked down at the white landing-craft unloading in the anchorage they had secured one morning, they naturally felt that they were leaving behind something that was theirs. The hot weather was beginning, and the roads and constructed tracks across country, packed with moving columns of every type of war transport, were hidden under clouds of choking dust, through which the Division passed. Dust infiltrated through eye-shields and clothes, masked the perspiring faces, and was particularly bad for the motor-cycles. The Division went into " hides" north of Caumont. It was quite different country from the *campagne* : this was the *bocage* that stretches south and west from Bayeux. From above it appears almost continuous forest, but on entering it you discover a labyrinth through small fields and orchards surrounded by high-banked hedges and trees. Apart from a few main roads, these innumerable, narrow, mud (now dust) tracks run like tunnels through tall thicket hedges, connecting the farms and hamlets. Farther south it all opens up again into pleasant open pasture and corn land, with occasional forests and hills.

It would have taken more than the densest cloud of dust to smother the irrepressible spirits of the men on that journey : they felt it was good to be alive. And a temporary Divisional Headquarters had not long been established at La Belle Epine before a message was received from I Corps, under whom they had fought till now, saying : " Your last vehicle passed the Start

Point at 2300 hours, 10 minutes late. Very many congratulations
on your staff work and march discipline. For a divisional move
on one road starting at 0800 hours, to lose only ten minutes was
first class."

Already the brief hour of relief was over ; the Division was
being committed to the battle, and once more the Infantry faced
the apprehensions that sicken most men before going into an
attack, that diminish mercifully once the action starts. First 185
Brigade moved under command of 11th Armoured Division on
the morning of the 3rd, then the rest of the Division with 4th
Armoured Brigade under command came into the line between
11th Armoured Division on the left and the Americans. They
had come south through the remains of Caumont, and across the
main Caen-Avranches road at St. Martin des Besaces. Here 11th
Armoured Division had just captured Le Bény Bocage. Vire had
been entered only to be temporarily recaptured by two S S
Panzer Divisions. Meanwhile General Patton on the extreme
right had entered the interior of Brittany and was thrusting
south for the Loire, " his flying columns meeting negligible
opposition."[1]

It was the precarious nature of General Patton's supply
route that now governed the enemy's strategy and encouraged
them in their attempt to drive westward to Avranches and the
coast, cutting off the United States Third Army from its maintenance beaches in the north. The enemy had at last resolved
to bring reinforcing Infantry Divisions from his Fifteenth Army
across the Seine, using them to replace his armour in the Caen
sector. This armour came to the aid of Seventh Army troops
struggling to prevent a collapse of the front in the Vire sector,
and was now massed near Mortain, a formidable striking force.
Their drive for the coast, only twenty miles over the level plain
of which they had full, tantalising view from the hills at Mortain,
was launched on August 7th, and Mortain was not many miles
to the south of the Division's front. To protect the flank of the
great panzer thrust, Seventh Army counter-attacked on the
Divisional front late on August 6th.

That day 9 Brigade were advancing, and 3rd Recce Regiment
were out in front, able to do their proper job for the first time

[1] Supreme Commander's Report, p. 52.

since they came ashore. The advance through the *bocage* on a front about five miles broad just missed the town of Vire, which was included in the left American boundary. On the main Caen-Vire road, about six kilometres north-east of Vire, the Infantry dismounted from their lorries and cut off on foot to the left. Before them on the left was Montishanger, a wooded hamlet on a hill, then the sparkling river Allière, a small tributary of the river Vire, ran all across the front. Beyond that the ground rose again behind Vaudry village on the right, and this slope was crossed first by the railway from Vire that ran east and later turned south to Flers, then by the dead straight road running due east from Vire to Vassy. The next road, just over the Vaudry height, ran from Vire south-eastwards to Tinchebray and Flers, and this road, once gained, became the Divisional axis.

Montishanger was occupied by the K.O.S.B.s at 10 that morning without opposition. Patrols reached the river south of Le Pissot and reported the bridges blown. At 5 p.m. a Brigade attack across the river was ordered, to start at 6 p.m. At 6 over they went, with shells exploding along the line of the river and small-arms fire from enemy paratroops waiting beyond. The K.O.S.B.s met very heavy opposition, and owing to the speed with which the attack was mounted and the fact that the bridge at La Houardière was blown, they were almost completely without support. One troop of the 44th Royal Tanks (from 4th Armoured Brigade) reached them late in the evening, and their very gallant attack on C Company's front saved the situation. From A Company one complete platoon was missing, and before the K.O.S.B.s consolidated that night they had lost a great many of their best officers and men, killed or wounded.

Meanwhile B and C Squadrons of the 3rd Recce Regiment had been pushed ahead of 9 Brigade to seize and hold the high ground if possible. Their A Squadron was keeping in touch with Americans on the right, directed upon Vire. B Squadron were heavily and consistently shelled at the crossing, and those who got across were pinned down on the far bank. C Squadron looked as if they might have better luck. They managed to work a Carrier Troop across under Lieutenant Turner, and an Armoured Car Troop under Lieutenant Snelling probed round

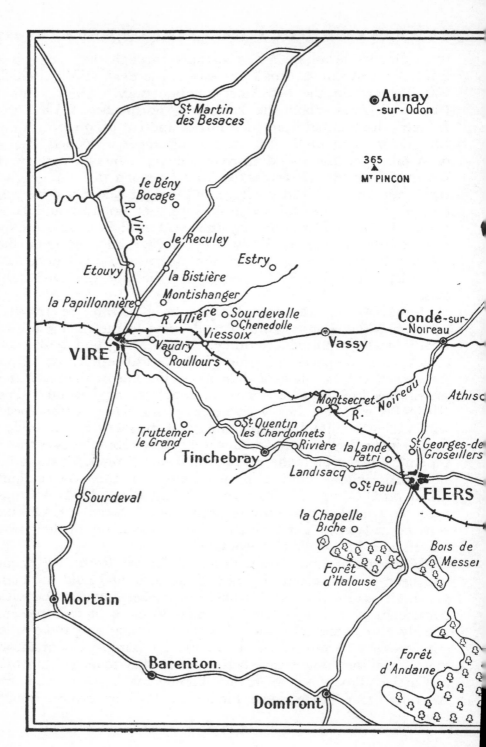

to the left and got across to Burcy. These two troops pushed boldly forward but ran into strongly-held positions, and when they returned to the firm base Carrier Troop, Turner was amongst those missing. Another Carrier Troop and an Armoured Car Troop made some ground on the left flank, but met the same impenetrable opposition and had to withdraw. Snelling won the M.C. for his exploit.

Near Burcy 9 Brigade adjoined 185 Brigade, on whose front that evening 10th SS Panzer Division counter-attacked. The attack came in at Sourdevalle, a scattered hamlet midway between Burcy and Chenedolle. By great good fortune it was launched just as the Norfolks were in the act of relieving the 3rd Monmouths of 11th Armoured Division, so that both Battalions were on the ground together. They formed a composite force, the Normons, and beat off the enemy. The hero of the Sourdevalle epic was Corporal Sidney Bates, whose V.C. was the first to be awarded to a member of the Division during the campaign ; but, alas, it was posthumous. It would be impossible to imagine a worthier, finer "descendant" of John Bates, Shakespeare's typical young soldier with Henry at Agincourt, who in the end says of his King, after the usual misgivings and apprehensions as they wait for the trumpet to sound in the cold dawn : " and yet I determine to fight lustily for him." The citation of Sidney Bates' supreme gallantry and self-sacrifice, submitted to and approved by the King, reads thus : the attack in strength by 10 SS Panzer Division near Sourdevalle " started with a heavy and accurate artillery and mortar programme on the position which the enemy had, by this time, pin-pointed. Half an hour later the main attack developed and heavy machine-gun and mortar fire was concentrated on the point of junction of the two forward companies. Corporal Bates was commanding the right forward section of the left forward company which suffered some casualties, so he decided to move the remnants of his section to an alternative position whence he appreciated he could better counter the enemy thrust. However, the enemy wedge grew still deeper, until there were about 50 to 60 Germans, supported by machine-guns and mortars, in the area occupied by the section.

" Seeing that the situation was becoming desperate, Corporal

Bates then seized a light machine-gun and charged the enemy, moving forward through a hail of bullets and splinters and firing the gun from his hip. He was almost immediately wounded by machine-gun fire and fell to the ground, but recovering himself quickly, he got up and continued advancing towards the enemy, spraying bullets from his gun as he went. His action was now having an effect on the enemy riflemen and machine-gunners, but mortar bombs continued to fall around him.

" He was then hit a second time, and much more seriously and painfully wounded. Undaunted, he staggered once more to his feet and continued towards the enemy, who were now seemingly nonplussed at their inability to check him. His constant firing continued until the enemy started to withdraw before him. At this moment he was hit for the third time by mortar-bomb splinters and sustained a wound that was to prove fatal. He fell to the ground but continued to fire his weapon until his strength failed him. This was not, however, until the enemy had withdrawn and the situation in this locality had been restored."

He died of his wounds two days later. His memory is not likely to fade from the minds of the men who knew him ; indeed that is true of all men who die fighting. The Normons had won the day, the two battalions re-formed and the relief was completed. It is an interesting coincidence that the Norfolks were similarly involved in the composition of the Norsets in Mesopotamia in 1917, though that was a much less temporary combination. In the Sourdevalle counter-attack the Norfolks lost 32 killed and 144 wounded.

The next day Von Rundstedt struck for Avranches, and so it is perhaps not surprising that 9 Brigade's attempt to push south of the railway was repulsed. They were joined that day by Lieutenant-Colonel C. L. Firbank, who took over command of the Lincolns, as Colonel Wilson had been wounded during the night, and by Lieutenant-Colonel Dominic Browne, who was appointed Brigade Commander, both coming from Div. H.Q. As one of the G IIIs was ill, the remainder of the G Staff were particularly hard pressed that day. They preserved sufficient sense of humour to record : " Liaison with United States V and XIX Corps on right very good, though rarely successful in discovering where U.S. forward troops really are ! " A Squadron of the Household Cavalry Regiment was under command of the Division, and one troop was used as a private " Phantom " with U.S. troops—forward !

The next day, 8th August, Lieutenant-Colonel W. F. H. Kempster assumed the appointment of G.S.O. I, and Operation *Walter* (named after him) was planned. Already the Americans reported substantial German forces cut off at Mortain, but the counter-attack persisted, so that a voluntary enemy withdrawal on the Division's front was considered highly improbable. Remnants of 3 and 5 German Para´ Divisions were known to be opposing, and it was presumed that the infantry and tanks of 10 SS Panzer Division that counter-attacked 185 Brigade were still there. Immediately south of Vire 363 Infantry Division was opposing the U.S. troops. The Division would advance on to Vaudry and astride the straight Vire-Vassy road, with a view to reorienting and advancing south-eastwards down the Tinchebray road, with the Americans abreast on the right.

Op *Walter* on the 9th was completely successful. 185 Brigade were back under command and with 9 Brigade got their objectives quickly. It was now quite customary for 9 Brigade to advance on the 9th of the month ; on that day they had entered Caen in July and Cambes in June. Op *Wallop*, a two-brigade attack on Tinchebray,[1] was immediately planned at Div. Headquarters, while offensive patrolling was kept up by battalions all the afternoon and evening. Persistent probing by the K.O.S.B.s and Ulster Rifles discovered the enemy in strength at Point 262, and Brigadier Browne warned his battalions that night that patrols " must literally sleep with the enemy," so that quick action could follow any withdrawal. It was estimated that a battle group of 10 SS Panzer Division occupied Chenedolle, and that elements of 3 German Para Division were in Roullours and Viessoix as 8 and 185 Brigades were concentrating for *Wallop* the next day, which was one of tremendous heat.

The 11th dawned with a dense ground mist so that the air-support programme had to be scrapped, but the Brigades moved off and made steady progress. It was the closest country entered

---

[1] A battle at Tinchebray in 1106 won Normandy for England.

so far and difficult to work through. To begin with, there was little or no enemy opposition—just isolated groups that sometimes fought and sometimes tried to make off. The 3rd Recce Regiment reported Viessoix ("Old Socks" to them) clear, and the East Yorks reported a counter-attack "a small affair" that did not worry them unduly. From the Lincolns, now in the southern suburbs of Vire, an enemy strong-point was skilfully stalked by Lieutenant Bush, whose patrol inflicted heavy casualties on the enemy. Bush's right arm was broken by machine-gun fire, but he refused to withdraw. He was awarded the M.C. The advance continued slowly and surely on the 12th, the South Lancs astride the main road and the East Yorks moving round to the left, 185 Brigade consolidating Hill 312 to give the Gunners the best possible O.P.s. There was some opposition at a rise in the main road and Major Neville Chance took some carriers forward. His C.S.M., Coombes, was killed after a gallant action, but soon the South Lancs reported all companies on their objective with signs that the enemy had pulled out in a hurry. The Gunners were engaging transport moving down the road. All the time the bag was contracting, shrinking round the Germans. That afternoon came the startling news that General Patton's 3 Army had turned *northwards* from Le Mans and had recce elements in Argentan ; meanwhile the Canadians were pressing south down the Falaise road against iron resistance. The mouth of the bag began to close.

At half-past six that evening General Whistler spoke on the line to 8 Brigade Commander, Brigadier Cass : " It looks as if the Boches are leaving. You will get on to *Pepper* (X-roads at Coquard, Point 279) with the Suffolks. Thereafter go forward with a Squadron of 3rd Recce as escort to give them a good kick-off in the morning." On the right the Americans were thrusting down on to Le Coudray and Truttemer le Grand, and if the Division was going for Point 279 they offered to help by putting something on to Point 275. At 7 p.m. Brigadier Cass was giving out his orders at Brigade H.Q., when a stray shell landed beside them, wounding nearly every member of the O.Group but the Brigadier. The calmness of his reaction— " Send for the Seconds-in-Command "—is reported by eye-witnesses to have excited some admiration.

It was getting dark when the Suffolks began to advance, commanded now by Major Allen. Without much trouble they reached the cross-roads shortly after midnight. D Company was then ordered to patrol as far forward down the road as possible. They were stopped a few hundred yards farther on by a machine-gun, and attempts to outflank it drew fire from the left. At the same time a body of paratroopers tried to outflank the company. After a clash in which D Company took three prisoners for the loss of two dead, they returned from their patrol ; it was obvious that the road was held in fair strength. Throughout the night and following day the Suffolks were accurately mortared and casualties mounted. " The highlight of 9 Brigade's day " was the discovery of 13 German dead, with among them a woman dressed as a paratroop N.C.O. At 3.15 p.m. the General held an O Group at 9 Brigade H.Q. and ordered 8 and 185 Brigades to continue the advance with limited objectives.

Ahead and on the flanks the Division was overlooked by high ground—the watershed from which the river Vire flowed down to the north-west and the Noireau flowed east into the Orne. The attack was to start at 8.30 that evening. The plan was comprehensive and included the support of a squadron of Churchills for each attacking battalion and the fire of an A.G.R.A. as well as the Divisional Artillery. The moment the barrage started the enemy answered with a very heavy counter-barrage that pinned down 185 Brigade and in 8 Brigade " caught B Company of the Suffolks fair and square, killing all three Platoon Commanders, the C.S.M. and one Platoon Sergeant." However, they re-formed and advanced in the face of the enemy Defensive fire, and in the failing light C and D Companies went through on to their objectives. The tanks, whose co-operation had been excellent, returned to harbour. D Company, having had no sleep the previous two nights and after twenty-four hours' continuous shelling, pushed on alone. A patrol of four Germans (one an officer) approached the leading section, who allowed them to pass and took them prisoner from the rear. Farther on, more Germans were heard as they approached from two directions to challenge each other. A section of Suffolks opened fire and dived for a ditch. Grenades were thrown by the Germans at their own men, and the section withdrew. By this time the flanking formations had been outstripped and the Suffolks had a wedge a mile deep in the defences of the enemy, who, according to prisoners, had received 200 reinforcements a few hours before.

It was now 4 a.m. on August 14th and D Company had been withdrawn at least half a mile to form a firm base, while A Company were ordered forward to take up a position this time on the left of the road. This they did, silencing machine-guns and taking prisoners, including a motor-cyclist. The escort was surprised to come under fire on the way back with the prisoners ; it was long after daylight, when the mist had cleared, that it dawned on A Company that in the dark they had come two or three hundred yards too far. Which accounted for the orchard that they failed to find on the map, and that contained between thirty and fifty Germans to their fifteen (including three wounded). They withdrew smartly, finding more enemy in their rear, taking prisoners and clearing the enemy from positions in the hedge-rows well away to the east of the main road. Here a raw re-inforcement is alleged to have remarked : " There's a German walking down the lane ahead. What do I do ? "

The Battalion now consolidated. News of B Company began to come from the R.A.P. Those who had survived that first barrage had gone in to clear a wood, but no intelligible account of this action was obtained, as those who survived were wounded, including Vaughan, who had assumed command, who was the only officer left, and was severely wounded in the head. That night the Suffolks took two hundred and fifty prisoners. They were shelled and mortared all the next day.

But 14th August was a beautiful summer's day, with the sky full of the sound of aeroplanes, and already the Corps Commander had rung up to say that a general German retreat was on, and that at Flers VIII Corps would be pinched out of the battle. During the afternoon a hot and dusty 76th Field Regiment rejoined the Division and 8 Brigade from the area of Bayeux ; there they had spent a week hastily refitting with 25-pounders in place of the cherished Self-Propelled 105 mm.s with which they had landed on *Queen Red* Beach. Each of the Field Regiments had to make this deeply regretted exchange in turn as the Americans were experiencing a shortage of 105 mm.

ammunition and could supply us with it no longer.   That afternoon, for the first time since 1940, 25-pounders of the Division shelled the enemy, and that evening the Commanding Officer of the 76th Field Regiment was ambushed and shot near St. Quentin les Chardonnets by the Germans while he was visiting the two forward battalions of 8 Brigade. Mervyn Foster was a very fine soldier and remarkably exacting commander, whose contribution as an Artilleryman to the planning and success of the early stages of the assault was never properly recognised. During the evening Colonel Hugh Merriman, commanding the 3rd Recce Regiment, ordered a two-squadron advance on Tinchebray and beyond, to begin next morning.

At last they made their long-anticipated break-through. After preliminary trouble with mines, C Squadron on the right moved quickly over the last mile or so into Tinchebray. At 9.30 the N.C.O. in charge of the Suffolks' water-cart had arrived at Battalion H.Q. " a little late but somewhat excited." It appears that he had missed the track leading to Battalion H.Q. and had gone straight on down the road, nearly to Tinchebray, and at no time had any enemy been encountered ! An attack on St. Quentin by the South Lancs with armoured support was in consequence called off. Instead the Suffolks sent *Kenforce* and *Perrettforce* under Captain Mayhew and Lieutenant Perrett to search and clear the road and track running across the Divisional front. They found only five very weary Germans, whose boots were worn through to their feet with marching. The 3rd Recce Regiment were in Tinchebray ten minutes ahead of the U.S. 102 Mechanised Cavalry, their opposite numbers in U.S. 2nd Infantry Division. (Colonel Merriman records in his regimental history that the commander of that Regiment " still owes us a Staghound on this one ! ") In Tinchebray the river bridge was blown. On the left, B Squadron had reached Montsecret quickly but by a very exposed route, and on reaching the bridge came under intense fire, their commander, Major Gaskell, being killed.

Overnight the East Yorks and South Lancs got across the river without opposition. At 8.30 a.m., 16th August, the Suffolks set off up the Flers road, consolidating at La Rivière, high in the hills, and sending Ken Mayhew on with three sections of his carrier platoon. Meanwhile, at 10 o'clock, C Squadron of 3rd

Recce Regiment started off along the same route, the other squadrons working swiftly forward on either flank. After investigating the village of Landisacq and finding two German Mark IV tanks ablaze with exploding ammunition at the bridge, Mayhew decided to push on with one section of carriers into Flers, which they entered with the leading Armoured Cars of C Squadron shortly after midday. That night's Divisional Intelligence Summary recorded : " A rare honour has this day fallen to the Division. It has captured a town ahead of the B.B.C."

Chapter Five

THE ADVANCE INTO THE LIMBURG LOWLANDS

FLERS HAD BEEN bombed in the D-day attacks on French communication centres,[1] but the people were overjoyed at the entry of a British D-day Division, and generous with kisses and flowers. The day after the entry into Flers, the General published a special message :

TO ALL RANKS

As far as this Division is concerned a phase of the main operation of this campaign has been completed.

You should be extremely satisfied with the part you have played. Your training in England was directed entirely towards the success of the assault landing. This was splendidly carried out by all parts of the Division.

Since then you have fought a variety of actions. You have fought alongside Canadians and Americans. And you have advanced every time until the enemy was soundly beaten, and is now in full retreat.

You have had great experience of battle, and now realise how much more there is to learn.

I am most grateful for your efforts, and very, very proud of your achievements so far.

(Signed) L. G. WHISTLER, Major-General,
Commander,
3 Brit. Inf. Div.

France, 17 Aug 44

" Until 17 August," says General Eisenhower's Report, " there was a steady seep eastwards through the gap, but then came a convulsive surge to get out . . . Road discipline among

[1] Since then the Germans had looted and burned down the whole centre of the town.

columns fleeing toward the Seine became non-existent, and vehicles plunged madly across the open country in an effort to avoid the blocked roads. Our air forces swept down upon the choked masses of transport, and there was no sign of the Luftwaffe to offer any opposition . . . Allied guns ringed the ever-shrinking ' killing-ground,' and while the SS elements as usual fought to annihilation, the ordinary German infantry gave themselves up in ever-increasing numbers. By 20 August the gap was finally closed near Chambois . . . The lovely wooded countryside west of Argentan had become the graveyard of the army which, three months earlier, had confidently waited to smash the Allied invasion in the Normandy beaches."

The Division had come through not only the invasion, but the whole period of development that was made possible by the successful amphibious assault ; all this without rest, with scarcely a pause, yet with increasing pride and undiminished vigour. Before the invasion it had been considered likely in high quarters that casualties in the Ouistreham landing would be so severe and the effort so exhausting that after holding the bridgehead for about a fortnight surviving troops would have to be brought back to re-form in England. At Flers, after ten weeks, the Division was directing its thoughts and energies to the assault-crossing of the Seine !

By the 18th, the Sappers had the Tinchebray-Flers road open for two-way traffic, and the 3rd Recce Regiment reported clear the extensive Bois de Messei, between Flers and Domfront, thought by civilians to be concealing at least 200 Germans. At 10 a.m. the Army Commander, General Dempsey, visited Div. H.Q. by Air O.P., and by 11.30 the Divisional Commander had flown to a conference at 21 Army Group. As a result the Divisional O Group met, in happier circumstances than they were used to, and on the 20th the Division concentrated in the countryside round Flers and prepared to practise crossing rivers. Training began next day. To aid and supplement battalion training the Div Training School under Major Ted Kilshaw was established on the 26th : it was to remain permanently on the Divisional establishment and follow the Division on its travels like the Div Club—at a respectful distance.

But by the 20th one of General Patton's flashing spearheads

had reached Fontainebleau, while the U.S. XV Corps established
the first bridgehead, and within ten days bridgeheads were linked
up across the length of the Seine. The Division, at its training,
was consoled by the thought that " there's always the Rhine."
They were glad of their training long before the Rhine was
reached. But perhaps a certain feeling of impatience was understandable. The fact remained that the Division now had a large
proportion of new reinforcements who could only benefit by
practice with seasoned warriors. The change after two and a
half months of the wantonness of war was hardly unwelcome.
Indeed the Lincolns have placed on record the admission that
" without warning we found ourselves settled in a small peaceful
French village, surrounded by friendly and admiring inhabitants.
As soon as we realised the implications of this strange turn of
fortune we began to take advantage of it. We turned out our
kits and spruced ourselves up. We marched down the street in
the approved smart and soldierlike manner, and so great was
the transformation that no earthquake occurred when somebody
mentioned Blanco."

And though the weather—for a time the only enemy—became
wet and spoiled life for those who had no barn-roof over them,
Flanagan and Allen, Florence Desmond, Kay Cavendish and
other ENSA entertainers arrived in Flers and did their best
to compensate for the cheerlessness of the rain. 17,000 soldiers
had some form of organised entertainment during the. week,
though the AQ complained of the usual administrative difficulties
in entertaining the entertainers, which in practice could only be
done by turning over to them the entire resources of an officers'
mess : never grudged, but inconvenient.

On 30 August came a warning order from VIII Corps : the
Division was to move within the next four days. The move from
Caen to the Vire front had seemed a wonderful journey, but it
was nothing, a mere step, compared with the advance into
Limburg, which was the next achievement of the Division.

It was true of the Division as of the rest of the Allied
Expeditionary Force, that its most remarkable achievement in
the period between the break-through and the consolidation along
the German frontier was administrative, logistical, *Q* instead of *G*.
From Flers till the battle for Overloon in mid-October the only

real fight the Division had was in the assault-crossing of the Meuse-Escaut Canal. Not but what the G staff had their hands full after the crossing, with the advance on Weert and all the subsequent daily moves and redispositions. But naturally at a time of such prodigious advances, the most vital problems were those of transport and supply. The spotlight was turned on to R.E.M.E. and R.A.O.C. and especially on to the R.A.S.C. For the drivers it was an effort comparable with D-day, in fact it was their great moment.

The first move was to take the Division 150 miles. It began on 3 September. On Divisional moves, Provost would work ahead blazing the trail with triangular signs for the rest to follow. On this occasion others had been before and the route was labelled EYE, with occasional triangles for reassurance. There must have been thousands of these signs left beside the roads of Europe, on trees, houses, hedges, derelict tanks and even on haunches of dead horses where a German gun-team had been caught at a cross-roads. The most famous sign, 240 UP, marked the main L of C from Arromanches to the coastal plain of N. Germany : the triangles extended to Bremen. One wonders if any remain, and if they serve to remind people of the men whose sign it was.

From Flers the route by-passed to the south the worst of the Argentan-Falaise shambles, leading to l'Aigle by way of Ecouche, Médavy and Nonant les Pins. From then on the roads were better, through Verneuil, Breteuil, Conches, Louviers and over the Seine to Les Andelys, above which town the units were to disperse among the prosperous villages. At every fourth hour of the day and night the whole column, stretching for miles, would pull in to the side of the road for half an hour's rest and " brew-up." There was no restriction on vehicle lighting, and all through the night the rumble and clatter and bright lights kept the people of the towns and villages at their bedroom windows, watching the sight that seemed too good to them to be true. By day they lined the streets waving and watching and throwing all the fruit they could lay their hands on. The moment a truck halted the children would crowd round demanding " Cigarettes pour Papa," and then, if they were boys, would as often as not light up for themselves. In this respect U.S. troops had an unfair advantage with their apparently unlimited cigarettes and bon-bons, though it was the experience of the Division that the popularity of the British soldier survived any such material disadvantages. It was no luxury trip, however : the Division had been reinforced to 10 per cent over established strength and no troop-carriers were available. The second-line transport had to ferry the surplus loads, and nobody was left behind in Flers.

On approaching the Seine from Louviers, the first sight of the long islands of poplars, the familiar picture of the chalk cliffs, the romance of our Richard the Lion Heart's great Chateau Gaillard standing on guard above Les Andelys, and, not least, the nearness of Paris, must have lightened hearts that were already lighter than they had been for a very long time. And so the short sojourn by the Seine was carefree and happy. The Div Club, now an institution, moved into an hotel in Les Andelys that had been used by the Germans. There were several dances given, much to the delight of the demoiselles. In Les Andelys the *entente* was exceedingly cordial. For two or three days all units sent a few lucky troops into Paris for the day, but this excellent scheme had to be abandoned when Paris was placed out of bounds to all British troops.

The main employment of the Division was training, needless to say, and the general overhauling of equipment. At the same time Commanders and Staff were studying river-crossing and counter-mortar problems. There were signals courses and all sorts of exercises. There were three indications that the campaign was still being prosecuted—four if the B.B.C. news is counted : it was certainly listened to with intelligent, professional interest. The other three were the despatch of a Squadron of 3rd Recce Regiment to Amiens to clear a wood from which a 2nd Army column had been shot at ; the move on the 9th of the Divisional Engineers to the area of Brussels (freed on the 3rd), where they were temporarily under direct command of 2nd Army ; and thirdly, the magnificent work of the Division's Transport Platoons.

The Division was at this time providing fourteen Transport Platoons (including six first-line Platoons) for third-line duties. These duties included the maintenance of VIII Corps Troops numbering 7 to 8,000, as well as the maintenance of the temporarily over-strong Division. (VIII Corps were moving a daily pack of 120,000 gallons of petrol, oil and lubricants from the Maintenance Area at Bayeux to No. 3 Army Cushion at Arras.) The roadhead was by no means fixed at Arras but grew ever more distant. Unfortunately, the records of the mileages covered do not exist, but some idea of the strain on the drivers (two in each lorry) may be gathered from the fact that they kept up the job non-stop for three weeks. During the period they only sustained one major traffic accident. "At each end of the journey, though thoroughly tired, the drivers simply said : ' This is what we came over here to do,' and started off again," recorded C.R.A.S.C., Lieutenant-Colonel A. K. Yapp.

Of the administrative staff of Divisional Headquarters, the Heads of the Services saw the campaign right through from the planning in Scotland to the military occupation of Germany. At Les Andelys Lieutenant-Colonel Hugh Hinton succeeded Lieutenant-Colonel Rea as AQ ; a few days earlier Major Val Lloyd had succeeded Major Watt, and Major John Baines came as DAQMG in succession to Major Woodrow Wyatt, and then the AQ's team was to work together with hardly any change for the rest of the campaign.

The first job that confronted them came in the form of another warning order on 10th September : the Division must stand by to make a very long move. Every platoon of trucks was out on what the drivers called " the Bayeux Bash," and there was " a first-class petrol crisis, the sum total available being about 7,000 gallons. Accordingly, ' Gadforce ' was mobilised under command of Captain Gadsby of 48 Div. Troops Company, to make the quickest possible run to Bayeux and back to collect petrol." ' Gadforce ' consisted of a platoon of very strange vehicles. " Office-lorries were stripped, Quartermasters' stores vehicles and workshop trucks emptied, captured German vehicles made roadworthy. Each vehicle had a trailer, of no very orthodox size or shape. Drivers were office clerks, batmen, sanitary men, all very composite. The result of the ' Gadforce ' foray was 40,000 gallons of petrol inside 24 hours, and not a single accident to a vehicle. Following this episode, many clerks, sanitary men and issuers applied to become ' drivers i/c ' ! "[1]

[1] Colonel Yapp's account.

This was only the beginning of the excitement. Now the information was received that the move would be one of practically 300 miles to the area of Peer and Petit- (or Kleine-) Brogel in the extreme north-east corner of Belgium. Each unit would spend two days " on the march," and the whole Division would be moved between the 16th and 19th. The Division would be provided with eight extra Transport Platoons for troop-carrying, but there would not be the slightest chance of ferrying. The task of the Divisional R.A.S.C. itself was " to troop-lift one Brigade, and arrive on the same lift prepared for battle, carrying four days' supplies, seventy-five miles petrol, two hundred and fifty rounds per gun of 25-pounder ammunition, and an augmented second-line Small-Arms Ammunition." With the exercise of considerable art and ingenuity it was done. The exact methods that so succeeded always remained something of a mystery, but by various measures, including the overload of a ton on all vehicles, and the use of 25-pounder ammunition boxes as seats in the Troop Carriers (compo-ration boxes had been carried this way on the previous journey ; it was thought that troops would find it easier to resist the temptation to open the 25-pounder cases to see what was inside), the equivalent of six hundred and sixty 3-ton loads in troops, ammunition and supplies were carried forward.

On the 16th the journey through northern France began : it was like a fabulous Royal Progress. Before, the admiring gaze of the populace had been gratifying. Now, as they drove through Albert and Bapaume, past Bourlon wood and the great, well-tended fields where the dead lay from the time of the Four Years War, so many men out of all our families, troops found the enthusiastic welcome excessive and very moving. Near Mons, just across the Belgium border, they stayed for a few hours, consumed some beer brought out by the Belgians and some food and slept a little, and drove on again. Past Nivelles and Waterloo they entered the Forêt de Soignes, regretfully forking right to miss Brussels and make for Louvain, twelve miles due east of the capital. Here was the line of the great rolling plain that some of the old members of the Division remembered occupying in 1940, when the Division's, and the country's, fortunes were so different. What a change had been brought about in the course of four years !

A change was to be remarked, too, in the present situation as the Division pressed out to the north-east, through Diest and over the Albert Canal to Helchteren and on to Peer and Petit-Brogel. It was a change that had nothing to do with the substitution of Flemish for French place-names or the transformation in the local architectural or agricultural methods. It was that the ground had been recently fought over ; farms were still smouldering, tanks stood burnt-out beside the road, invariably the horses and cattle sprawled in the fields with their legs stuck in the air.

9 Brigade and a Squadron of the 3rd Recce Regiment arrived in the area on the 17th, the day chosen to launch Operation *Market Garden* with the object of establishing the Airborne Corps astride the rivers Maas,[1] Waal and Neder Rijn and driving XXX Corps north to the Zuider Zee. XXX Corps had a small bridgehead over the Meuse-Escaut Canal near Overpelt three or four miles to the north-west of Petit-Brogel. The three Airborne Divisions dropped that morning near St. Oedenrode, Nijmegen and Arnhem, and the Guards Armoured Division pushed north from the canal bridgehead up the solitary road linking Eindhoven, St. Oedenrode, Veghel, Grave, Nijmegen, Arnhem, Apeldoorn and the Zuider Zee. They were held up at Valkenswaard, seven miles short of Eindhoven, by strong opposition.

The 3rd Division and the 11th Armoured Division still made up VIII Corps, whose part in the *Market Garden* plan was to operate on the right of XXX Corps. As at Vire, the Division was on the flank of the 2nd Army, next to the U.S. 1st Army, but now, instead of working just across the road, 1st Army was concentrating on the bitter struggle for Aachen and the Roer bridgeheads, some miles away to the east. And XXX Corps were bound northwards. Possibilities for VIII Corps to the north-east were almost unlimited.

8 Brigade arrived next day, the 18th, while 9 Brigade spent the afternoon in preparation for the assault-crossing of the Meuse-Escaut Canal at Lille St. Hubert : one Class 9 and one Class 40 Bridge were needed in the Corps sector. They had little time for reconnaissance, but made the most of it. The assault was to be

[1] The lower Meuse, once it has left the Ardennes and entered Holland, takes the Dutch name of Maas.

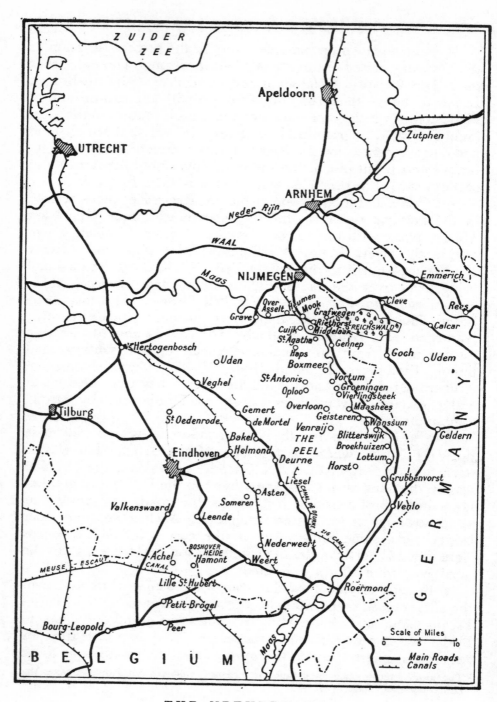

THE NETHERLANDS

made at midnight by two rifle companies from both the Lincolns and the Ulster Rifles. Gaffikin and Baudains, Commander and Second-in-Command of one of the two Ulster Rifles companies (the latter was in England as recently as the 15th convalescing from a wound gained at Troarn), dressed themselves in borrowed civilian clothes, wandered nonchalantly through the fields and finally made their way down to the canal under the noses of the enemy on the other side ; they returned, having fixed a crossing place and the routes to it, as well as having in their minds a complete picture of the canal, its banks and the ditch and stream on their side of it. It was about as awkward a waterway for the manipulation of assault-boats as could be imagined, though not unlike the majority of canals in the Netherlands, with its banks rising above the surrounding pancake and walled with concrete in the Lincolns' sector.

It was a pitch-dark night, but neither wet nor cold. After a hot meal the leading companies were on their way down to the canal at about 10 p.m., confident. In the assembly areas detachments from the K.O.S.B.s, the reserve battalion, came to help erect the storm-boats. The Ulster Rifles were anxious about the non-arrival of their boats as midnight approached, but they came just in time. At 11.45 the Artillery programme started and the Germans replied with accurate mortaring. At this stage Rifleman Greene, a batman of B Company of the Ulster Rifles, behaved with great courage. " While forming up with the boats," Ken Bradshaw writes, " mortar fire came down once more, and the men went to ground. With great coolness and far surpassing his normal duty, he continued to erect the assault-boats, at the same time urging others to do likewise. His great example produced the necessary effect."

For the first time in the campaign the operation was assisted by " artificial moonlight "—low-angle beams from 474 Searchlight Battery. (During the winter this " phenomenon " appeared almost nightly in the sky, to aid patrols and sometimes, perhaps, to persuade the Germans that our patrols were out where none were.) At midnight, after some very heavy, tiring work getting them over the first stream and up the steep bank and with mortars causing considerable trouble to Major de Longueuil's company, the boats entered the water and the crossing was made. The Lincolns met the stiffest opposition on the right, from small arms and a 20 mm., but all companies were across within the first quarter of an hour. The training had not been wasted. A house on the Lincolns' front was set on fire and the crossing area brightly lit by the great flames. Immediately the Pioneers got to work on the rafts and the Signallers on their cables (both Battalions testify to the excellence of communications during this operation : wireless and line were more than ever vital in view of the water obstacle).

The blown bridge had crossed from Lille St. Hubert north into the little village of Broek, beyond which was a level-crossing and a cross-roads. Gaffikin got his company round Broek to a point on the road between the village and the level-crossing, then attacked Broek from the *north* to the surprise of the Germans. As soon as they cleared the village back to the canal, work began on the main bridge.

The Sappers had lost no time. 246 Company were responsible for building the Class 9 Bridge. They had already lost Lieutenant Cadwallader, who had been killed by an anti-tank gun while reconnoitring the canal the previous afternoon. Lieutenants Boyse, Field, Duncan and Borrowman crossed with the assaulting companies. Borrowman was seriously wounded, and Sapper Smith, who had been with him, was taken prisoner, to be recaptured in Broek by the Ulster Rifles, together with the five Germans who were escorting him and upon whom the tables were satisfactorily turned. Despite the enemy fire, construction of the bridge was begun at 1 a.m. It was open to traffic at 7 a.m., although still subject to sniping, which sank two of the boats. Its span was 160 feet.

The Class 40 Bridge was in the hands of 17 Field Company. It was begun as soon as Broek was cleared, and though it was getting light, a thick mist concealed everything till ten o'clock. They record : " The bridge was finished by 5 p.m. without a casualty. In fact it all worked out as the book says it should. The Company received personal congratulations from General Dempsey, Commander of 2nd Army."

A 3.30 p.m. 8 Brigade were ordered to cross the canal on the right of 9 Brigade. This crossing was opposed more strongly than was expected, and the East Yorks found A Company of the Lincolns having serious trouble with some Germans in a wood who proved to be SS Officer Cadets out for battle experience. " See that you assist them to gain it," said the C.O. of the East Yorks when he heard. Thirty-two of the Officer Cadets revised their intentions and surrendered next morning.

185 Brigade had now arrived in the area, and the Division was complete. They were three-quarters of an hour behind schedule. The total vehicle casualties were found to be just over 1 per cent and the average distance covered in the two-day march from the Andelys area was 280 miles. The Div Club, despite a determined effort to establish itself in luxury in Brussels, was prevailed upon to move into an ex-German Panzer billet in the village of Peer. To have been grounded beside the Seine on the 16th and astride an enemy-held canal at the Dutch border on the 19th was an accomplishment with which everyone in the Division had a right to be pleased, not least the Divisional R.E.M.E. Since the arrival at Flers, Brigade workshops had been working to an inspection and repair programme that ensured any necessary " stitch in time " decarbonisation or repair to approximately ten vehicles a day in each workshop. Apart from the excitements of experiment and conversion (they had turned captured German tanks into A.R.V.s for their own use, mounted mortars on the floor of all 3rd Recce Regiment's half-tracks so that they could be fired on the move, and then designed pent-houses for the half-tracks with " canvas obtained by C.R.E.M.E. in Paris ") their main source of excitement was front-line recovery, and that only concerned certain men at the time of an attack or shortly afterwards. But they found their justification as well as that of all the drivers responsible for the daily maintenance of their trucks, in the complete mechanical success of transporting a Division out of the permeating dust of Normandy into the sand-dunes and marshes, the *heides* and *peels* of Limburg.

The K.O.S.B.s occupied Achel on the morning of the 20th and 8 Brigade advanced due east. As they entered the little township of Hamont, the Suffolks' leading sections were met with peaches, apples and pears and estimates of the enemy in the town, varying in strength between none and a hundred. As it was, they took sixty prisoners, who could have hindered the liberation more

seriously had they not been deserted by their officers and all but
three of their N.C.O.s. Hamont then fell to the undignified
business of the indictment, unavoidably summary, of its collaborators, and women were publicly shamed with their heads
shaven. A touching feature of the freeing of Hamont was the way
the entire population paid homage to Private Hollis of the Suffolks,
the only soldier killed in the advance that morning, who was
buried with full civic honours, his coffin draped with the Belgian
flag, covered with flowers, and followed by several hundred people
to his grave.

That morning 11th Armoured Division passed through 9
Brigade, driving north and reaching Leende by 12.15. The 3rd
Recce Regiment were protecting the flank at villages with the
remarkable names of Dorpleen and Groot Schoot. The weather
had been unsettled for two days now, and at Arnhem the position
of the troops at the bridge was critical. At Nijmegen that evening
a small force, including tanks and infantry of the 1st Grenadiers,
pushed the bridge and crossed the 600 yards span to join up with
the U.S. paratroops. The commander of that force, Lieutenant-
Colonel E. H. (Eddie) Goulburn, came to command 8 Brigade
the following month.

On the morning of the 21st, 8 Brigade were directed to cross
the Dutch frontier and advance due east to occupy the town of
Weert. The Suffolks led, followed by the East Yorks and the
76th Field Regiment. The Gunners had a day of drill-order
" fire and movement " such as they thought only possible at
Larkhill, and as they leap-frogged forward with the infantry
they derived considerable amusement from the looks on the faces
of the marching sections on either side of the road. Their own
F.O.O.s wore the most pained expressions as they plodded along,
18-set on back, passing and repassing their own guns as gun
position after gun position was prepared and occupied.

The road soon petered out altogether and the way led east,
first through villages and farm-tracks, then over a waste of sand-
dunes, the Boshover Heide, stretching five miles to Weert. This
was not the normal approach to the town, but the most direct.
Weert lay on the main Eindhoven-Venlo road at the intersection
of railway and canal, but the main road ran in from the north-
west and the tow-path from the south-west. The first enemy

spandaus opened up on the Suffolks as they approached the railway from the dunes late in the evening. As the attack went in on these positions the sight of Colonel Craddock striding down the track wearing his S.D. cap in preference to a helmet greatly heartened the men. While they were establishing themselves astride the railway, their objective for the night, they heard a series of loud explosions and knew that the Boche was destroying the canal bridges.

At 3.15 a.m. the C.O. ordered the Battalion forward to the canal at Weert. Despite the rather early hour, a terrific reception was waiting, with the leaders of the local resistance movement and all the townsfolk, and everywhere the colour orange, on favours and frocks and flags, in memory of an earlier War of Liberation, when Spanish troops had trampled across the Netherlands. The Dutch patriots had now organised an efficient telephone service to the south and east of the town, and information poured in to the effect that the enemy was establishing himself along the line of the canal that ran almost due north through Nederweert to Helmond.

This information was confirmed later in the day by 3rd Recce Regiment, who had exploited to Nederweert, and by the Gunners, who found that the great belfry of Weert church had already been converted for use as an A.R.P. fire-watchers' post and dominated the country for miles around—an unusually comfortable O.P. until the Germans decided that it was a suitable target for an 88 mm. It was soon learned that 11th Armoured Division had a bridgehead over this canal at Asten and were operating in the area of Helmond and Deurne. In the afternoon the Commander-in-Chief visited Div. H.Q. at Hamont. General Montgomery outlined the trend of the future operations of 21 Army Group to the Divisional Commander before he left. It was while he was at Div. H.Q. that the news was received that enemy infantry and tanks had cut the axis of XXX Corps between Uden and the Maas bridge at Grave. That night 185 Brigade was ordered to relieve the 11th Armoured Division astride the canal at Asten.

The Division now faced east, had their backs to the vital XXX Corps axis, and were committed to a front that widened daily. They were determined that there should be no severing of the axis on that front. The plight of the men at Arnhem became more hopeless as the weather grew blustery and bleak. Men cursed the weather and remembered their own feelings in mid-Channel. And when some huge supplies of German rations were captured up at Oss, and distributed in place of the accepted compo rations, they were cursed too, though it was obvious that they were saving some hundreds of trucks journeys of some hundreds of miles back and forth to Normandy. The German pork and beans and cheese were palatable and you would have thought they would have been acceptable, if only for the change : they were emphatically not. It cannot be denied that the *Knackebrot* was intolerable.

In cold wet weather, 8 and 185 Brigades and 3rd Recce Regiment patrolled the front ; the friendliness and enthusiasm of the Dutch continued in an almost embarrassing degree : at this time the G Ops Signals log bears constant witness to the assistance they gave the forward troops.

Moves and rumours of moves were continual. The K.O.S.B.s group moved out in front of 185 Brigade to Liesel. In the Weert area the South Lancs crossed the canal, while 3rd Recce Regiment patrolled the canal right up to Helmond and beyond. Then, on the 25th at last light, the East Yorks were ordered to Gemert, still farther north, and the rest of 8 Brigade were relieved by 4th Armoured Brigade, while they followed the East Yorks north to Bakel and De Mortel. On the 26th a very rare incident (because their appearance was rare) was the shooting down of a Messerschmidt 109 near Zomeren, which was in the middle of a Divisional front extending 35,000 metres north and south. The next day it was to be extended north and also east another 16,000 metres to St. Anthonis and held as a firm base while 11th Armoured Division advanced to the river Maas. Arrangements were made and the GOC had given out his orders when, in the middle of the night, VIII Corps rang up to say the 11th Armoured Div. operation was postponed forty-eight hours. This involved a rapid readjustment of Brigade plans, but the result was a quieter day for the whole Division than it had known for some time . . . until 5.45 that evening, when Corps rang up to say that all elements of the 3rd Division must be clear of Deurne, Liesel and Asten by 8.30 the next morning This was to make way for the

United States 7th Armoured Division, who announced their intention of sweeping down through Overloon and Venray to Venlo. " Elements of the 3rd Division " were clear by 8.30, all excepting the covering troops, who stayed to furnish the Americans with details of tank " going," bridge and canal reconnaissance and certain facts they had noted about the enemy.

The 29th was passed in ominous quiet at Div. H.Q., and, sure enough, an L.O. arrived at midnight with a note from the Corps Commander to the GOC, inviting him to a reconnaissance the first thing next morning. At 6.30 a.m. General Whistler set off on reconnaissance north of the Maas in the Nijmegen area with the Commanders of VIII Corps and 1 Airborne Corps and General Gavin, the Commander of 82nd U.S. Airborne Division, who had made the descent near Nijmegen. That day, the last of September, plans were made for the preliminary moves of two Brigade Groups over the Maas on the 1st October, to be ready for an operation on the 2nd/3rd. Three O Groups were held as details of the complex traffic and concentrations plans successively became known. Allowances had to be made for the full operational scope required by U.S. 7th Armoured Division, for the move of 231 Brigade across the river and for the heavy demands of XXX Corps maintenance. 8 and 185 Brigades would cross, and also the 4th Tank Battalion of the Coldstream Guards, which came under command from 6th Guards Tank Brigade : they had operated and trained with the Division at Vire and Flers.

On 1st October they crossed the Maas bridge at Grave and turned east along the bank. The road was extremely narrow and the sides gave way into deep dykes on either side. They came to Over Asselt and then Heumen, where they crossed the southern end of the Maas-Waal Canal. Nijmegen was five miles to the north beside the Waal River, and most of the narrow neck of country between the two waterways was in our hands, despite violent Panzer counter-attacks. A mile ahead to the east a pine-forested ridge rose to 70 metres (a Dutch mountain range) and sloped down, then rose again into the massed pine-trees of the great Reichswald whose edges marked the German frontier. In the southern end of the first forest ridge, next to the Maas, the line was held by the 82nd U.S. Airborne Division, who had landed from the air exactly a fortnight ago. In this wood, near the Mook and Middelaar halt on the Nijmegen railway, 8 and 185 Brigades and the 4th Tank Coldstream Guards arrived in pouring rain. 9 Brigade, the 33rd Field Regiment and 3rd Recce Regiment, stayed west of the Maas in the area of Haps, and just across the river had remarkably good flank observation of the least German movement—to the special satisfaction of 33rd Field Regiment.

East of the Maas the 82nd Airborne Division were attacking next day in the low ground alongside the river from Mook south to Middelaar and Riethorst. All that day the Divisional Artillery fired in support of this very determined attack, which was costly but completely successful, and the Germans who were routed from this area found it costlier. The Division's gunnery was appreciated.[1]

Now Operation *Gatwick* was contemplated. It was intended that the Division should clear the Reichswald with the 15th (Scottish) Division on the right and 43rd (Wessex) Division on the left. On the 3rd, VIII Corps Commander visited Div. H.Q., and General Whistler told him he reckoned the wood on the slope at Kiekberg would be his chief problem, capable of absorbing a brigade by itself. He thought he would have to put a brigade straight at this with a second brigade at Grafwegen on the left edge of the western tip of the Reichswald, and the third brigade would then be put on to St. Jansberg, the wooded ground overlooking the Corps bridges that would have to be built before the operation could succeed. That afternoon and early next morning 185 Brigade relieved the American Glider Troops, not without interference from a watchful enemy at Heikant.

On the 6th the full programme of complicated reliefs was ordered. The congestion in the close area and the limited capacity of the roads were reminiscent of the conditions in the Normandy lodgment area. On the 7th, after due consideration, the Army Commander decided that the operation would absorb too many troops in view of the current operations farther west to clear the Antwerp approaches. Operation *Gatwick* was therefore postponed and the 3rd Division was ordered to

[1] The Ops log at H.Q., R.A., recorded on Oct. 2nd that 454 Battery of the 76th Field Regiment had fired the first of the Division's shells on to Germany. This was inaccurate : reference to the War Diary of 20th Anti-Tank Regiment reveals that B 4 gun of 41 Battery fired a round into Germany at 4.10 p.m. on Oct. 1st. It was not yet seventeen weeks since the first was fired at the German beach defences.

recross the Maas to take part in the elimination of the enemy pocket west of the river.

Clearing the Reichswald was a job most men had regarded with more foreboding than relish. It was one of the least attractive stretches of the Siegfried Line.[1] The Division was on the very site of the catastrophe of Mook Heide where an earlier Dutch Liberation Army of fifteen thousand men had been caught and outmanoeuvred by a Spanish force. It was from this rout that the leader of the resistance movement, William the Silent, had received that worst-of-all news of his gallant brothers : missing, believed killed. The line was handed over to the 43rd Division together with detailed reconnaissance information that had been obtained by vigorous patrol activity over the last two thousand yards to the frontier. The cost to the Division of this information was ten officers and eighty other ranks during the first week of October.

[1] The GOC's famous description of the Reichswald is appropriate but unprintable.

Chapter Six

OVERLOON AND VENRAIJ

" This ill-digested vomit of the sea. . . ."
ANDREW MARVELL, on the Netherlands

THE BULK of the German force that fled from Normandy withdrew behind the Siegfried Line. But as they saw an opportunity to establish outposts they emerged and quickly prepared a forward line, a line whose farthest positions protected a bridgehead west of the Maas. This was where the river wormed its way northwards and westwards in poor imitation of the snake-like progress of the Rhine round into the North Sea. They meandered together in land that lay level with the sea and seldom rose to the eminence of 30 metres. The Germans on our side of the Maas held a position that in the south, opposite Venlo, made full defensive use of the waterlogged *Peel* areas through which ran the Deurne Canal. The northern part of their bridgehead, in the area of Overloon and Venraij, gave them not quite the same degree of natural protection. It is true that here their front was covered by the *Molen Beek*, a stream that was an effective obstacle to any vehicle, and by the morasses of the *Vierlingsbeeksche Heide* and *Overloonsche Heide* ; but in addition to the road running from Oploo, there were subsidiary farm-tracks that, unnavigable as they became in wet weather, did connect Oploo with the village of Overloon and the town of Venraij. The Germans were determined to hold these last two places, and therefore surrounded them with mines.

Up to the 9th October, when the Division began to concentrate in the neighbourhood of St. Anthonis and Oploo, and the U.S. 7th Armoured Division was relieved, the Germans had held out successfully. The " After Action Report " of the U.S. Armoured Division reads : " After nearly a month's pounding against the fortress of Metz, 7th Armoured Division went north to aid in an end run play around the Siegfried Line in the vicinity of Holland.

The Division was given the mission of clearing the enemy resistance in the PEEL SWAMP region (*sic*) . . . The OVERLOON battle was a costly one, and during the first six days of October the Division suffered 452 battle casualties (killed, wounded and missing), also 35 tanks and 43 other vehicles." The 3rd British Infantry Division watched unappreciatively as the Americans pulled out and drove away to the south. Their misgivings were justified : in the seven days between the 12th and 18th October their own casualties in men were almost three times as many as those the Americans had suffered. But by the 18th they had taken Overloon and Venraij.

The VIII Corps plan (Operation *Constellation*) was to clear, in four phases, all the enemy from their Maas bridgehead. The plan for the first phase (*Castor*) was for the 3rd Division to attack south-east on to Venraij and draw the largest possible force of enemy to meet them. Then, when the enemy was fully engaged, three other Divisions would strike east (*Pollux, Sirius and Vega*), from Brexem and Weert to Roermond and Venlo, cutting off the enemy's retreat at those two crossing-places. Every effort was to be made to mislead the enemy into thinking that operations were limited to the Venraij area !

The Division's part was planned at Headquarters on the 10th and orders given out that afternoon. Operation *Aintree* (Division favoured this more terrestrial code name : the stars were all very well for higher formations) was to begin next day. But a slow, soaking drizzle had been descending all day, and in the evening the operation was postponed 24 hours. That meant that the Infantry and their supporters had the whole of the 11th in which to consider the battle that lay ahead.

There would be two phases in the operation : the first the capture of Overloon, the second the capture of Venraij. 8 Brigade would complete the first, securing Overloon, opening up the road in from Oploo, and exploiting a mile forward down the Overloon-Venraij road. 9 Brigade would be prepared to carry out the second, clearing the Laag Heide woods to the right (south-west) of Overloon, then advancing over the *Molen Beek* into Venraij. 185 Brigade would be ready to assist in either phase and exploit the success of the second. It was obvious that this onslaught through mines and mud against a strong force of Germans would call for the very fullest support. The fire power of the 25th Field Regiment and all the guns of the 11th Armoured and 15th (Scottish) Divisions and 8 A.G.R.A. was added to that of the Division's three Field Regiments. The Divisional Sappers, with the heavy responsibilities of developing the forward routes and the crossings over the *Molen Beek* and gapping the minefields, were joined for these tasks by the Flails of A and C Squadrons of the Westminster Dragoons and by A.V.R.E.s of 617 Assault Squadron of 42 A.R.E. The 4th Tank Battalions of the Grenadier and Coldstream Guards came to join the Infantry, and during the afternoon Wing-Commander Tollemache, G.C., reported to Div. H.Q. to set up his Forward Control Post : the Division would have the close support of two Typhoon Wings as well as a preliminary destructive programme for Medium Bombers.

At 11.20 on the morning of the 12th, thirty-six Marauders of XIX U.S. A.A.F. attacked Venraij, while Typhoons of 83 Group, R.A.F., were going for known enemy positions. These Typhoons had a most successful morning, roving the sky in packs of four, rockets bristling from the leading edges of their wings. Over the target they pounced down one after the other, rocketing out of existence anything in their line of fire. Bombing attacks on the bridges at Venlo and Roermond were called off at the last moment, and to this is attributed much increased resistance as reinforcements arrived.

The guns, massed in the flat fields south of Oploo, were now splitting the sky and making the earth tremble. First, 8 A.G.R.A. (four Medium Regiments, one heavy, and one heavy A.A.) opened up at 11 o'clock, and the three Divisional Artilleries joined in at 11.30. The din grew indescribable as hundreds of shells a minute were slammed into the breaches and trajected volleying through the sky towards Overloon. One unfortunate observer flying an Air O.P. above the forward assembly area was hit by a medium shell and disintegrated in mid-air.

At the moment of midday the guns switched to the Opening Line of a barrage, and after 15 minutes the guns lifted as the Infantry of the Suffolks and East Yorks, supported by Churchills of the 4th Tank Coldstream Guards, advanced over the Start-Line. They had to cross half a mile of desolate land to reach the village, the Suffolks on the right making for the western and

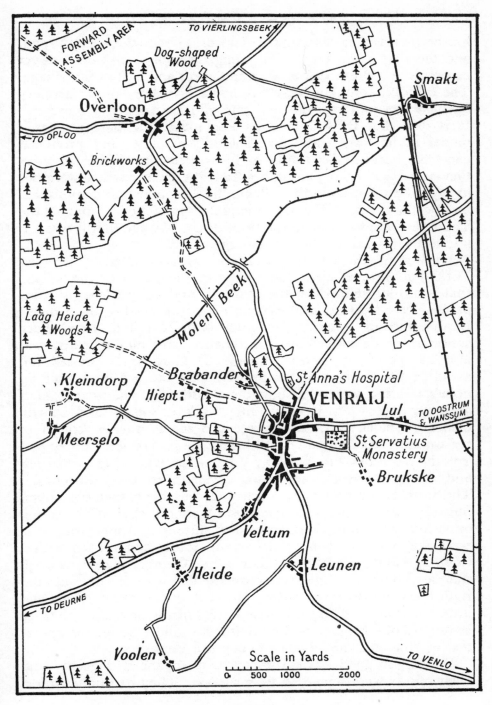

OVERLOON AND VENRAIJ

southern parts as far as a small brickworks beside the Venraij road, and the East Yorks on the left going through some woods to get across the Vierlingsbeek road in the north and east of the village. The Suffolks complain that " progress was slow, as the artillery barrage was timed to lift at a rate of 100 yards in 5 minutes." It is true that their follow-up close under the barrage was a model of how such advances should be made, and produced excellent results. According to the statements of the prisoners they sent back, enemy casualties from the great barrage were not heavy, as the houses in the village, though almost all demolished, had cellars that afforded adequate protection : but " the Tommies were so close on the heels of the barrage that it was too late to start fighting when we emerged."

It was on the left that resistance was strongest. The East Yorks had first to clear the woods to the north of the village that were dog-shaped on the map. C and D, the leading companies, were held up in the north edge, the head of the " dog." In this opening stage of the attack both Battalions were under considerable defensive fire from enemy guns and mortars, and also hampered by mines. C and D Companies pressed on, avoiding the thickest of the minefield on the left, and after an hour's fighting were well into the " body " of the wood. Half an hour later they were sending back prisoners, and shortly before 2 o'clock D Company reached the south-west corner of the wood : " D Company could advance no farther, as they had lost their officers and C.S.M., suffered several other casualties, and at the moment were being commanded by a Corporal." The Suffolks and East Yorks were now just short of their objectives. Steadily they fought their way into Overloon, against decreasing opposition that was soon confined to sniping and mortaring. At 5 o'clock A and D Companies of the South Lancs, each with a troop of Churchills of the 4 Grenadier Guards, passed through the East Yorks and Suffolks to clear the first wood on the Suffolks' right flank immediately south of the road at Overloon. They met little opposition. By dusk Overloon was firmly held and the three Battalions of 8 Brigade had established a solid base for the operation of Phase 2 : the advance to capture Venraij.

So far, so good. The Infantry had advanced doggedly and their efforts were rewarded with success. They had only limited support from the Churchills, which had been stopped by mines until, late in the afternoon, Flails got them forward. The weight of the Artillery support had effectively kept many German heads down until the Infantry were upon them. The Middlesex had joined the Gunners in this, for once firing as a battalion, with all three machine-gun Companies in a line along the forward edge of a wood, and close behind them, in a clearing, all the mortars of D Company : that day they fired 3,800 bombs and 300,000 rounds of Mark VIIIz machine-gun ammunition. The Field Regiments added a new trick to an already extensive repertoire (including the firing of shells filled with propaganda leaflets) by firing what were known, sardonically, as Joker Targets. This was the joke : a " cab-rank " of rocket-firing Typhoons patrolled the sky, weather permitting, while one of their officers worked on the ground with a Gunner officer at either Brigade or Battalion H.Q. : the Infantry reported the position of an enemy strong-point in their way, the Gunner agreed with the Airman the exact time when the Artillery would fire a few rounds of red smoke at the strong-point, and the Typhoon pilots given this time, and a brief description of the target by wireless, watched out for red smoke and did the rest. Our own troops saw the joke and laughed loudest. The Germans never did have much of a sense of humour. The I.O. of 76 Field Regiment and Flight-Lieutenant O'Brien of 404 Squadron once performed the jape within 7 minutes of the Infantry request : the good people of Overloon are having to build a new church in consequence. That they were glad to sacrifice their church may be easily inferred from the fact that in 1946 they have included in their programme of rebuilding a war-museum as " a monument to honour the memory of the British soldiers who sacrificed their young lives at Overloon," and have written to the Division, through the Netherlands Government Information Office at The Hague, for a full account of the battle that was fought in their gardens and in the ruins of their homes : even in the churchyard where their own dead lay.

Interrogation of the day's haul of prisoners showed that the enemy was disposed substantially as the Intelligence staff had predicted. The German 180 Infantry Division was in the line opposite. It was not a very good Division, and the Divisional

Battle Group Walther was sent to strengthen the Overloon front.
Div. Battle Group Walther contained a number of battalion
battle groups formed from German Air Force units and paratroops. Such was Battalion Paul in Overloon. It provided 109
out of the total of 147 prisoners taken by 9.30 that first evening.
Its strength was apparently not much more than 250 before the
attack, but they were experienced fighters, several of them wearing
the Crete armband. Their officers under Hauptmann Paul all
saved themselves (these battle groups and some higher formations
each bore the name of their commanding officer). The commander of No. 1 Company, Hptmn. Bockmann, came in for
some caustic comments from his men. He had, until recently,
been a *Luftwaffe* pilot, and his rare visits to his forward sections
had been made, they said, at almost Luftwaffe speed. 8 Brigade
had dealt with Battalion Paul very well, and were ready to deal
with Battalion Kerutt on the right if necessary, or Battalion
Hoffman on the left. The doggedness of their advance has been
remarked : it remains to add that, despite heavy shelling during
the night and the restriction imposed on movement by mines
that had been laid with typical German excessiveness, tails were
well up.

The next day was Friday, the 13th. 8 Brigade stood fast,
while 9 and 185 Brigades spent the day clearing pine-woods, a
sinister occupation in itself, without the dark potent that inevitably
attaches to that date. From Overloon, belts of woodland extend
eastwards and round to the south and south-west. The one road
to Venraij runs through them to south-south-east. 185 Brigade
were given this road as their right boundary and would advance
to the south-east, while 9 Brigade over on the right went south.

After the most difficult reconnaissance of mine-free tracks
from their assembly area, the Ulster Rifles attacked at 9 a.m.
Passing through the South Lancs of 8 Brigade—who had got into
the northern edge of the wood at first light that morning—the
Ulster Rifles were soon acquainted with some of the handicaps
of this sort of fighting : " In some places the wood was thick
enough to be impenetrable, in others it did not exist at all.
German positions and abandoned equipment testified to their
recent occupation. Snipers were encountered at once, neces-
sitating a thorough searching of every inch of ground : mopping

them up was inevitably a slow, laborious process. . . . Farther south it was more uniform, with pine-trees of medium size, hedged about with foliage and undergrowth through which a way could be forced without undue difficulty. Throughout the wood were soft, sandy tracks, treacherous for vehicles because of their nature and because they were often beset with mines. Neither these tracks nor the shape of the wood itself bore much relation to the map, even with a revised trace from an air-photograph, so that one of the principal difficulties was finding the way." Thus the speed of the operation was reduced, but by 1 o'clock Major Bird reported D Company in the left-hand forward edge of the wood.

Twenty minutes later the K.O.S.B.s advanced into the wood on the Ulster Rifles' right, clearing up to the edge of the wood on their right with Churchills of the Grenadiers supporting them on the exposed right flank. They got through to the forward edge of the wood without much difficulty, though they were shelled and mortared hard and the Churchills had to be Flailed through a minefield. As soon as they began to emerge from the southern edge of the wood they came under cross-fire from enemy machine-guns, two of which were stopped by Lance-Corporal Harmon. He crawled under fire towards the nearest enemy post, threw two grenades in, rushed it with his Sten, killing two Germans, then immediately went on to treat the next post likewise. The co-operation with the Grenadiers was excellent at this stage. Corporal Forrest, who had spotted a German section stalking one of the Churchills with bazookas, ran forward firing his Sten : he killed two Germans, and when the other five withdrew he tracked them down to their fox-holes and took them all prisoner. Then it grew dark and the mortaring increased.

Over on the left in the woods east of Overloon the Warwicks and K.S.L.I. had had similar experiences. The K.S.L.I. soon discovered that the edge of the wood on the map was quite different from the edge of the wood on the ground, and Y Company only got on to its area after much wandering about among the close firs. But both battalions cleared their areas of the enemy and were level with 9 Brigade along the southern edge of the wood at nightfall. That night orders were given out for the

Division to continue the advance next day, the 14th : in 8 Brigade the South Lancs were to drive north-east to Schafferden on the railway, a mile short of the Maas at Vierlingsbeek, while the Norfolks continued the 185 Brigade advance south astride the Venraij road and the Lincolns crossed open ground in front of the Ulster Rifles, and K.O.S.B.s to enter and clear the next strip, the Laag Heide wood.

The South Lancs' account, austere as ever, is restricted to the statement : " The operation was effected by each Company operating successively with limited objectives, and by 1800 hours the ground was secured and 102 prisoners taken, C Company being responsible for 83." That is all. The same day Major W. A. Waller, M.C., assumed command of the battalion. But the picture of the Lincolns' attack on the other flank is more detailed. Burton had taken a patrol out at 4 a.m. to bring back information about the dyke that ran across the middle of the open stretch between the two woods, but was brought back himself badly wounded before he could get near the ditch. · So at first light Major Smith took B Company forward without the information. They met the usual small-arms fire and advanced to deal with it. As they reached the dyke German Defensive Fire came crashing down, and in a few minutes the Company had suffered such losses that Major Smith, who was under orders not to become too heavily committed, gave the signal to withdraw under cover of a smoke-screen : a disastrous start to a day's fighting.

Now a full battalion attack with a troop of Churchills and a barrage from the Divisional Artillery was planned, and that afternoon the Lincolns advanced as the Ulster Rifles had done at Cambes, as 8 Brigade did at the chateau : to a watcher it was awe-inspiring. As they approached the dyke close behind their own barrage, down came the German mortar and shell-fire upon them, this time perhaps more intense than before. They continued to advance. " Those who fell were left to the care of those whose job it was to look after them, and the rest pressed on. There was no cover—only the soft sandy soil to lessen the effect of the murderous rain of shells." The Germans who were waiting in the wood were unfortunate : some threw down their arms and ran for their lives. They belonged to the battalion battle-group Kerutt. The wood was soon cleared down to within a quarter of a mile of Kleindorp, a hamlet two miles due west of Venraij, and just short of the *Molen Beek*. Among the Lincolns' dead were Major Smith, and D Company Commander, Major Dawson, who was just back after having been wounded near Cambes. Their C.O., Colonel Firbank, had gone in with the rest, firing his Sten, directing them, encouraging them wherever a cheery word was wanted. For his own courage and devotion to duty he was awarded the D.S.O.

Between the 8 and 9 Brigade advances, the Norfolks advanced that day astride the Venraij road. From the start of their attack at 7 a.m. they met stiff opposition that included artillery concentrations observed from Venraij church steeple. They were surprised to find the road-bridge intact over the first dyke (the same one that was proving so fatal to the Lincolns along to the right). By last light Colonel Bellamy had managed to manœuvre all four companies into a fairly compact formation about 400 yards short of the *Molen Beek*. After seven separate onslaughts by Typhoons the troublesome Venraij church at last started to burn. It was a day of unsettled weather, the clouds now low with drizzle, now breaking into a clear sky : flying conditions were bad, but improved. During the day it became clear that a separate operation was needed by another formation to clean up the area east to the Maas while the whole Division concentrated on Venraij. 11th Armoured Division, who had so far been providing a firm base for the Division, were to commit 159 Brigade in the area of Schafferden on the 15th,[1] relieving the South Lancs. That day the 3rd Division paused to draw breath and prepare for the next day's battle : their action was limited to patrolling. The Typhoons were busy attacking ferries on the Maas. And at Div. Headquarters the crossing of the *beek* and the final assault on Venraij were being planned.

The *Molen Beek* was a much more formidable obstacle than could be appreciated from a glance at the map. It was a stream no more than 10 feet wide, but the banks were 4 feet high and sloping, so that the effective gap was about 25 feet. In addition, the approaches were almost impossible across low-lying water-

[1] It was in this Brigade's attack here on the 16th that Sergeant George Eardley of the 4th K.S.L.I. won the V.C.

logged ground. The road from Overloon and the few tracks along to the right that led up to it had been broken up and cratered by the Germans, who had also sown the whole area with mines—even the bottom of the *beek* where it was shallow enough for wading. 185 Brigade were to cross in the area of the main road and advance into the northern part of Venraij, while 8 Brigade were to pass down through 9 Brigade in Laag Heide wood, cross the *beek* and enter Venraij from the west to clear the southern part of the town. Venraij was the size of a typical English market-town, as it might be in the Fenland. Its main streets ran north and south. Its northern " parish," 185 Brigade's objective, was called Brabander.

Success depended first on ability to bridge the *beek*. This was one of the responsibilities of the C.R.E., Lieutenant-Colonel R. W. (" Tiger ") Urquhart. He had under command 617 Assault Squadron as well as the Divisional Companies. To establish two tank crossings 617 Squadron mounted two Small Box Girder Bridges on Churchill A.V.R.E.s and rushed them up ready for use the following day. For the Infantry crossings, 2´10 feet of kapok (floating) bridging was obtained—sufficient for four bridges on each of the four battalion fronts. The battalions chosen for the assault were the Suffolks, East Yorks, Warwicks and Norfolks. The 4th Tank Grenadier Guards were to support 8 Brigade, the 4th Tank Coldstream Guards 185 Brigade. The largest force of bombers the Division had ever seen filled the sky that evening on its way into Germany to destroy more of the enemy's sources of armament, and the sight did much to cheer up the tired soldiers, who had personally very little to look forward to in the coming day's battle. The weather grew worse that night. Few men slept. Ammunition had to be got to the guns ; tanks and bridging equipment had to be got right forward along defective roads in pitch darkness. " We got our orders after dark," recorded the Norfolks, " and in the usual streaming rain the unhappy Company Commanders made their plans while, with hooded torches, we struggled to read our maps."

The Infantry kapok bridges were a success : the tank bridges —through no fault of the Sappers, whose pluck was beyond praise—were with one exception a failure. The last consignments of kapok were received by the Infantry at 4.20 a.m. The assaulting troops carried it forward to the *beek* and launched it with the aid of the Sappers. 185 Brigade crossed first, silently, and by 5 o'clock the Norfolks had two Companies across beside the Overloon-Venraij road, the Warwicks two Companies across half a mile along to the right. A small counter-attack against D Company of the Warwicks was beaten off after a hand-to-hand fight. Otherwise there seemed to be little opposition. Work was immediately begun on the banks in preparation for the heavier bridges, while the Infantry formed up on the Start-Line across the *beek* for their advance to the Brabander outskirts of Venraij. The first two attempts by 617 Squadron, R.E., to approach the *beek* through the quagmire and lay bridges across in the Norfolk area both came to grief. By this time the enemy had guessed what was going on, and brought down heavy fire along the line of the *beek*. At the Warwick crossing on the right, Sergeant Finan of 617 Squadron drove his A.V.R.E. with its girder bridge held out in front like a great, ill-balanced fire-escape, down the track through the minefield to the cratered edge of the stream. On dismounting, he saw that the release cables for his bridge were gone. Under intense fire his demolition N.C.O. climbed on to his shoulders and released the bridge, which dropped well. This was the only tank bridge across the *Molen Beek* for the next 24 hours. 4th Tank Coldstream Guards got two troops over it to help the Warwicks, when it, too, began to break down. After strenuous efforts to repair it with logs the Squadron was eventually all across.

If the Sappers were not lucky, the Norfolks certainly were. They began by advancing straight across a minefield, without realising it, and miraculously without a single detonation. Until the Warwicks had beaten off the counter-attack against their D Company, the Norfolks had to wait in very exposed marsh, accumulating casualties. Then the Warwicks' A and C Companies crossed the *beek* and both Battalions advanced. This was at 7.30, and the Divisional Artillery laid down a barrage for them. The German guns and mortars were already firing as fast as they could reload. Though a Tiger tank was giving trouble, the German Infantry were now feeling the effect of the barrage. Under it the Warwick advance was as exemplary as that of the Suffolks on to Overloon. By midday their A Company were established in Brabander.

8 Brigade's attempt to get tanks over the *beek* were even more steadily frustrated than 185's were. The Suffolks and East Yorks had marched out from Overloon at about 3.30 a.m. At 7.30 the Suffolks were approaching the *beek* with their kapok, and A.V.R.E.s were Flailing the approach for tanks. As elsewhere, the banks were boggy and Flailing was slow. B Company came under heavy machine-gun fire and were held up. For the tank-crossing three A.V.R.E.s were available, each carrying, not a box girder bridge, but a fascine—an enormous bundle of chespaling that in this case would be dumped bodily in the stream to form a solid bridge, but which had the additional use, when unrolled, of a firm carpet that could be laid in a mud-track. Unfortunately one of these tanks became stuck before it could get into position to drop its fascine into the *beek*. The other two went up the track cleared by the Flails, but the second A.V.R.E. became immovably bogged in the *beek* itself. The third fascine alone was not adequate to bridge the obstacle. There was no course but to send back to the Armoured Brigade H.Q. for the box girder bridge that was held in reserve. It would take time. B Company were already in difficulties, their Company Commander wounded. The rain was descending

" Steady as the sand in an hour glass on this day,"[1]

and the cold soaked into the bone.

Despite the fact that for some hours they would have to do without the support of the Churchills or of their own carriers and anti-tank guns, Colonel Craddock decided to pass C and D Companies through B Company and over the *beek*. They crossed at 10 o'clock, but their progress was slow, with intense enemy fire coming at them from the right. Going forward himself to visit C Company, Colonel Craddock was crossing the corner of a field when he had a foot blown off by a *schu* mine. In his comparatively short time as their commander he had endeared himself to officers and men of the Battalion, and his appearance among the forward troops at difficult times had proved a main factor in

[1] *Third Ypres*, Edmund Blunden.

their successes. Once again Major Allen found himself in command at a critical time.

C and D Companies continued to press forward, though both lost their Company Commanders. New thrusts were planned by the Brigadier to start at 3 p.m., when the new bridge would be in position and the Churchills streaming across. At 3 the new bridge *was* in position, but the first two tanks to cross were bogged down in the soft ground on the far side, so was a third, and there were no more attempts at that point. But the East Yorks now crossed over the Suffolks' kapoks and moved out to the left flank. Their Commanding Officer was suffering from a wound received earlier, and Major J. D. W. Renison, T.D., took over the command, which he was to hold for the rest of the campaign. " Banger " King succeeded him as Second-in-Command. By nightfall the Suffolks had reached Hiept, a hamlet three-quarters of a mile to the west of Venraij. On their left flank the East Yorks were level with them.

Farther along, on the extreme left, the Norfolks had advanced a thousand yards, to reach the woods outside Brabander. Since they joined the battle two days earlier they had been hard hit, losing 211 casualties, including five Company Commanders. The Warwicks, in Brabander since their morning advance behind the barrage, found themselves in a salient that was continually counter-attacked, shelled and mortared. They held their ground and later managed to push on another 200 yards towards Venraij. In the evening C Company fought their way into the grounds of St. Anna's Hospital on the left. Many prisoners were taken. Shortly after dark the East Yorks arrived on the right and the two Brigades were linked up.

That night the Sappers were working at full pressure. At the Suffolks' crossing-place, 246 Field Company constructed a 40-foot Trestle Bridge with a firm track approach and improvised an additional brushwood and steel crib causeway. No. 1 Platoon of 253 Field Company built a similar trestle bridge at the break in the Overloon-Venraij road, to be known as the Forth Crossing. No. 2 Platoon, together with all other troops available, laid down culverting to fill the gaps, working furiously. Bulldozers scoured the area for rubble, R.E.M.E. Recovery Tanks tugged away at bogged Churchills, while everyone else

collected logs and faggots. It must have been quite obvious to
the Germans what was going on, and they sent over shells to
add to the difficulties. Late in the evening the Warwicks discovered that St. Anna's Hospital was an asylum containing 1,700
incurable female lunatics. The message from the F.O.O. with
the Warwicks was received over the air at the gun-position as
" two thousand bad women," and caused much speculation
amongst the Gunners. Conditions in the hospital were pitiful.
The A.D.M.S. (Colonel W. A. Robinson had just succeeded
Colonel R. D. Cameron, M.C.) and Civil Affairs immediately
organised relief.

That night's Div. Intelligence Summary reproduced a marked
map captured from the Germans during the day, indicating
three successive lines at which they apparently intended to stand
and stem the advance. The first of these ran through Maashees,
on the river, south-westwards through the northern outskirts of
Venraij. The Division was practically up to it at all points.
They crossed it at all points during the day, the 17th, but progress
was slow. The only new enemy identification was 2nd Battalion
of Regiment Hardegg : the battalion had apparently been
rushed north from the Maeseyck front where the rest of the
Regiment were engaged. In the early hours, orders were given
out and the attack continued. The K.S.L.I. had moved up
behind the Warwicks overnight, and daylight revealed the
battalion completely surrounded by a series of minefields ! They
therefore delayed their attack until 8.30. By the middle of the
morning, with a squadron of the 4th Tank Coldstream Guards,
they had reached the V-shaped wood on the Warwicks' left. At
the start of their attack it looked as if the tanks would be held
up by a minefield. Lieutenant Aldridge, the K.S.L.I. pioneer
officer, walked ahead of the tanks prodding for the mines, with
no cover from intense enemy shellfire, " showing the utmost
gallantry." For this he was awarded the M.C.

By 10.30 the Suffolks had been held in the wood just beyond
Hiept and were under heavy rifle and machine-gun fire at cross-
tracks only five hundred yards west of the town. At last their
Churchills got across the *beek* and joined up with them, loosening
up the battle. By midday the East Yorks, on the left of the Suffolks,
confirmed that they had one platoon in Venraij. At one o'clock

they reported two companies in, street-fighting, " with plenty of Germans to deal with." That afternoon Brigadier Cass ordered the Suffolks to face right and clear all the woods west of the town. This they had achieved as far south as the new hospital in the woods beside the main Merselo-Venraij road at the end of another day's painful slogging. The South Lancs had moved up behind the East Yorks and were ordered to enter the town at first light. The K.S.L.I. had rapidly cleared the V-shaped wood and with the Warwicks consolidated in Brabander.

At 4 o'clock on the morning of the 18th, the seventh day of the operation, the Artillery opened up with two hours of Victor targets (for every gun within range)—a most impressive noise, which heartened the tired Infantry. At 6.45 the South Lancs passed through the East Yorks into the north-west corner of the town. There was heavy shelling, but as they advanced through the main streets into the southern part they found that most of the Germans had gone. There were mines at all the approaches and exits, and in the southern area the South Lancs overran and captured a 75-mm. gun while the Germans were still firing it. The Warwicks, who at 2 a.m. had sent a patrol through the north-eastern quarter of the town into the Monastery of St. Servatius and found it clear of the enemy, came under heavy machine-gun fire later in the morning as they advanced to occupy it ; it was now quite a familiar trick of the Germans to withdraw at night and infiltrate back into position just before dawn. The monastery had a main block and a series of out-buildings connected by glass corridors, and stood at the enemy edge of the town on the road that led east into the villages of Lul and Oostrum. At midday the Warwicks were established inside and in the grounds, whose far wall was for many days the front line. There was persistent and concentrated enemy shelling and mortaring, crashing into the monastery, shattering the glass in all the corridors. The monks behaved with fine self-control in conditions that soldiers, not used to the tranquil life of the *Klooster*, found quite disturbing. The whole town was consolidated by midday, and the Suffolks were completing the clearance of the woods to the south-west.

The weather improved slightly, so that Typhoons could spend the afternoon strafing the Germans. These last had withdrawn to defend the line from Smakt down through Oostrum to Veulen and Amerika, villages on the edge of the desolate *Peel*. 8 Brigade now adjusted Company positions to face due east, while 185 Brigade went back out of the line for a seven-day period of rest and training. To the left of 8 Brigade that night, 9 Brigade and the Household Cavalry Group, including 3rd Recce Regiment, were holding the river line right up to Cuijk : together they were disposed against the enemy on a front of sixteen miles. A week of fighting that will not be easily forgotten by members of the 3rd Division had come to an end.

At the end units received a Special Order of the Day by Lieutenant-General Sir Richard N. O'Connor, K.C.B., D.S.O., M.C., Commander of VIII Corps. It reads :

3rd BRITISH DIVISION

I would like to congratulate you all on the very fine performance you have put up during the recent operations against Venraij.

All of you have taken your share in this success, but I must particularly congratulate 185 Brigade on the magnificent performance of bridging the Beek north of Venraij with all the elements against them.

In this fighting you have shown grit and determination, and you have gained the knowledge that you are a better man than the enemy.

It is probably the first action of a good many of you, and I feel that you have made a great start and have thereby gained my full confidence.

(Signed) R. N. O'CONNOR,
Lieutenant-General,
Commander,
VIII Corps.

16 Oct 44.

8 Brigade were the first to admire this feather in 185 Brigade's cap, but at that time they felt that their own advance on Venraij against all the elements had not been the less magnificent for having been made without Churchill support such as the Warwicks

had. The Suffolks were left with 12 officers present, about a third of their proper strength. Indeed it is small wonder that all three Brigades and all nine Battalions felt particularly jealous of their own honour just then. To discriminate was perhaps generous but unwise : the order was dated the 16th, and the battle had yet two days to run before Venraij fell.

But now it was the Corps Commander's turn to feel hurt. It was at this point in the Corps plan (*Constellation*) that the three other Divisions in the Corps were to have driven due east to Venlo and Roermond, cutting off the escape of the German formations facing the 3rd Division. At this critical moment a Division was urgently needed on the 's Hertogenbosch sector, and it had to come from VIII Corps ! This departure of the 15th (Scottish) Division meant that the whole Corps plan came to nothing. It is reasonable to suppose that had it been fully operated then it would have succeeded, and with four Divisions instead of the seven that were required before Venlo was reached a month later. It was a great pity, because, as General O'Connor wrote in his comments to the Army Commander, " The first part of the plan worked very well. The clearing of Overloon and Venraij by 3rd British Div. was a fine achievement, as the enemy held strong positions, heavily mined, and frequently behind an anti-tank obstacle. He fought well to start with, but was gradually worn down by the dogged fighting qualities of 3rd Div. and eventually considerable numbers began to surrender. . . ."

This was an Infantry battle. As a demonstration of the way a British Infantry Division fights in adverse conditions it was eminently successful. In cold and wet and mire and sand-dunes and dark pine-woods and minefields that were a perpetual nightmare, but with the fullest possible support from all the supporting arms, the Infantrymen advanced and took every objective. That was all that mattered to them : the Corps plan gave them little worry. They were necessarily more interested to learn how Germans defended woods, how they sited their spandaus, how to detect and disarm mines, and how to live in the ground. And they were very thankful for what assistance they got from the Sappers, the tank crews, the mortarmen and Gunners : they felt a particular admiration during this battle for the Typhoon Wing of 83 Group of the Tactical Air

Force. They felt bloody, but on the whole unbowed. 8 Brigade had lost all three Commanding Officers, and, on the average battalions lost three Company Commanders each. So it was with 185 Brigade : the Norfolks lost four and the Warwicks three of their Rifle Company Commanders. But the survivors addressed themselves to their duties and carried on : 185 Brigade reorganising, resting and training for a week, while the other two Brigades held the line and started sending out patrols east towards the river. The Division's connections with Overloon and Venraij were by no means ended, though when Venraij was taken the most unpleasant chapter in their history was over.

Chapter Seven

WINTER: THE MAAS RIVER LINE

Discover the soldier
Here by the inundations of the Maas,
At one with nature and at variance
With the elements
That ever since one grey, immortal dawn
On the blazing Calvados coast
Have belaboured constantly
The fighting men.

War has suspended
Even the cultivation of the soil :
Cows are not milked nor sluices attended—
The Stygian Maas
And the cold *beeks* have left their appointed course.
Here you can see despair,
The glimmering waste of years,
Sense the frustration.

The pines are silent,
Deserted the excavations among the dunes,
Trappings and traces of the unnatural Germans
In lonely mist.
Only the quiet nook in the shell-splintered wood
Restores the sweet sense of rest
Where men were gently laid
Beneath the earth.

The wearied sentry
Sees only the devastation of the day,
The puppy that survived, and licked his hand
And won his heart
So long deprived of affection : stares at the blackness
Over the evil river ;
Recovering, remembers
Another country.

As SOLDIERS the British are famous for, among other things, their irrepressible cheerfulness and their refusal to be dominated by a formidable environment any more than by a formidable enemy force. In Burma, the Chindits proved themselves better at jungle war than the Japs, who were, one would have thought, more nearly in their own element. Static in Holland, as autumn dissolved and the dark winter descended over heath and bog, the 3rd Division's humour stood the strain, though it is as well to record that there were moments when men were, thoroughly, depressed. The Division could afford to admit this, because it had just won a battle that was fought with medical charts as well as maps—the battle of morale.

The importance of this local battle may be judged from Montgomery's summing-up in his despatch. Lord Montgomery writes : " No account of this campaign would be complete without some mention of the truly remarkable success of the medical organisation. But it must be remembered that there were two factors which contributed greatly to the results achieved : probably no group of doctors has ever worked on better material ; and secondly, they were caring for the men of a winning army." The despatch continues : " Commanders in the field must realise that the medical state of an army is not dependent on the doctors alone. Their efforts are immeasurably facilitated when morale is at its highest, and of all the factors which ensure a high state of morale, there is none more important than success." If more were needed to emphasise the importance of the point, it is to be found in the closing sentences of this significant despatch : " High morale is a pearl of very great price. And the surest way to obtain it is by success in battle."

In general terms, then, the situation is clear. Under the GOC, the G (Ops) staff wins a battle, thereby helping the Medical staff to keep morale high, which in turn helps the G (Ops) staff to win the next battle. So that the battle the Medical staff must constantly fight is that of morale. In the 3rd Division this battle was very well documented, as befitted so important a battle. The Divisional Monthly Medical Bulletin, compiled by the A.D.M.S., contains a wealth of interesting analysis to show the progress of this fight, as well as all the points of purely professional interest. The bulletin was a reliable scientific gauge of the Division's spirit month by month, and if it had not been for the danger of such statistics falling into the hands of the enemy the distribution of this bulletin down to sub-units might (on the Field-Marshal's hypothesis, since the R.A.M.C. were fighting a winning battle) have proved another factor of success. It was perhaps seen by too few people at the time, but the object was achieved.

The main medical victory in the Division was over the incidence of " battle exhaustion," and was fought immediately after the battle for Venraij. The measure of success was striking. To state it at once, a simple addition sum shows that during the six months' campaign that followed the Venraij battle and included the hellish battle of the Rhineland, the Division had only 127 " battle-exhaustion " casualties over the whole period : this was exactly half the number sustained during the one week of onslaught on Overloon and Venraij.

Exhaustion cases are hard to define, and vary from the few men who take fright during the first two or three hours of battle, and who can hardly be considered genuinely " exhausted," to men who arrive in the R.A.P. shaking all over, looking older than they should, staring, and tending to dive for cover at the slightest noise. In addition there is the case of the man who is *physically* exhausted from hard fighting, lack of sleep, and who, as a result of his experiences, no longer has complete control of his nervous system. We have already noticed the Norfolks' report of such casualties under the foul conditions that followed *Good-wood* in July. There were altogether too many men with one or other of these symptoms during that week in mid-October, and the problems faced by the Divisional Medical staff were how to deal with these cases *during* battle, and what preventive measures to take *between* battles. The former was their own professional concern, the latter is of general interest, particularly in view of the astonishing success of those measures, which were based on conclusions drawn from the recent fighting.

It was recognised that the general conditions of the battle had been the worst possible—cold, wet weather ; inability to dig proper slit-trenches owing to the waterlogged ground ; a prolonged battle with not very rapid progress and, worst of all, the continual fear of mines, encountered in large numbers for the first time. These conditions could hardly be improved by the

A.D.   M

R.A.M.C. But there were two factors that did suggest a definite course of action. One was the marked shortage of officers—particularly Company Commanders, but Battalion Commanders and Junior Leaders as well ; this coupled with a high proportion of reinforcements in the ranks. It has to be remembered that the total number of men lost to the Division between D-day and the start of the Overloon battle was 10,000, and that as the great majority of these were Infantrymen in the Rifle Companies who only represent one-quarter of the 17,000 men in the Division, the loss of 10,000 men probably represented two complete turnovers in the strengths of each Rifle Company : that there were men in the Rifle Companies who had survived since D-day is explained by the fact that many of the casualties occurred among the reinforcements themselves. It was this factor that the Corps Commander had recognised in his Special Order of the Day to the Division when he said : " It is probably the first action of a good many of you. . . ." The second factor that led to a line of action lay in the relation of obvious battle success and ground gained to the various exhaustion figures.

During the seven days the average ratio in battalions of Exhausted to Wounded was 1 to 3. In the case of the Lincolns, where the ratio was 1 to 22, a probable explanation is that the bulk of the casualties were sustained during their one magnificent attack, when satisfactory progress was made. The Ulster Rifles, on the other hand, though in the same Brigade, endured a long period of inactivity during which, though casualties were low, the nervous tension was high owing to intense enemy shelling and mortaring and the necessity to send patrols against the enemy, who yielded no ground. The Warwicks were to be congratulated on their figures, which showed against the highest number of casualties one of the lowest proportions of exhaustion cases (1 to 10). These and other similarly revealing points were talked over by General Whistler with the Brigade and Battalion Commanders and with the senior medical officers, and the plan adopted probably owes most of its success to the wholehearted way in which Commanders and everyone else who recognised the importance of this psychological problem co-operated at once to solve it.

Many of the measures themselves were not new : those

designed to "keep men's minds occupied" were inevitably quizzes and talks concerning the war, on other fronts as well as theirs, and it would have been hard to draw other than optimistic conclusions. Too much talk about demobilisation, details of which had (unhappily in this respect) recently been announced in Parliament, was not encouraged : men who thought all the time in terms of demobilisation would not be inclined to take a chance in battle. Out of the line, after a period of rest of not more than two days, hard physical and battle training was to be resumed. The most important measures related to "making the reinforcement feel at home !" The men who went ashore on D-day started off roughly equal. Reinforcements were now arriving at units with the feeling that they were inferior to the older members of the battalions. To overcome this a seasoned soldier was picked to keep an eye on the newly-joined reinforcement, to give him what tips he could during training and in the line, and to help him over the difficult time of his first battle. Officers and N.C.O.s got to know them and their capabilities as quickly as possible, though officers and N.C.O.s were often new themselves. The value of regimental discipline was appreciated as never before.

The results of this well-conducted "battle" were very soon apparent, and the indications were more positive than pinnacles drawn on medical graphs. It should be clear that, though the R.A.M.C. made an accurate diagnosis and helped to prescribe the remedy, everyone had a part in the rapid recovery and immunisation for the future—not least the "patients" themselves. And before we return to life in the line we may note Colonel Hinton's observation : that in the winter months only about 15 per cent of Q work is operational, while the rest must be devoted to the questions of Ordnance stores, NAAFI and accommodation, "comforts never mentioned in training establishments or text-books." He reckoned the feeding of forward troops the worst of all winter problems, and welcomed an increase in the rations of oatmeal and cooking fats. As an attempt to solve the difficulty of keeping food hot, a small petrol cooker was created by the Div. Catering Adviser from empty 25-pounder cartridge cases, 2,000 of these being mass-produced in the R.E.M.E. workshops by Christmas-time. During November, the wettest and most dismal November known on the Continent for many years,[1] warm woollen socks, pullovers and Balaclava helmets arrived from the women at home ; that they were appreciated is certain from the grateful mention of them in each unit's records. Unfortunately the entertainment that was arranged daily for approximately 5 per cent of the Division did not, for a variety of reasons referred to later, get the same warm reception.

In the town of Helmond, some twenty miles behind the line, the Div Club was now established in what had been a modern factory-workers' club. The Dutch helped to stock it with many luxuries, and readily produced beds, bedding and washing facilities for 250, and built a stage. There was a cheerful and fairly homely atmosphere about this place as men came back to spend 24 hours' leave or stayed for the night on their way back to Brussels for 48 hours. It so happened that the first major action in the Maas pocket following the capture of Venraij was a counter-attack, at first light on October 27th, aimed by 9 Panzer Division through Meijel to Deurne and Helmond, where a few bombs were dropped : this determined attack from the south-east succeeded temporarily in penetrating the positions of the unlucky U.S. 7th Armoured Division,[2] and for a moment the Div Club was threatened ! The permanent denizens of the Club, such as Bernard Rigby, the Education Officer, found the news particularly disturbing, though indeed the whole Division stood, even more than before, on the alert. This was the last local German attempt to interfere with the northern L of C and to distract our forces from the Scheldt estuary.

The main military operations of the autumn and winter were first the clearing of the mouth of the Scheldt to open up the port of Antwerp, and then the battle of the Ardennes. The 3rd Division had no part in either of them. For nearly four months after Venraij the Division was committed to holding a relatively peaceful but far from pleasant stretch of the line—16, and later 22, miles of it : during one period of regrouping they were

---

[1] It is a galling tradition that the British Army should be thus handicapped towards the end of its campaigns. It can never be forgotten how, in 1917, the weather bestowed upon us the wettest autumn for twenty years.

[2] Seven weeks later the U.S. 7th Armoured Division were struggling to hold St. Vith in the full flood of the Ardennes break-through.

covering a front of 27 miles. For the first month, until 22nd November, the line ran three-quarters of its length along the left bank of the Maas, between Cuijk and Vierlingsbeek, and the remaining quarter, through Smakt and the eastern edge of Venraij, was where the advance had stopped in October. The long sector north of Vierlingsbeek was held by the Household Cavalry Group, consisting of the 2nd Household Cavalry and 3rd Recce Regiments, with two Squadrons of the Inns of Court Regiment. The 3rd Recce Regiment held the right of this sector, including Vierlingsbeek, Groeningen and Vortum. On their right the front facing the German pocket was held by two Brigades. In conformity with the morale battle it was found possible to hold one Brigade back out of the line almost throughout the period, and at the same time the other two Brigades managed to keep a Battalion in reserve.

The chief characteristics of the first month were a constant downpour of rain (lashed from time to time by a howling gale), frequent patrols both ways, a rigorous daily harassing programme by the Divisional Artillery and the Middlesex, and stoic work on " Fir Track " and the almost unrecognisable roads in the Divisional area by the Sappers, who also added a few minefields wherever they could find a gap in the existing German ones. Brigadier Cass, who had commanded 8 Brigade so successfully since that assault on D-day, was badly injured on one of these while partridge-shooting, and had to be evacuated. (One thinks of the Duke of Wellington, who was unable to resist giving chase to a hare in the course of one of the Peninsular battles ; no mine was exploded, but the senior officers with him were very surprised.) Brigadier Cass was succeeded by Brigadier E. H. Goulburn, D.S.O., who had commanded the 1st Grenadier Guards at Nijmegen.

The Division's patrolling was vigorous and valuable, and soon revealed, or rather confirmed, the enemy's identity and position. The enemy's patrols also had a certain value, since they occasionally provided prisoners and gave the Division an idea of the sort of men they were facing. In 9 Brigade one example of this was on November 1st, All Saints' night, when the sentry on the right flank of A Company of the Ulster Rifles saw three men in the darkness, and, not being satisfied with

their reply, he opened fire with his Sten-gun. The patrol withdrew, but one of their number reappeared a few minutes later
" dancing about the company's slit-trenches, crying : ' Tommy,
come out ! ' " He had misdirected his invitation, which merely
evoked a stream of small-arms fire. Next morning a body was
found in a ditch in front of the company lines. A further indication of the mood of the enemy was the sight next day of the first
V.2 weapons to be launched before the eyes of the Division. As
these projectiles ascended vertically into the sky they left a trail
of white vapour, and from that day the bearings and timings of
these were collected from all over the front and sent back to
Corps, but it is doubtful if they were close enough for the bearings
to have been of use. It was hateful to watch these things making
for Antwerp and London and to be unable to prevent them.

8 Brigade's patrols also produced useful information, and to
start with, patrolling on both sides was so intensive that night
skirmishes were frequent. The South Lancs' historian says, with
rare expansion in a regrettably naked narrative : " As our own
patrol activity increased the enemy's decreased, and towards the
end of the third week several of our patrols had reached the line
of the railway and a most comprehensive picture of the enemy
posts had been built up. In this place Lieutenant Wright, M.C.,
M.M., and Lieutenant Rennie, M.C., of C Company, especially
distinguished themselves, until both were wounded on mines on
the 22nd, the latter going forward to rescue the former." Even
so, such scanty treatment of a period of personal enterprise and
at least one instance of heroism, in a *Battalion* history, is
lamentable.

Apart from the local intelligence that was thus being gained,
considerable interest during that period attached to the broader
estimate of German capabilities which was made regularly at
this time in the Divisional Intelligence Summaries. O.C. Rowntree, the G III (I), who had issued that first vital estimate of the
Norman shore defences, was still summarising our own and enemy
activities and issuing a very intelligible account almost daily.
From these it was clear that the main German preoccupations
at the moment were trying to form a reserve of crack troops
while staving off current penetrations (principally in the Aachen
area). This, after the defeat in Normandy, involved them in a

vast general reorganisation, and " the 16-year-olds (next year's class) were largely eaten into, and industry combed near to scalping." But the result of the effort was that 50 new Divisions appeared, 20 of them in the west. A typically interesting Summary was produced on 19th November, showing that the Germans had had to bring their reserve of crack troops, the newly-formed Sixth Panzer Army, across the Rhine, " to defend, if necessary, the crossing of the Roer River," which was being steadily approached by the U.S. Ninth Army. By coincidence (for it was this Sixth Panzer Army that a month later broke through with Fifth Panzer Army into the Ardennes, employing numbers of troops dressed in American uniforms), this Summary also reproduced a letter captured by a flanking formation and addressed to Para Regiment Hübner from H.Q., LXXXVI Corps, stating : " The Führer has ordered the fmn of a special unit of a strength of about two bns for employment on recce and special tasks on the Western Front. . . . Personnel will be selected from volunteers who fulfil the following requirements. . . . Knowledge of the English language and also the American dialect and especially their military technical terms. . . . Captured clothing, eqpt, weapons and vehs are to be reported and collected for the eqpt of the above special troops. . . ."

These Summaries were frequently rounded off with an amusing tailpiece. On the 20th November the latest German propaganda leaflet was reproduced under the heading *Hard Times Indeed*. It is a curious affair. On one side was printed in German, above the forged signature of General Eisenhower, the following imitation Safe Conduct Pass : " The German soldier who carries this safe conduct is using it as a sign of his genuine wish to go into captivity for the next ten years, to betray his Fatherland, to return home a broken old man and very probably never to see his parents, wife and children again." On the reverse side was the following prize example of Teutonic wit, this time in English : " Dear Friends, We are returning your age-old dodge, after having made the necessary rectifications with sincerest thanks. It was highly amusing, and we must commend you on your efforts. But please refrain from molesting us further in this direction. It should be obvious to you that the ideals for which 90 million Germans have fought (according

to Churchill) ' like lions ' for over five years cannot be so very
rotten that we could be lured into surrender through mere ham
and eggs.   Hoping that we can rely on your sagacity to comprehend, we remain as of old with Heil Hitler !   Hard times,
what ? "

At least this served to demonstrate that the Germans were
grown concerned with the numbers of desertions from their
ranks.   Another tailpiece of that week was well worthy of
Charivaria.   It reprinted the following extract from 21 Army
Group Local Electrical and Mechanical Engineers Instruction
No. 1 (General G. 953), under the heading *Change of Lubricants
—Tracked and Wheeled Vehicles and Static Engines* :
" 1.   Following a study of meteorological reports there is
evidence to indicate that low temperatures will be encountered
during the winter months . . ." and added brightly : " Investiga-
tions at this H.Q. by much less highly qualified experts suggest
that it may also be wet."

Finally, through these Summaries it could be seen how, on
the one hand Brandenberger, General der Panzer Truppen, was
having to write : " To the Officers of Seventh Army . . . We
are fighting directly under the eyes of our people. . . . All habits
which may have been understandable in enemy territory must
disappear. . . . Be an example More than Ever. . . ."   While
on the other hand, as on the evening of 21st November, General
Eisenhower was calling for " an all-out effort," with Allied
armies pressing down all three of history's great routes into
Germany—Belfort, Metz and the Ruhr.   It was now apparent
that the Germans were ready to fight it out *west* of the Rhine.
This suited the Supreme Commander well.   Any large-scale
penetration of Germany beyond the Rhine would obviously be
a much easier proposition once we had closed up to the left bank
and smashed the German forces west of the river.   So the intention
was now to close to the Rhine.   The advance from Aachen on to
Cologne was making relentless progress.   For the present nothing
could be done in the north.   We have seen how the 3rd Division
were extended almost to the point of insecurity.   A direct advance
across the Maas to the Rhine or a drive south-east from Nijmegen
would have been impossible without taking troops from the
Aachen attack and switching them to the north. . Rather than

do this, the Supreme Commander continued for the time being to stretch the formations in the Low Countries, so that 21 Army Group extended as far south as Maeseyck, where their line crossed the Meuse and turned east to join the U.S. Ninth Army in the Geilenkirchen sector.

So far from being in a position to concentrate to cross the Maas, the 3rd Division had not yet reached it on the southern quarter of their front. They were to reach it with less trouble than they anticipated, though a few score of perverse Germans gave them trouble enough. As part of the Second Army plan for the final elimination of the Maas pocket, the Division was to attack eastwards to the river in line with other formations farther south which were now advancing on Venlo. By the middle of November battalions were on their legs again if not actually spoiling for the next fight. The three Brigades were all fitted into the line (which now ran as far south as Veulen), and ready for the word " Go," when on the night of November 21st the Germans made a very noisy demonstration in the Smakt area, and also in front of 9 Brigade, with machine-guns and mortars and fighting patrols. This probably meant their withdrawal. Next morning a civilian reported to 8 Brigade that the enemy had retired across the Maas, and patrolling throughout the day seemed to confirm his statement. During the day 15th (Scottish) and 11th Armoured Divisions reached Maasbree, Sevenum and Horst in the south, and the 3rd Division was ordered to advance, with due caution, next day.

The weather on the 23rd, the first day of this advance, was abominable. A week earlier the ground had been visited by the first heavy frost of winter and had since been softened by a cease-less fall of rain. Deep mud was everywhere and under it lay the schumines the Germans had planted. They had also felled trees to block the roads and booby-trapped the trees. The roads were cratered. The bridges were blown. The sickening scent of dead cattle filled the air as usual. The Germans appeared to have left.

Next morning, however, as the probing forward continued, Major Read, commanding Z Company of the K.S.L.I., was informed by a runner from one of his patrols that the enemy had fortified a house in the village of Meerlo. He at once took up the rest of his Company, made a very skilful reconnaissance under fire, and led a successful attack. For this he won the M.C., and Sergeant Gillett, who led a charge into the house, won the M.M. Nine Germans were killed and the tenth taken prisoner. Meerlo had a few houses on either side of another Molen Beek—this time the *Groote* Molen Beek. The *beek*, running south-north, also divided the village of Wanssum in two before entering the flooded Maas ; and running as it did directly across 185 Brigade's front, it had been given to them as the limit of their advance. Just here the inter-divisional boundary was rather untidy. A glance at the map facing p. 147 shows the Maas flowing up from the south-east and a wedge of land between its left bank and the right bank of the *beek*. Towards the tip of this wedge was Wanssum wood, the scene of a later exasperating episode. On the side of the wedge that flanked the Maas stood the village of Blitterswijk. For the moment it is sufficient to notice that the inter-Divisional boundary was so arranged that this wedge in front of 185 Brigade was left to be cleared by the 15th (Scottish) Division sweeping up from the south.

That day, as the K.S.L.I. occupied the part of Meerlo that lay west of the *beek*, D Company of the Norfolks patrolled to the western half of Wanssum village, dealing with the slight opposition they encountered. On the left of the Norfolks, the Suffolks had closed right up to the river and found, with one notable exception, their area clear. The civilian problem, difficult throughout the winter months, was at this point critical. In the fairly quiet northern sector, where the 2nd Royals had taken over from the Household Cavalry, civilians were flocking back with their belongings and their cattle to live in the line rather than in crowded areas farther back. They appeared to think that, as non-combatants, they were immune from bullets and shells and mines. They quite failed to understand that they could not be allowed to wander backwards and forwards to the very brink of the river if there was to be any sort of security against German infiltration. In fact here it was now reckoned harder to ward off civilian infiltrations from the rear than German patrols from the front. In the southern sector as the Division closed to the river the situation was pathetic. The Germans had taken many of the inhabitants of Overloon and Venraij back across the Maas with them to dig defence works. Several escaped and were streaming back. In addition there were refugees from the river-line and others who had been deported from Northern Holland. The scene in the slush and pouring rain was unbearable. Within twenty-four hours of the advance from Venraij hundreds of exhausted civilians had arrived in the Monastery of St. Servatius. From there the R.A.S.C. Companies transported them back twenty miles or so to a dispersal point where a civilian organisation took care of them.

One of the dispossessed was the Baron Weichs de Wennee, a Chamberlain of Queen Wilhelmina. He reported to the Suffolks that the Castle on the river-bank close to the village of Geisteren, a summer residence of the Queen, was now occupied by some sixty German officer cadets. Colonel Goodwin, now recovered from his Normandy wound and back in command of the Suffolks, decided to storm the *Kasteel* (as it was generally called) the next day, after it had been " prepared " by Typhoons and the Divisional Artillery. That night a patrol approaching the Castle from the village found the road covered by the floods, and it was suspected that in the middle of the floods the road passed over a bridge that was now demolished ! The other road approaching the Castle along the bank from the north was not itself flooded, though everything on either verge was, and in any case it was in view from the other side of the river.

Early next morning a Suffolk standing patrol spotted ten of the Germans making off towards the village, and immediately opened fire on them. Some fell and the rest ran back into the Castle, sending stretcher-bearers out to collect four. The Suffolk attack was timed for 2.30 p.m. and the Artillery fired a pre-liminary concentration. At the last moment a sudden hailstorm prevented the Typhoons from attacking. Advancing down the road from the north, D Company, under Captain Thomas, soon came under enemy shell-fire, and, about 600 yards from the Castle entrance, were held up by very heavy machine-gun fire. They could not deploy because of the deep floods on either side of the road ; nor could they move forward. The attack was called off at 4.30 and Thomas skilfully extricated his Company from an extremely difficult situation. Then for four days the Castle was bombarded by Typhoons, by Heavy, Medium, Field

and Anti-Tank guns, by tanks and by mortars, until it was a
total ruin. And by day the watchful Battalion snipers claimed
several victims. On the night of the 28th a patrol from D Company again approached and was again kept at bay by heavy
small-arms fire. So the next night the Divisional Artillery fired
to cover the noise of the bringing up of assault boats. Unfortunately this drew Defensive Fire from the enemy's guns which
holed every craft just as C Company were about to embark.
After a three hours' wait fresh craft arrived, and C Company
crossed the flood waters in the early hours of the last morning in
November. Not a sound came from the enemy as the Company
approached the Castle. They touched down in silence. The
enemy had vanished. They left behind them only bloodstains,
a few weapons, signs in the wine-cellar of extensive junketings,
and the sad shambles that· symbolised the German legacy to
Europe.

At Div. H.Q. it was noted on November 25th in the General
Staff War Diary that " the Kasteel receives press and radio
publicity out of all proportion to its military significance." It
was a corresponding lack of proportion that had been the
Division's principal grouse in the bridgehead days when, for
example, the 51st (Highland) Division's arrival had been
announced by the B.B.C. within a few hours of that event and
several days later came the news that " the 3rd British Infantry
Division are now fighting in Normandy "—as if it was they
who had followed in the wake of the 51st instead of the other
way round. This proportion is fairly adjusted in the C-in-C's
despatch where the space devoted to the military achievements
of the respective Divisions may be taken as the proper scale of
their news-claim if not of their news-value. There was nothing
more to the Geisteren affair than has been stated. Admittedly
it might make a good story if the German version could be
obtained, though their explanation might equally well spoil it.

On November 30th the 3rd Recce Regiment went back into
Divisional reserve and 185 Brigade moved north to assume
responsibility for the vast northern sector of the Division's river
front. 8 and 9 Brigades each took a share of the area vacated by
185 Brigade, but a much heavier responsibility had already
been allotted to 9 Brigade. The 15th (Scottish) Division had

discovered a strong pocket of resistance in the Wanssum-Helling-Blitterswijk wedge between the *beek* and the river, and before they had time to eliminate it they were sent south to attack Blerick, opposite Venlo. The task fell to 9 Brigade, who deputed the Ulster Rifles.

Their attack was carefully prepared, with reconnaissance on the ground and recent air-photographs studied by the Company and Platoon Commanders concerned. It was timed for 5 a.m. on the 30th. Darkness was essential, as there was no covered approach over the marsh. But at 5 a full moon showed up every movement at a distance of 200 yards, while a keen wind cleared the clouds away. C Company on the left ran into heavy opposition in the hamlet of Helling and suffered several casualties. Major Bird's Company, advancing from Blitterswijk along the Wanssum road, soon came under machine-gun fire, but by rushing in and throwing grenades the first three objectives—two windmills and a thick wood—were taken before daylight. During the day the 33rd Field Regiment engaged several targets in the Helling area, while D Company's snipers accounted for eight Germans. The next attack began at 1 a.m. on December 1st, again betrayed by the moon. A number of machine-guns opened up on the left, low and accurate, and including captured Bren-guns that were confusing. The same thing happened when Bird's Company crossed the road to clear a wood to the north. Here, under heavy and sustained fire, Lance-Corporal Rossiter ran forward into the open to pick up Corporal Carroll, the wounded commander of another section that was pinned to the ground. Placing him over his shoulder, he called to the others to follow, and ran back to the wood. The Germans seemed determined to hold on to their bridgehead, and by this time the Ulster Rifles were being badly shelled from over the river. During that day the Germans in Wanssum were well repaid in kind, and Henry Taylor, the F.O.O. of the 33rd Field Regiment with D Company, " who never ceased trying to silence the enemy's guns or to neutralise his ground defence, and who was outstanding for his cheerful and tireless assistance," was awarded the M.C. So, also, was Major Bird.

In the early hours of December 2nd, Rifleman Irwin of D Company held his fire as a German patrol approached, until they were almost on his position. The enemy managed to bring down Defensive Fire and retire, with one groaning exception who was brought in. Having " got his man," the Rifleman " had breakfast and went off to Brussels." This patrol was evidently intended to cover the German withdrawal from their bridgehead. Later that morning, as plans were completed for a two-battalion attack supported by two squadrons of Churchills, a reliable civilian arrived with the news that the enemy had crossed the river. Wanssum was occupied by the Ulster Rifles that afternoon.

The Division now held a series of rather scattered positions among all the riverside villages on the left bank as far downstream as Cuijk : their names—Geisteren, Maashees, Vierlingsbeek, Groeningen, Vortum, Sambeek, Boxmeer, Beugen, Oeffelt, St. Agatha—are sufficient to recall many memories to members of O.P. parties, Support Companies, Rifle Companies, Squadrons of the Recce Regiment. In fact there can be few members of the Division to whom they are not familiar. The river itself was normally about 150 yards across, but now it had overflowed and its average width was three-quarters of a mile. Its normal level was about 4 feet below its banks, and it only needed three days' heavy rain in the Ardennes to produce a rise of 12 feet. There were regulating barrages (one was at Sambeek) that in normal times kept this main north-south waterway navigable, but even if these had not been under fire in no-man's-land it is doubtful if they would have coped with the floods resulting from the recent weeks of rain. Fortunately there were special winter flood-dykes at varying distances from the river, but in some places even these had been swamped. And the villages were sited respectfully along this winter river-line.

Early in December the northern group of Armies was getting ready to close up to the Rhine. While on the Aachen-Cologne front, the ten American Divisions pressed east on an average frontage of two and a half miles per Division, the British Second Army released XXX Corps to concentrate in the north for the drive down through the Reichswald and the country between the Maas and the Rhine. This release involved the 3rd Division in a further stretch south almost to Venlo, though in the north they lost the village of Boxmeer and those beyond—and, incidentally, the useful rest areas of St. Anthonis and Gemert—to the Canadians.

They gained Ooijen, Broekhuizen, Lottum, Houthuizen and Grubbenvorst, and occupied this extension of the line on December 16th. South of the Aachen front the Eifel sector was held almost as lightly as the Maas sector—and there was no protecting river. There on the 16th the Germans made their desperate attempt to cut through to Antwerp, and XXX Corps was used to ease this situation in Eifel. By their outbreak the Germans postponed the Rhineland offensive a month, or perhaps six weeks. They also protracted the 3rd Division's long watch over the river.

The routine in the river-line was dreary. It is an understatement to say, as Ken Bradshaw does, that " in many respects it was a position without undue appeal ! " He goes on to describe how living conditions for his battalion in the line were slit-trenches that flooded too easily and then gradually caved in, and how they were spread out over a wide expanse of marsh and wood that took two hours to walk round on foot. At the time of the regrouping in December the Commander decided to risk holding the line once more with two brigades and the Royals Group forward and a brigade in reserve. The full benefit of the training and general " maintenance " thus made possible for units out of the line was apparent when the Division went into the full-scale offensive in February. At the time it meant " an unending round of sentry-go and stand-to " for the forward platoons. Bob Moberly records for the Middlesex : " Single sentry on each post during the short days, double sentry during the long nights, stand-to at dawn and dusk, and whenever an enemy patrol was expected near at hand. It was usually very quiet at night, and ears and eyes were strained for any sign of movement. Now and then a trip-flare would go up, but they were often false alarms, set off by the wind or by a stray cat."

Guy Radcliffe, Adjutant of the K.S.L.I., explains how, " if they were in a village, cellars could be used for sleeping by day. But by night it was slit-trenches for anyone who could sleep after guards and patrols had been found. Where there was no village the whole life of the Company was led in slit-trenches and dug-outs. Successive occupants would improve them until they became tolerably comfortable with lined walls, solid roofs, and stoves. But these long hours of standing about in the cold or huddling in ill-lit dug-outs were a great test of morale. It was annoying to read of the way front-line troops had constant entertainment. The nearest mobile cinema show involved a journey back through the mud that took about an hour on foot or half an hour in a truck, while regular cinemas and shows were back at Deurne, Helmond and Eindhoven—involving freezing journeys of one and a half or two hours in the back of a lorry over awful roads—not to be undertaken unless very browned off. As reserve battalion life was better. Even then the main entertainment amenities were nearly as far away, though we did have one adventurous ENSA team who visited us and were nearly shelled. The Mobile Bath was available once a week in the line, but not all men could be spared from Companies to bath in that one day."

Fortunately units changed round once every week or ten days : they naturally grumbled at being thus " always mucked about," but it stopped them from growing too despondent. Some rearward units were actually no better off. There was hardly a habitable dwelling in the whole of the Divisional gun area. At one time the sight of all the C.V.s, caravans and bivouacs of Div. Headquarters in a hopelessly waterlogged field beside the Oploo-Overloon road could be relied on to prompt derisive and very disrespectful comment from men returning from the front.

Drab December was interrupted by two important announcements and an anniversary. The news that U.K. leave would start in January concerned everybody, and provided the main topic of conversation and thought. The *Daily Telegraph* and *Daily Mirror* hastened to assure D-day men and their families that they could expect to be reunited not later than February, and it was therefore no surprise to several members of the Division who had landed on D-day to find that they would not be going home on leave before May. Jack Harrod, Adjutant of the Lincolns, recorded : " The fact that L-of-C troops were placed on an equal footing with themselves raised no more than the typical soldiers' grumble, especially when it was made known to them that the GOC and even the Corps Commander had taken up the cudgels on their behalf, though unsuccessfully." It need not be assumed that even Lincolnshire men felt at home in Nord Brabant and Limburg, though Harrod does say that the river line " from Vierlingsbeek to Lottum became as *familiar* to Lincolnshire men as any reach of Witham or Welland ! " The second piece of news only directly concerned 185 Brigade. It was that their Brigadier Eric Bols was leaving them on being promoted to command the 6th Airborne Division. They were losing an admired and well-trusted Commander. As their G Ops Log puts it, it was " unexpected and upsetting. A farewell party was hastily organised."

The anniversary of Christmas Day was quiet. Most Logs have Nothing to Report but a Happy Christmas. It was a fine day, crisp with a hard, sparkling frost. There were special extra rations of pork and turkey and Christmas pudding and fruit, and cooks excelled themselves. Troops in the line made what relay arrangements they could. Those who knew they were due for relief in a day or two held their rations and celebrated out of the line. On Christmas Eve there had been several reports of revelry on the far bank, reaching a drunken pitch, and next door on the right the 11th Armoured Division reported sounds of German vomiting. It was wondered if the enemy were getting their celebrations over on the 24th in order to be able to spoil the 25th, but Christmas Day was quiet. General Whistler said all that it is necessary to say of the occasion :

A CHRISTMAS MESSAGE TO ALL RANKS OF THE DIVISION

I wish to send you my best wishes for the sixth war-time Christmas.

During the last six months the Division has fought splendidly, and has added to its high reputation. From the moment when you first touched French soil as the spearhead of the Invasion you have been almost constantly in action. Very largely due to your efforts during those first critical days, a large part of German-held Europe had been freed of the enemy. Since then you have been in the forefront of many hard battles.

I wish to say a special word to the Infantry. Splendid as has been the support given by all arms of the Division, it is that small number of men in the Rifle Companies of the

Infantry Battalions who have to take ground and hold it. In spite of heavy casualties, they have never failed to take their objective and retain it. Their determination and steadiness under fire had been beyond all praise.

All of you will be thinking of your homes and families on Christmas Day, and regretting the fate which has placed you so far from them. But your families would not have it otherwise until this job is finished. They are rightly proud of you.

We must all draw spiritual inspiration from this Christmas season for the great effort which will be required from us in the Spring.

Good luck, and God bless you all.

> (Signed) L. G. WHISTLER, Major-General,
> Commander,
> 3 Brit Inf Div.

24 Dec 44.

The Germans said all that it was unnecessary to say in a pamphlet picked up and suitably disposed of by the Division's neighbours :

HELLO, BOYS !

Did you have a merry Christmas eve in Blerick and Baarlo ? A little uncomfortable, cold and humide ? And then—the longing to your family, to all your loves at home and furthermore the bad news from the First American Army ! And you was thinking in the last months : " Christmas at home " . . . You may believe that we had a merry Christmas—with the good news from the great " winter battle " from Belgium. We dare say, that you are a little disappoint, and therefore we had the only wish to give you a little Christmas-box. But may be, that you don't know nothing from our great attack ? No wonder, General Eisenhower has stopped all the news from the Western front . . . (Then a garbled German version of the news). That's all for today, SO LONG, AND A HAPPY NEW YEAR !

During the usual time-lag between Christmas and the New Year very little happened in the Division, but " the good news from the great winter battle " was that the Germans had been halted : it was the Germans who " didn't know nothing." There were a few raw, foggy days in which the roads iced over, making driving as difficult as it had been in the mud, and much more dangerous. New Year's Eve, like Hogmanay a year earlier in Inverness, was " a bra' bricht moonlicht nicht," cold, and exciting. " Just before midnight the last shell of the old year fell in Venraij," noted Bob Moberly, and a few minutes later the far bank of the river blazed up in a fantastic firework display : flares, coloured lights and tracer went up, and the noise of bugles was added. The Germans were saluting the year of their defeat.

They were determined to keep it up, and shortly after break-fast the air above the Division was full of Messerschmidt 109's and Focke-Wulf 190's, flying very low and very fast. 92nd Light Ack-Ack Regiment, who since June had despaired of ever seeing the Luftwaffe again, and had been practising shooting at ground positions across the Maas, engaged the enemy enthusiastically. That morning some 800 planes raided Allied airfields in Belgium and Holland in their last great extravagant sortie. The first wave to pass over the Division made for Helmond. There they appeared to be met by British fighters and there were " dog-fights " all over the sky. Enemy aircraft—some of which bore R.A.F. roundels and markings—kept breaking off from the air-fights and flying back towards the German lines at a height of about 30 feet. They paid a fair toll to the 92nd Light Ack-Ack Regiment, who destroyed eleven and damaged three. A single gun of Dog Troop, 318 Battery, destroyed three planes outright and had a share in a fourth. On this day their Regimental Commander, Colonel Bazeley, left them to command the 7th Field Regiment, in place of Colonel Tapp, who was going out to the Far East : it was at this time that troops in the B.L.A. got the feeling that " Burma Looms Ahead."

The Division was comparatively busy on January 1st, shooting down enemy aircraft and rounding up the crews who baled out. The same morning one of the Field Regiments received the entire Australian crew of one of our own bombers. Their plane had been crippled over the Dortmund-Ems Canal, and they had just managed to get back to the right side of the front line before

having to jump. Meanwhile the enemy just over the river
were busily preparing a crossing in force, which they called
Operation *Snowman*, though no snow fell till the day of their
withdrawal, a week later. They had been able to send patrols
over without great difficulty as the Divisional line was so
thin. After dark on New Year's Day a whole Company
crossed from Well to the wood north-east of Wanssum. This
village, where the Ulster Rifles had had so much trouble, was
now in the keeping of D Company of the South Lancs. The
Company in the wood, and another force that landed west of
the *beek*, then attacked Wanssum from the north, south and
east. With the Wanssum garrison were Lieutenant Ken
Baxter and his mortar O.P. Party and a machine-gun platoon
of the Middlesex.

Shortly after midnight an Infantry Corporal ran into Baxter's
O.P., a small house, with the news that a suspicious party of
men were coming up the road. As they approached, " Baxter's
party opened fire from the doorway and the Germans scattered.
The whole Infantry platoon which normally defended the area
of the O.P. had gone out on patrol. Baxter therefore posted two
men on the first floor with a Bren (which jammed after the first
few bursts), collected the other three and his batman and took
up position at his O.P. They were seven, armed with rifles and
a pistol, against twenty-five, armed with bazookas, machine-
carbines and grenades. The enemy tried to rush the house, and
Baxter shot one of them through the head with his pistol, at
point-blank range. The enemy then started to rip the ground
floor to pieces with bazooka fire. It was impossible to get to the
telephone on the ground floor, which had probably been put
out of action anyway. ' Oxo,' the platoon dog, was the only ally
on the ground floor. He thoroughly disapproved of the whole
proceedings, ran out of the door, and was not seen for two days.
The fire-fight continued for twenty minutes, and the party were
nearly out of ammunition when the enemy withdrew." Baxter
won the M.C. for " great coolness, gallantry and leadership,"
and Private Orme won the GOC's certificate for gallantry. In
other parts of the garrison there were similar incidents, and after
a while the enemy withdrew.

All seemed quiet next day, and extensive sweeps of their area by the South Lancs revealed no sign of the enemy on their side of the river until a patrol at dusk went to the jetty opposite Well and was fired upon from the neighbouring wood. This was the first indication that the enemy had established positions, which were pin-pointed by later patrols, but an attempt by C Company during the night of the 2nd to clear the wood was unsuccessful owing to enemy defensive shelling. Later the German Artillery trace was captured : that it was prepared by their Corps H.Q. gave some idea of their deliberate intentions. A fighting patrol from A Company found the wood still occupied on the night of the 3rd/4th. It was left undisturbed the next night, but at first light on the 6th, supported by a diversionary attack by D Company, A Company began an operation to clear the wood. Under cover of artillery smoke they reached the edge of the wood, to be met by such a concentration of machine-gun and shell-fire that they were forced to withdraw with heavy casualties. At ten that morning C Company relieved the depleted A Company in sleet and Arctic conditions, and kept the wood under observation.

Snow began to fall on the 7th, and twenty-four armoured troop-carriers (*Kangaroos*) arrived. (*Kangaroos* had first been used on the 7th August to take the Canadians right in among the German positions before Falaise. When the Americans could spare no more 105 mm. ammunition the S-P guns of the Divisional Artillery had been converted to this use, and several of them were later found knocked out near Falaise still bearing their triangles and R.A. signs.) Early on the morning of the 8th, while the Suffolks were boarding the *Kangaroos*, Lieutenant J. B. Smith of 20th Anti-Tank Regiment was carrying out a diversionary operation with his troops. He and his men were well aware that their armour was not proof against a direct hit from the guns over the river, but they manœuvred in full view of the enemy, drawing the weight of their fire. The enemy gave away the whereabouts of many of his gun and mortar positions, which were duly neutralised when the Suffolks advanced. Smith won the M.C.

That morning the snow was freezing on the roads and the *Kangaroos* were skidding badly. This delayed the attack, which, when it went in, was effectively screened from the German bank by a sudden heavy snowstorm. But only twenty prisoners were taken. According to them the main body had made off across the river as soon as they heard the tanks approaching from Venraij. That was the end of an episode which was given much prominence in German propaganda, but which had not the least tactical significance : it was an effective nuisance.

For another two and a half weeks the banks of the Maas lay deep in snow, and men led an Eskimo existence. On the 10th, 27 degrees of frost were recorded. The same day white camouflage snow-suits were issued to men on patrol. The infantry were helped out with their patrols between Wanssum and Geisteren by the Middlesex. The 92nd Light Ack-Ack Regiment supplied a garrison for Groeningen. In the northern sector the 3rd Recce Regiment had relieved the Royals and had two Dutch Resistance Companies under command. Though untrained and still suffering the effects of undernourishment, these Dutchmen were tremendously keen, and their No. 2 Company drew the first blood in the Recce Regiment's area, shooting up a patrol of four in Vortum and taking one prisoner.

Since the beginning of December each Brigade had had twelve light assault boats in which reserve battalions could practise as watermen. On January 26th the 3rd Division went over to offensive patrolling on the German side of the Maas. The East Yorks had the honour of providing the first reconnaissance patrol, which though it suffered some casualties when an enemy patrol was bumped on the *near* bank, crossed over safely and returned with the information that was required. On the 28th, in the early hours, the 3rd Recce Regiment sent over a recce patrol supported by a fighting patrol opposite Sambeek. The former, under Lieutenant Hodgetts, killed two Germans between the river and the Afferden lateral road, while the latter inflicted a number of casualties on the enemy who approached them near the lock-gates, and brought back a prisoner for interrogation. Next evening Lieutenant Cray with two others from the Suffolks crossed on reconnaissance and withdrew safely with their information, though under fire most of the time. The last patrol to make contact with the enemy in January crossed under Lieutenant Moon of the South Lancs and captured two prisoners with no loss to themselves. Throughout the period Dutch civilians, including women and children, were making this perilous crossing to get away from the Germans. One night the burgomaster of Well brought over a whole boatload. Another night two Dutchmen brought over a Major of the U.S. Eighth Air Force who had spent four months without detection behind the German lines. Some men, incredible as it may sound, swam the icy floods and reached the British lines safely.

By now the Germans had lost their Ardennes salient, and many of their best troops and tanks and planes into the bargain. The Allied offensive to reach the Rhine was imminent. It was planned that when the great drive began down from Nijmegen through Cleve and the Reichswald (Operation *Veritable*), the 3rd Division should assault across the Maas and take the *Veritable* enemy in rear. This would be Operation *Ventilate*. Planning for it began on the 30th under Major-General A. Galloway, C.B.E., D.S.O., M.C., who was commanding the Division during the temporary absence of General Whistler on a few days' hard-earned leave in England. This planning was slightly complicated by the fact that on the 31st January there was a welcome rise in temperature and the thaw set in : visitors at first had no difficulty in splashing through the slushy roads and dirty yellow lanes that led across the white monotonous marsh to Divisional Head-quarters. But soon these approaches became rivers of mud, and their edges and middles collapsed under a strain for which they were not designed.

During the third co-ordinating conference for *Ventilate*, which was being held in Horst on February 3rd, a D.R. arrived with orders that the Division was to be relieved by the 52nd (Lowland) Division and to move into reserve in the area of Louvain, except-ing 185 Brigade, who would move to G Trials Wing of the 79th Armoured Division near Maastricht to assist 33rd Armoured Brigade in perfecting the technique of assault river crossings. Advance parties from the Lowland Division would arrive on the 5th.

Meanwhile the Suffolks sent another patrol across the river. Cray went again, with Captain Harris and six others. They crossed as a fighting patrol opposite Geisteren. They wirelessed back full reports on the ground and on two enemy encounters.

After searching two houses, about a thousand yards back from the Maas, voices were heard, and twelve Germans, including an officer, were seen carrying a rubber boat. Fire was opened up at them by the patrol at ten yards range, and all fell. No fire was returned, and they were probably nearly all killed. Returning to the river the patrol ran into a position containing at least two machine-guns manned by eight men. They were engaged at five yards range, and five of the occupants were killed or wounded. After this it was found that Cray was missing. Harris and Private Spendlow stayed to look for him while the others returned to the boat. After waiting half an hour—none of the three had returned —the others reluctantly recrossed. At 5 a.m. another patrol crossed to look for the missing men. No trace was found, and though careful watch was kept the following night, nothing emerged either then or later concerning their fate.

The last patrol to cross from the 3rd Division was provided by the Ulster Rifles. They had already made a most satisfactory reconnaissance with a patrol under Lieutenant Hancock of five enemy-occupied houses near Lomm. On the night of February 4th Lieutenant Beavan took a patrol across to bring back a prisoner from here. Across the swollen river they were amazed to see a man carrying a shovel of blazing coal from one house to another while three men walked down to a position Hancock's patrol had told them about. An ambush was prepared for these three, but, not two minutes later, two more Germans walked into it. They were disarmed, hurried away to the river, and proved very informative.

These patrols were in all cases given the closest artillery support, and every possible precaution was taken against an emergency. The Field Regiments were kept in action without more than about ten days' rest throughout the period. Counter-Mortar, Counter-Battery and Harassing shoots were fired off daily, and in that respect the enemy was effectively dominated. At the end of the period the Artillery O.P.s had an intimate know-ledge of the habits of the Germans across the river, and this, with the results of the Infantry's patrols, was handed over to the Lowland Division.

Before the relief took place, the South Lancs and the Middlesex played off the final in the Divisional Football Competition on

February 5th, on the De Valk ground, Venraij. " The Middle-
sex goal had some narrow shaves, but Phipps played an outstanding game, carrying their side on his broad shoulders : then
Mason and Howey scored, and the final result was a win for the
Middlesex, 3–1." That day the Lowland Division's Advance
Parties arrived, after a journey over terrible roads, from the
Geilenkirchen sector. The relief was greatly complicated by
the fact that there were only two routes open to the Division :
Horst-Venraij-Deurne and Overloon-Oploo-Deurne. These,
despite everything the Sappers and Pioneers could do, were
practically impassable. However, they began to pull themselves out of the mud on the 6th, and by the afternoon of the
8th they had all left the area. The South Lancs record that
it took them seven and a half hours to cover the twelve miles
to Deurne !

From Deurne the road was well known : through Helmond
and Eindhoven, across the Escaut Canal, and along " 240
DOWN." It was the way they had taken for the brief pleasures
of 48-hours' Brussels leave. The target date for Operation
Veritable was February 8th, and that day, " despite weather
conditions that could hardly have been more unfavourable,"[1] it
was duly launched as the Division left the line. They had the
feeling that war had released them only for a few moments, and
would soon reclaim them. They were not wrong.

When they first arrived in Flanders the previous September,
the Divisional Artillery had noticed the number of Artillery Ranges
marked on their maps in the neighbourhood of Bourg-Leopold,
Belgium's Aldershot : the Gunners had commented rudely then,
as they did now that they found everyone else (except 185
Brigade) billeted near Louvain and Brussels while they remained
within easy reach of the ranges of Lommel. But, wherever they
were, the Division were quick to win the friendship of the local
inhabitants, while they cleaned the Maas mud off their vehicles
and themselves and started training again. 185 co-operated
with a will in the production of landing-tables and schemes for
marshalling and bank control : these, with hardly any alteration,
were used with manifest success in getting the assaulting Divisions
across the Rhine a month later.

[1] Supreme Commander's Report, p. 107.

They were away from the war a fortnight. On February
22nd, recce parties were suddenly ordered forward to stage at
Tilburg. The Division was to relieve the 15th (Scottish) Division
in Germany, near Goch. XII Corps would arrange the move of
185 Brigade. The only communication with Corps was by High
Power telephone, " but by 9 p.m. it became apparent that the
main body would move on the 24th."

Chapter Eight

THE RHINELAND OFFENSIVE

'' Onward led the road again
  Through the sad uncoloured plain
  Under twilight brooding dim,
  And along the utmost rim
  Wall and rampart risen to sight
  Cast a shadow not of night,
  And beyond them seemed to glow
  Bonfires lighted long ago.
  And my dark conductor broke
  Silence at my side and spoke,
  Saying, ' You conjecture well :
  Yonder is the gate of hell.' ''
                              A. E. HOUSMAN

ON FEBRUARY 24TH the long convoys of lorries, tracked vehicles, gun-tractors, trailers—all painted with the triangular sign—again moved forward across the desolate southern wastes of the Netherlands. Within a few hours of leaving the warmth and the friendliness of their rest-areas, the 3rd Division were approaching the Maas at Gennep, this time to cross over on the longest Bailey Bridge they had seen. Three or four miles farther on they came to the German frontier.

XXX Corps had begun the offensive a fortnight ago. Five Divisions, supported by over a thousand guns, had advanced through the Siegfried Line, through terrible conditions of forest and flood, clearing the whole Reichswald, and finally capturing the town of Goch to the south. On the 15th, II Canadian Corps had assumed responsibility for the completely amphibious operations on the left, flanking the Rhine, and were now developing an attack on Calcar. The great offensive, *Veritable*, had been designed to strike the Germans between the two rivers from the north at the same time as a blow was delivered by the Ninth American Army from the south. The Americans, under Montgomery, were to have crossed the River Roer on the 10th and

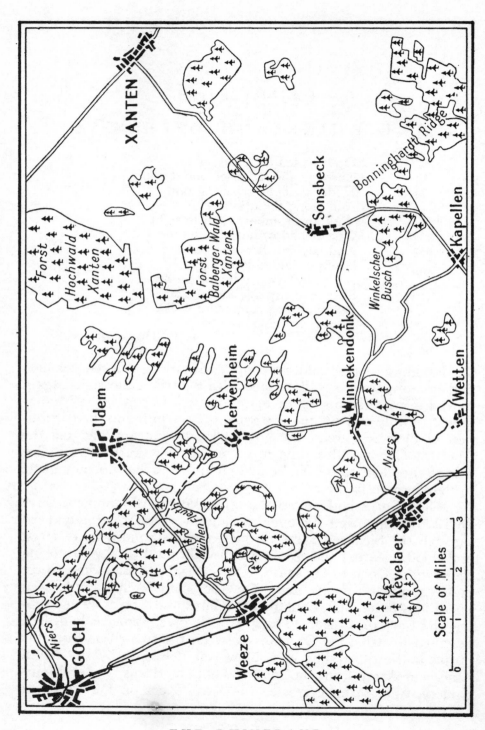

THE RHINELAND

driven north to meet the British and Canadians. Between these
two Armies the Germans, who were still trying to watch the Maas
river-line (their idea was for us to attack from the west, not from
the north and south simultaneously), would be crushed. But on
the 10th the Roer was so swollen that Montgomery had to hold
back the Ninth Army : it had just been released on the 23rd, the
day before the 3rd Division was brought into the northern Army.

The result of the delay in launching the southern offensive
was that the Germans put their main strength and their reserves
in the way of the advance from the north : three Infantry, four
Para, one Panzer Grenadier and two Panzer Divisions were doing
all they could to stop the British and Canadian Divisions. They
made good use of the deep defences of the Siegfried Line and of
the appalling ground, and for once they had massed as much
artillery as we had, confronting us with 1,054 guns, according to
the 21 Army Group estimate. They did not prevail, and their
preoccupation was turned to admirable advantage by the U.S.
Ninth Army once they had established their bridgehead north of
the Roer. And so, while the 3rd Division was on the point of
engaging in what both Eisenhower and Montgomery have
described as some of the fiercest fighting of the whole war, there
was comfort now in the thought that the enemy's rear grew daily
less secure as the American advance gained momentum, and that
his very reluctance to give ground in the north made his destruction certain.

The Division entered the battlefield at Gennep opposite
Oeffelt in the northern sector of their old river-line. At Gennep
the River Niers wandered into the Maas from the south-east. The
whole topography of the battlefield conformed with the general
north-west, south-east direction of the Rivers Maas and Rhine
that bounded it. The main roads and railway ran through
it that way, and roughly down the middle of it meandered the
stream of the Niers. Farther over towards the Rhine a fairly
continuous ridge also ran parallel : the northern part was called
Hochwald Xanten, the next part Balberger Wald Xanten, and
then after a gap, in which stood the village of Sonsbeck, came the
Bonninghardt ridge. Xanten is the birthplace of the fabulous
Siegfried, and the " lay-back " positions of the Siegfried Line
were based on the length of this ridge. The arrival of the 3rd

Division was part of a general regrouping in the north for Operation *Blockbuster*, in which II Canadian Corps on the left was to break through the enemy defences between Calcar and Udem, smash the Hochwald Line and exploit to Xanten, while XXX Corps advanced and swung round on the right of the Canadian Corps.

Across the Maas and past Gennep the Division entered the enemy's country and drove thoughtfully along the southern edge of the Reichswald. At least the Germans who lived here knew now the pleasures of total war. Any house that had been missed by the bombs and shells was liable to be blown down by the Sappers and bulldozed into a military road. They also knew fear. But to know fear and the horror of war was not likely to be enough. They also needed to be taught the rudiments of self-confidence and the point of peace. That must wait. Through complete devastation the Division made its way until the sound of guns reached their ears. At a distance it was a continuous reverberation, and as they approached the rubble that was heaped on the site of the town of Goch they came right in amongst the perpetual bang and crack of the gun-areas. Goch was still being mentioned in B.B.C. news bulletins.

The 15th (Scottish) Division held the line of the main Goch–Calcar road a mile or two to the east of Goch. In the past fourteen days they had borne untold privations, advancing waist-deep in mud and water, with five miles of their main supply-route submerged at one point near Kranenburg. Then the 3rd Division relieved on the 24th and 25th February, in thickly wooded country. 9 Brigade took over from the Brigade holding the lateral Goch–Calcar road. Forward and slightly right of them 8 Brigade, with a squadron of the 3rd Recce Regiment, relieved two Brigades in the woods, as far forward as the lateral Goch–Xanten railway branch-line. On their right flank 8 Brigade had the River Niers, that flowed from Geldern in the south-east up through Wetten, Kevelaer and Weeze to Goch and Gennep. The little town of Udem stood away to their left. Despite the general north-west, south-east tendency of the roads and physical features of this part of the Rhineland, the only two roads in the area through which the Division was to advance south-*eastwards* ran from Udem diagonally *across* their front : the first went south-*west* to Weeze, the second south to Kervenheim and Winnekendonk. Kervenheim was the 3rd Division's objective. To reach it the Udem-Weeze road had to be crossed. The Division's axes of advance were two soft, saturated sandy tracks leading south-east through the woods.

General Whistler's plan for this operation, known as Op *Heather*, was for 9 Brigade to advance through the woods on the left to secure the left (Udem) half of the Udem–Weeze road, for 8 Brigade to advance on the right to secure the Weeze end of the road, and for 185 Brigade, at present in reserve, to advance then through 9 Brigade's positions and capture Kervenheim. *Heather* was to begin at 7 a.m. on the 27th. 11th Armoured Division, the right-hand formation of II Canadian Corps, would be operating on 9 Brigade's left ; and on 8 Brigade's right, just across the Niers, the 53rd (Welsh) Division would be attacking Weeze. 53rd Division's operation closely concerned 8 Brigade, whose objectives on the Udem–Weeze road included a vital bridge. This was where the road crossed the *Mühlen Fleuth* before entering the town of Weeze. The *Fleuth*, a narrow tributary of the Niers, assumed a significance comparable with that of the *Molen Beek* in the battle for Venraij. If 8 Brigade could take the bridge intact, the 53 Recce Regiment would cross it on the 28th, the morning of 53rd Division's attack on Weeze, and take the town in the rear.

The Commander-in-Chief remarks in his despatch that the enemy had built up to about the equivalent of eleven divisions ; " in particular their paratroops fought magnificently." In front of the 3rd Division, but not exactly facing them, were all three battalions of 7th Para Regiment, fighting under command of the 8th Para Division. They were facing Udem, expecting the 3rd Division to come bowling down the Udem–Weeze road. The attack through the woods caught them off guard. They soon recovered, and seemed to bear in mind the final exhortation of Von Rundstedt, C-in-C West, who addressed them as " My valiant fellow-combatants," and went on : " Through your perseverance the general attack of the enemy must be shattered. With un-shakable confidence we gather round our Führer to guard our People and our State from a destiny of horror." The amazing Germans persevered all right. It was a good thing they did.

They helped unintentionally to get it over quickly, and enabled Eisenhower to write afterwards that " the war was won before the Rhine was crossed."

So the 3rd Division was going into the last full-scale pitched battle of the war ; probably, in view of atomic bombs, the last of all time. There were still some hard battles to fight, but not on the intense scale of this Rhineland offensive. The Division had under command the 6th Guards Tank Brigade, a Squadron of Flails, a Squadron of flame-throwing *Crocodiles*, and a Squadron less a troop of A.V.R.E.s. The support of the Divisional Artillery was strengthened by that of the Field Regiments of the Guards Armoured, 51st (Highland) and 53rd (Welsh) Division, as well as by that of the heavier guns of higher formations. The division, thus augmented, was only a fraction[1] of the force of the two Corps that were concentrated between the two rivers on a front that was never more than twenty miles broad.

February 26th the Division spent preparing and patrolling. On the left, 11th Armoured Division began their attack in the afternoon. 9 Brigade's Start Line was reconnoitred by Captain Baudains of the Ulster Rifles. As he crawled forward to examine the bodies of a British tank crew lying on the track, he caught a glimpse of a German steel helmet peeping over the top of a bank not thirty yards away. He immediately organised an attack on this position and " flushed out two very timid members of the Master Race, who proved valuable because, on being marched away down the track, they indicated with shaking fingers and terrified shouts of ' Minen, Minen,' that the main Brigade axis was mined." All units had retained a Dutch interpreter since the Venraij days : they proved extremely competent in the German language and in handling the Germans generally. The Ulsters' interpreter soon discovered the exact location of these mines, but as no Divisional Sappers could be spared from the desperate job of holding the main supply road together, they had to set about clearing the mines with their own resources. They did what they could during the night, and where the track was still uncleared it had to be by-passed bygoing through the wood. Throughout the period of waiting

[1] About one-eighth.

both Brigades were being shelled and mortared. It rained, and the sky was cheerless : Op *Weather* would have been a more suitable code name.

However, the attack next morning through the woods took the Germans by surprise. A great barrage—the Infantry described it as " ample "—preceded 8 and 9 Brigades, who were led on to their respective first objectives by the Suffolks and Lincolns. Through them passed the other two Battalions of each Brigade. The K.O.S.B.s' account gives a good idea of this stage of the battle. Since Colonel John Macdonald left them at Overloon (he was now G.1. at Div. H.Q.) they had been commanded by Colonel R. C. Macdonald, D.S.O. He writes : " At 7.30 we saw the Lincolns advancing. The barrage made a most heartening and impressive noise. We did not wait long before we were on the move behind the Lincolns, who seemed to be getting on well. As we moved up to cross the stream we saw the first prisoners coming back. There were about sixty of them, formed up in threes, and marching quite smartly to the rear, only looking pretty dazed . . . The enemy Defensive Fire had started, but I think the direction of our attack took him by surprise, as it fell mostly on our flanks . . . The Lincolns' attack was completely successful and enabled the Ulster Rifles and ourselves to form up as planned." The tanks of the Scots Guards arrived to support them, and at 10 o'clock the barrage started up again. Despite the density of the wood, the Company Commanders succeeded in " leaning " their companies against the barrage. The wisdom of this policy was soon apparent, as German positions were over-run wholesale before the defenders had recovered from the effects of our devastating artillery fire, and a large number of prisoners came back, obviously in a dazed condition. When the paratroop defenders of a group of buildings in a clearing proved stubborn, Lieutenant Simpson's platoon, led by himself and Sergeant Jaggers, rushed them, forced them out and made them prisoner. By eleven o'clock the forward companies had reported the line of the Udem–Weeze road captured. They had covered a thousand yards in exactly fifty minutes. " The barrage was due to pause on this line, and a good thing it was, as a German locality about sixty strong were dug in just beyond the main road, and they got the full benefit of the ten-minute pause. They were thrown into disorder and the whole lot fell to A Company, who had a fine picnic."

Advancing on the left of the K.O.S.B.s, three Companies of the Ulster Rifles were having an equally fine picnic, D Company alone claiming 80 prisoners. Purcell is mentioned again for the way he led his platoon of C Company forward in tremendous strides, capturing several posts with inspiring enthusiasm, winning the M.C. But on the K.O.S.B.s' right, the South Lancs, 8 Brigade's left-hand Battalion, met sterner opposition. This was by-passed by the troop of tanks of the Grenadier Guards supporting C Company, who " reached the main road but were picked off by bazookas . . . The leading platoon of A Company forced their way through the woods on to the road, but were picked off by machine-gun fire enfilade, and by snipers, across the road. The Battalion consolidated between three and four hundred yards short of the objective, the action having proved extremely costly, especially in officers. Among the killed were Major Carse and Major Watson, C and A Company Commanders, Captain Carmichael, and Lieutenants Slack and Helm."

The Battalion on the right was the East Yorks. Their action was epic. They had been given the responsibility for capturing the vital bridge across the *Mühlen Fleuth* which 53rd Division's Recce Regiment were to cross in the attack on Weeze next day. Like the South Lancs, they found that resistance increased after the first stages of the attack, but they reached the road by 1.30 p.m. From this point the road sloped down very gradually to the right, passed through a copse, and crossed the bridge not more than 500 yards away. C Company under Reg Rutherford were sent up with orders to seize the bridge, whose code name was *Donald*. By two o'clock this was done, against *comparatively* light opposition, and just across the bridge the Company based the defence of their bridgehead on Schaddenhof, a group of farm buildings in a clearing in the woods to the left of the road. The bridge, a solid Class 70 construction, had been prepared with four 500 lb. bombs for demolition, but by an astonishing piece of good luck the fuse had gone out. At 4.10 the Corps Commander, General Horrocks, wirelessed his congratulations to Colonel Renison on gaining *Donald*.

It was not long before the enemy made it clear that it had not been his intention to allow the bridge to be taken intact, or to expose the defenders of Weeze to an attack in the rear when it was imperative to hold that nodal point at least one more day if his troops still in the Maas River line were to be extricated. C Company were still busy organising the defence of the bridge, and had sent back for more small-arms ammunition when at 5.30 they were approached by an enemy tank that quickly withdrew. One section of the East Yorks' anti-tank guns crossed the bridge, without their Platoon Commander, who had been hit by a shell. The carrier-load of small-arms ammunition sent forward to replenish their low holding was also hit by a shell and never reached them. The only tank to cross the bridge with them was the Sherman O.P. taken over by John Ford, the F.O.O. of B Troop, 76th Field Regiment. He also provided the only means of wireless communication between C Company and the main force throughout much of the grim battle that now developed.

At 6.55 the 76th Field Regiment fired on " enemy forming up " in the woods just south of the bridgehead. This counter-attack by a Company of 1st Battalion 24 Para Regiment came on with tanks, and the Field Regiment continued to fire their S.O.S. Task without intermission until 10.55, when there was a pause before the enemy launched the whole of the 3rd Battalion of 22 Para. Regiment. At the same time the other Field Regiments were engaging further D.F. Tasks at the request of Major Burton Pirie, M.C., the Battery Commander with Colonel Bill Renison. Nearly everyone in the Division was anxiously watching the fate of C Company all night, but especially the Gunners, over whose wireless net came the terse, intermittent commentary. The dumping of ammunition that night was a frantic business, at one time guns having only ten rounds left, and consternation was general when it was heard that Ford had dropped the range until the rounds were falling right on to the Company position.

If the Gunners got desperately short of ammunition, so did C Company. After borrowing 3,000 rounds of ·303 from the Middlesex machine-gunners in the copse back along the road, they were reduced to the small reserve in Ford's tank.[1] B

---

[1] Just as the operator in the tank pressed his pressel switch an urgent voice said : " A hand will come in through the opening : fill it with ·303," and was transmitted over the Gunner net.

Company had been ordered up to Bussenhof, a cluster of
buildings 500 yards short of the main road, from there to get
through to the relief of C Company. But to begin with they got too
far over to the right, and meanwhile the enemy had crossed the
Fleuth and occupied the copse on the road. To make quite sure
that B Company got through, Colonel Renison went over to the
Bussenhof himself, placed the carrier platoon under their command, and told them to steer clear of the copse, which D Company
and the troop of tanks of the Grenadiers would deal with. C
Company had now been forced to pull into the tight perimeter
round Schaddenhof, and Rutherford had asked Ford to bring
the S.O.S. down about their own ears : enemy tanks were
penetrating right up to the walls of the house, while their infantry
got a foothold in the outbuildings.

About 9.30, as soon as it was learned that the carrier load
of ammunition had never arrived, the Second-in-Command,
" Banger " King, collected another carrier from Bussenhof and
loaded it with ammunition and spare wireless batteries. He met
the Colonel on the way to Tac. H.Q., who told him the enemy
in the copse would make it difficult for him to get through.
Banger said he was quite willing to take the chance. " He was
asked before leaving how long it would take him to get to the
desperate company (as they wanted to know). He replied :
' About ten minutes' good going on the main road.' " It was five
minutes later that Bombardier White, himself fatally wounded
soon afterwards, reported from Ford's O.P. the brief message :
" Banger's here." C Company could not have held out many
more minutes.[1] At that point Banger undoubtedly saved the
bridgehead, and was awarded a bar to the D.S.O. Soon afterwards B Company crossed to join C, and the Germans desisted
for a while.

B Company took over the defence of the right flank, their
wireless was added to the Gunner communications, and Maclean,
who was acting F.O.O. with them, took over the duties of

[1] It is a notable coincidence that (as the Fifteenth of Foot) the East Yorks earned
their Regimental nickname " The Snappers " at Brandywine under the condition
of a shortage of ball ammunition. Their C.O., learning of the acute shortage, cried :
" Snap and be damned," whereupon all available ammunition was handed to the
best shots, the rest running from tree to tree, snapping blank charges. The ruse
succeeded.

Infantry Officer. About this time D Company got into the copse : the Company Commander found he had fifteen men left when he came to consolidate. Meanwhile a recce party from the 6th Royal Welch Fusiliers of 53rd Division had come forward to make arrangements to relieve the East Yorks during that night. This did *not* appear practicable : indeed, the R.W.F. recce party lost two officers killed and three wounded.

Soon after midnight the enemy struck again for the bridge, this time with a battalion of paratroops. Now they pressed in from all sides and tanks overran one section position in the sandy bank in front of the house, one track actually passing over the Company H.Q. dugout. The Battalion anti-tank section were surrounded, but eventually succeeded in getting back into the farm, the walls of which were being subjected to bazooka fire. The artillery support was maintained, the guns firing as much as five rounds a minute for long periods. The entire Corps Artillery was called in. And again the counter-attack slackened. It intensified again about 3 a.m., and back over the bridge the copse was retaken, yet the Germans never tried to rush the bridge from this side, a suprising reflection in view of the terrific shelling with which their onslaught from the south was constantly met. The bridge was held, and at last, about 4.30 on the morning of the 28th, the attacks began to die down and the rate of gunfire was reduced. An entry in the East Yorks' Signals log : " 0440-0510—Brig and C.O." suggests that Brigadier Goulburn and Colonel Renison discussed at length the situation and the possibilities of relief. This began at 5.50, when a company of the R.W.F. supported by tanks reoccupied the copse and four East Yorkshiremen were found still in their positions—with four prisoners ! At 9 that morning three Welsh Companies got forward over the bridge and permission was given for B and C Companies to move back. Even then C Company were held down by increased enemy shelling, including close fire from an S-P on the west bank of the Niers. By midday the relief was completed.

That night the 76th Field Regiment fired 450 rounds per gun, and the other two Regiments must have fired almost as many, while all the available guns of the Corps contributed some 100 rounds each. Baglin, the Staff Captain R.A., acknowledges that the Division could never have produced sufficient ammunition without the great co-operation of the S.C.R.A. of 15th (Scottish) Division. But all who helped with the supply and dumping and firing of ammunition were sufficiently gratified by the thought that *Yorkshire Bridge*[1] had held, and without their efforts those two East Yorkshire Companies must have been wiped out. In the woods over the bridge eighty-three dead Germans were counted on the left of the road alone. These first twenty-four hours of Op *Heather* cost the East Yorks 8 officers and 150 others in killed and wounded.

"Dear Renison . . . Will you let all ranks know that I shall come and tell them as soon as I possibly can how moved I have been by their very gallant actions . . ." wrote General Whistler that day, the last of February, as the battle for Kervenheim continued. From the Udem–Weeze road the Warwicks and K.S.L.I. advanced across difficult country—woods, waterlogged clay fields, scattered houses, no roads to speak of—with at first little, and later considerable, resistance. When it grew dark, at about 6 o'clock, they were not far off their objective. Patrols that night penetrated right up to the outskirts of Kervenheim, and next morning, the first of March, the Norfolks also took part in the 185 Brigade attack. Colonel Bellamy had gone to 6th Airborne Division as a Brigadier under General Bols, and the Norfolks were now commanded by Lieutenant-Colonel F. P. Barclay, D.S.O., M.C. 185 Brigade were now commanded by Brigadier F. R. C. Matthews, D.S.O., " and so," comment the Norfolks, " with new commanders came new ideas, always a good thing."

The morning began badly with an enemy counter-attack, that B Company of the Warwicks with a troop of the Coldstream Guards only repulsed after very heavy fighting, and with the mortaring of the K.S.L.I., in which Lieutenant Aldridge, who " was

---

[1] Bill Renison writes : " It gave the greatest pleasure to all ranks when the Div. Commander ordered the Sappers to place a nameboard on the bridge with the East Yorkshire's crest and name. . . . A week later when I went back over the ground with Reg reconstructing the battle, the thing that most of all struck us was the bridge itself, a structure so insignificant that, as a newspaper correspondent later pointed out, you could drive over it any day without realising you had gone over a bridge at all. What more fitting comment could there be on the folly of war ! Intact as it was, it had soon ceased to have any meaning, but there are many of us who will never forget it."

quite the greatest character who served with us,"[1] was killed. The attack began and made good progress on the left, but the right, the more direct approach to Kervenheim, was bitterly contested. Here Private J. Stokes won the Victoria Cross but died of his wounds. He was a member of the leading section of 17 Platoon, Z Company, of the K.S.L.I. "During the advance," runs the citation, " the Platoon came under intense rifle and medium machine-gun fire from a farm building and was pinned down. The Platoon Commander began to reorganise the Platoon when Private Stokes, without waiting for any orders, got up and, firing from the hip, dashed through the enemy fire and was seen to disappear inside the farm building. The enemy fire stopped and Private Stokes reappeared with twelve prisoners. During this operation he was wounded in the neck.

" This action enabled the Platoon to continue the advance to the next objective, and Private Stokes was ordered back to the Regimental Aid Post. He refused to go and continued the advance with his Platoon.

" On approaching the second objective the Platoon again came under heavy fire from a house on the left. Again, without waiting for orders, Private Stokes rushed the house by himself, firing from the hip. He was seen to drop his rifle and fall to the ground wounded. However, a moment later he got to his feet again, picked up his rifle and continued to advance, despite the most intense fire which covered not only himself but the rest of the Platoon. He entered the house and all firing from it ceased. He subsequently rejoined his Platoon—who, due to his gallantry, had been able to advance—bringing five more prisoners.

" At this stage the Company was forming up for its final assault on the objective, which was a group of buildings, forming an enemy strong-point. Again, without waiting for orders, Private Stokes, although now severely wounded and suffering from loss of blood, dashed on the remaining sixty yards to the objective, firing from the hip as he struggled through intense fire. He finally fell twenty yards from the enemy position, firing his rifle until the last, and as the Company passed him in the final charge he raised his hand and shouted good-bye."

During the K.S.L.I. advance, Lieutenant Banks and Company

[1] Guy Radcliffe's account.

Sergeant-Major Olden also distinguished themselves at the head of their men. The Norfolk advance was equally fine and makes equally distressing reading. " At 4.15 a.m. a long snake of men wound their way along the track to the assembly area . . . At 9 o'clock the leading Companies crossed the Start Line. To the right were a strong-point and large farm called Murmanshof, and it was from these that we suffered out first set-back. A Company on the right suffered badly. Major D. W. Smith, M.C., was shot clean through the head, all the Platoon Commanders were either killed or badly wounded, only the Gunner F.O.O. remaining to control what was left." Captain George Haigh, M.C., of 16 Battery, the 7th Field Regiment, the Gunner in question, writes : " Most of the close quarter fighting I was not able to see in detail owing to the usual smoke and confusion. My operator and I were watching the battle from a shell-hole about seventy-five yards away from the farm. We were neither of us in very good form, having had about an hour and a half's sleep the previous night. Before long the Company Commander and two of his officers had been killed, and the remaining officer I last saw with a wound in the leg being carried away by two of his men. I could count only fifteen or twenty men remaining, who with the loss of their leaders and so many wounded requiring attention were already coming away from the farm. I assumed command of the Company, and gave orders to the only remaining sergeant to organise a defensive position. After my operator and I had helped some of the wounded I`returned to the carrier, and, after passing on what information I had, ordered the driver to ' brew up ' straight away, and this being done, we took some tea round to the remaining men."

The Norfolk D Company was now sent to work round the left flank through the K.S.L.I., as there was slightly more cover that way. B Company had not got on very far, but C Company were able to join up with D, and " a fingerhold was taken on the eastern extremities of the town." By three that afternoon " the enemy had had about enough and the key to the town had been won. Some house-to-house fighting took place with a few suicidal paratroops holding out. A factory fell to C Company and became a bastion from which to operate." The Lincolns were placed temporarily under the command of 185 Brigade, and helped to clear and consolidate the factory area. Late that night enemy resistance in Kervenheim ended.

Already 9 Brigade had been ordered to prosecute the advance next day to capture Winnekendonk, four miles south of Kervenheim. The Ulster Rifles and K.O.S.B.s with 3rd Tank Battalion of the Scots Guards, met only a few snipers as they advanced down the tracks to the right of the Kervenheim-Winnekendonk road. Later in the morning the 3rd Recce Regiment established contact with some enemy some 3,000 yards ahead, while Typhoons attended to an enemy pocket in Berberheide wood. The enemy had pulled back to a tight perimeter defence of Winnekendonk, which was to be taken by the Lincolns " as soon after 5 p.m. as possible."

They crossed the Start Line at 5.41, and then crossed 1,200 yards of open ground, where two of the supporting Churchills were knocked out before a third avenged them. Major P. H. W. Clarke, M.C., a Lincolnshire man from Binbrook in the Wolds, was killed by a grenade as he cheered his men on, but the rest did not waver. Once the village was reached, snipers fired on them from first-floor windows, and Spandaus shot through loopholes made in the walls at ground level. " Now the light was going fast, and the Infantry and tanks entered the village in billows of smoke, punctuated by the orange flashes of enemy 88 mm.s, and criss-crossed by lines of red tracer. It was a terrible spectacle.

" The Battalion had really got its teeth in and was not to be shaken off. While Battalion H.Q. was fighting its way into a house, the leading Company had reached the centre of the little town . . . The next day we took our ease, and saw the reward of our efforts as the Guards Armoured Division poured through ' our ' village."

Ahead of the Guards on the right—crossing and then recrossing the Niers—raced the 3rd Recce Regiment. With 185 Brigade following them up closely, they had been ordered to advance and capture Kapellen, " to give the Guards a clear run." The Recce Regiment's brief account reads : " On the 3rd March C Squadron had a good run through Kevelaer and Wetten, captured two demolition parties in the act of preparing charges for the Niers bridges, and was only held up just short of Kapellen by an S-P gun, a brilliant day being spoilt by the death of Lieutenant Ferguson, whose troop throughout played a prominent part. Their count of prisoners for the day topped the hundred mark, while one young member of the Officer Corps, very anxious for his luggage, even thumbed the Colonel for a lift.''

The road from Wetten to Kapellen led due east. This was the point at which XXX Corps wheeled left around II Canadian Corps, for that day the 53rd Division met the U.S. 35th Division in Geldern, three miles south of Wetten. The Americans had come up from the south at a good pace and all that was needed was for both Armies to face east : in the northern sector the paratroops were clinging bitterly to the Rhine corner opposite Wesel. When the Recce Squadron was held up it appeared unlikely that any further advance would be made that evening, as the Guards Armoured Division, cutting across direct from Winnekendonk to Kapellen, were not far past Winnekendonk when they found their way barred by an obstacle too wide for their own bridge-layers. But half an hour before midnight XXX Corps directed that the 3rd Division *would* capture Kapellen that night. At 1 a.m. Brigadier Matthews said his leading battalion was moving forward steadily and hoped to be in Kapellen soon. As the Warwicks were advancing, a patrol from the K.S.L.I. under Lieutenant Wright penetrated the town and reported it lightly held. At 5.20 the Warwicks were entering Kapellen, while on the left the Norfolks had completed a night infiltration by the whole battalion through a two-mile belt of the Siegfried Line— a big anti-tank ditch, well-laid wire, and a series of deep trenches to cover all approaches—to take their objectives, Haus Winkel, and a smaller hunting lodge in a wood, for the loss of one carrier and its driver !

The Division was now at the foot of the Bonninghardt ridge. The bridges in Kapellen were all found badly damaged. This meant a further delay for the Guards Division, but eventually they got away though the Norfolks' position in the Winkelscher Busch on the morning of the 5th, and General Whistler ordered 8 Brigade to screen their left flank from Sonsbeck with a strong patrol. As the Guards advanced over the Bonninghardt ridge, 8 Brigade stood ready to follow under their command to hold ground for them while the other two Brigades rested and the guns went on firing into the Wesel pocket. On the 8th II Canadian Corps warned the Division that they " *might* be required to pass through the Guards and the Lowland Division, as the latter were still stubbornly opposed." But the last opposition broke. On the 10th the Division was ordered to take over from the 43rd Division a stretch of the West Bank of the Rhine opposite Rees. They moved into position on the 12th. Fourteen days after the beginning of Op *Heather* the Division was watching the survivors of the Para Army across the River Rhine.

Chapter Nine

BEYOND THE RHINE AND THE EMS

" In planning our forthcoming spring and summer
offensives, I envisaged the operations that would lead to
Germany's collapse as falling into three phases : first, the
destruction of the enemy forces west of the Rhine and closing
to that river ; *second*, the seizure of bridgeheads over the Rhine
from which to develop operations into Germany ; and *third*,
the destruction of the remaining enemy east of the Rhine and
the advance into the heart of the Reich. This was the same
purpose that had guided all our actions since early 1944."
GENERAL EISENHOWER.

Now IT WAS spring, and in spring men's thoughts are not
naturally turned towards killing one another. But it is true that,
despite the new sunshine and almost summer warmth that
suddenly filled the countryside, the end of the war was the foremost thought with the men of the Division. Their main purpose
they shared with the Supreme Commander : to make the
Germans admit their defeat, and the sooner the better ; it was
already obvious to everybody but the most fanatical followers of
the Führer, who were open to only one method of persuasion.
To continue the application of that method, the Rhine, biggest
water barrier after the Channel, would now be crossed.

Knowing that another Division had been nominated to assault
across from the bank they held, the Division found themselves
able for once to indulge in the genuine pleasure of wishing they
had been chosen to lead the way ! There was no doubt now who
was dominating whom, and the Division had not lost any confidence in themselves since the day they set eyes on the French
beach from their craft rolling in the channel. But they had an
important part to play in the preparations for the crossing :
an unspectacular, fundamental part. Being used as a spring-
board off which two Divisions dived into mid-Germany one after
the other, and then plunging in after them, implied hard and
rapid work from everyone, and much resource.

The first task was to deny the enemy all access to the west bank, where the preparations for the assault proceeded at incredible speed. That only a fortnight elapsed between the end of the struggle for the Rhineland and the establishment of two Army bridgeheads north of the Ruhr is a superlative tribute to the supreme planners ; it is a tribute, too, to those whose job it was to see that there was no enemy interference with the plans and preparations, and that was the first of the Division's responsibilities in the area of the west bank opposite to Emmerich and Rees. The job naturally went to the three Infantry Brigades. There was not the slightest enemy interference with the mass of troops, guns and R.E. equipment packed into the area, nor is there any reason to suppose that any enemy patrol or agent who succeeded in penetrating the Division's river-line escaped death or capture.

The three Brigades were also pledged, and so were the Gunner O.P. parties, to keep close watch on all enemy activity east of the river, to mark down every movement. The Divisional Engineers undertook all R.E. responsibilities on the near side of the river. Thus the development, signing and lighting of all routes, for tanks, *Buffaloes*, and wheels, the filling-in of craters, the blowing of holes to provide " entries " into the river, all came under the supervision of the C.R.E. The Divisional Signals had the job of preparing the " beach " Communications on the west bank of the Rhine for the whole of the assaulting Corps. They had to bury fifty miles of heavy cable and a hundred miles of quad cable, and the Brigade, Field Regiment and Cable sections all became skilled in handling cable ploughs, bulldozers, and German horses !

Meanwhile, to spare the assaulting formations as much road congestion as possible and leave them as much accommodation, it was decided to despatch all A echelons and 700 vehicles of the Division fifty miles back to an overflow area west of the Maas. This was C.R.E.M.E.'s cue to suggest that all vehicles requiring engine exchanges or overhauls should be included in the 700. 185 Brigade Workshops attended to them in the friendly neighbourhood of St. Anthonis, in the Overloon area. The Ordnance Field Park and Mobile Laundry were also sent back, and there Ordnance established a dump for all winter stores and for the assorted junk (notably coke stoves and stove-pipes) that

since winter had adorned the transport of all units (notably
Field Regiments) on the move, so that they had come to resemble
something in *Sidings and Suchlike* drawn by the *Punch* artist Emett.
Since the Division's next operational role was likely to be a very
mobile one, 9 Brigade Workshops were grounded at this stage so
as to release twenty-five 3-ton lorries and a transporter converted
to carry 30 tons of ammunition in anticipation of the strain that
would be placed on the R.A.S.C. Transport Companies.

These Transport Companies had an extremely heavy dumping
programme on the four nights previous to the Rhine crossing.
In that time 18,000 rounds of H.E. and 4,800 rounds of white
smoke were dumped for the 25-pounders of the Field Regiments,
and 900,000 rounds of Mark VIIIz and 12,000 bombs were
dumped for the machine-guns and mortars of the 2nd Middlesex.
C.R.A.S.C. pays tribute to the sureness of the guides supplied
by the Regiments, whose co-operation with the drivers again
made a complete success of a difficult programme. All this
ammunition indicated business for the artillery and support
weapons. The C.R.A. would control a gigantic *Pepperpot* on
the evening of the assault, peppering the enemy bank with three
Machine-gun Battalions, a Tank Battalion, two Anti-Tank Gunner
Regiments, and three Light Ack-Ack Regiments. These included
the 2nd Middlesex, 20th Anti-Tank Regiment, and 92nd Light
Ack-Ack Regiment. In addition, the Divisional Field Regiments
would fire in support of the Highland Division throughout the
period of their assault.

Finally, all casualties that occured on the Highland Division's
front during their assault and the follow-through by the 43rd
(Wessex) Division on the right and a Canadian Brigade on the
left would be received by the Medical Units of the 3rd Division.
It may be believed, then, that between their arrival on the Rhine
bank on 12th March and the assault by the Highlanders on the
23rd all units of the Division were very actively engaged in their
various preparations. Spirits were wonderfully high, as they were
throughout the entire Allied Expeditionary Force. Battalions
had had all their casualties replaced the moment Operation
Heather ended : reinforcements were mostly nineteen-year-olds,
and impressed one Commanding Officer as " raw enough, but
dead keen." The Division displayed more than ever a self-

assurance and a competence that had grown out of experience both of the assault landing and of holding a river line, and that only increased in the remaining actions of the campaign.

If holding the Rhine bank was to be their job, it was one they knew well : when the time came, they did everything they could to give the Highlanders a leg across, watching their progress with as much concern as if their own units were engaged. Major-General Tom Rennie had recovered from the effects of his unlucky visit to Cambes wood in the Normandy beachhead days, and now commanded the 51st (Highland) Division with all the mastery of the complications of amphibious assault that he had achieved in command of the 3rd Division. Two other commanders in the Rhine crossing whom the Division looked upon as their own distinguished representatives were the Commanders of the 6th Airborne Division and, within that Division, the 6th Air Landing Brigade : Major-General Eric Bols and Brigadier Hugh Bellamy had fought from the Caen Canal to the Molen Beek with the Division, and doubtless Brig. Bellamy enlivened his G.O.C.'s conferences at 6th Airborne Headquarters with the persistence that was expected of Col. Bellamy at the daily conferences at 185 Brigade Headquarters.

The Division spent that fortnight beside the Rhine in conditions that contrasted completely, and very happily, with their winter vigil down by the Maas. The riverside villages were undamaged. Fields that had been flooded were drying in the stronger sun. The nights were shorter, and each morning found new buds on the fruit-trees in gardens where snowdrops grew. In this rural life was a fantastic illusion of peace. Though all battalions were forward in the river-line, each providing an average of five patrols every night and manning five O.P.s by day, battalion areas were very much tighter than they had been in the winter months, and large numbers of the men found themselves employed as bailiffs and herdsmen and house-agents. All buildings had to be emptied of their inhabitants and firmness shown to protesting, disgruntled females. They and the cattle had to be sent back west of the Cleve–Calcar–Xanten road. The demeanour of most of the civilians was one of servility and tractability, and there was little difficulty in handling them. But there were too few German herdsmen, and cattle tended to wander back to their home pasture : they took great exception to the dense and pungent smoke-screen generated by the Pioneers continuously all along the river. Most men found the smoke difficult to work in, but the only alternative was to work in full view of the enemy. Not that the enemy seemed to take advantage of any break in the screen : they lay subdued, though they were paratroops whom the Division had met in *Heather*, and they knew how to fight.

The Germans were delighted to think their livestock was being removed to a safe area—that is, until they heard it was being driven still farther back as a first payment for the beasts they had looted from the Low Countries over five years.

One of the contrasts that first struck the Division on entering Germany was that between the poverty of Limburg and the richness of the Rhineland, with its fat pastures and every cellar stuffed with hams, cheeses and preserves. After the cattle had been driven away there were still plenty of pigs, ducks and hens left. The East Yorks' Commander, writing of his experiences with his battalion, notes : " I suggested to Company Commanders that, with a little prompting, the troops might appreciate the advantages of an egg a day over one meal of chicken, but I was hardly prepared for the enthusiasm with which the whole battalion took up poultry farming ! "

At Battalion and Field Regimental H.Q. the Intelligence staffs were busy collating information from the O.P.s and passing it back to Brigade H.Q.s, who in turn sent it back to the Divisional " I " Staff, and so on. St. John Mann, the GIII (I), and his staff at Div. H.Q.[1] were equally busy keeping all units abreast of the news from the American front in the Saar Basin, where the " grand tactical co-operation " between General Bradley's 12th Army Group and General Devers' 6th Army Group brought about a destruction of German forces " on the Tunisian scale." Mann's Intelligence Summaries, circulated to the whole Division, kept up the high standard set by Rowntree. At this stage in his report the Supreme Commander first indulges in reflection : " Under these conditions the success of our operations appeared certain, a conviction I felt was undoubtedly shared by the German

[1] Div. H.Q. were established in the ancient Schloss Moyland, which had been damaged by nineteenth-century restorers as well as by twentieth-century gunners.

General Staff." I gather from M. Bertrand de Jouvenel that informed opinion in France—to go no further abroad—is convinced that the success of our operations was certain, *and* anticipated by the German General Staff, before 6 June, 1944. Whatever the German General Staff may have thought individually cannot easily be proved, since Hitler would not have liked his Generals to anticipate defeat, and they would not, therefore, commit any such apprehensions to writing, but there is plenty of evidence to show that the Supreme Allied Commander, though optimistic as any Commander should be before embarking on such an operation, did *not* regard victory as inevitable. One undeniable piece of evidence may be found in the footnote on p. 92 above.

But now there was no question : " the war was won " and the results of this certainty were apparent in the behaviour of visitors (both senior and junior) to the Division's O.P.s, who, regardless of whether or not they were screened by smoke, flashed their talc-covered map-boards in the sun like heliographs and in general gave a model demonstration " how not to occupy an O.P." Perhaps the most exact indication of the state of affairs was that such carelessness went unrewarded and the enemy appeared to be incapable of reaction.

Now our bombers roamed all over the Reich, paralysing its communications. In addition, for the seventy-two hours preceding the Rhine crossing, intense and sustained air attacks were made upon known enemy-defended localities (ranging from those spotted by the Division's O.P.s to one further back believed to be the H.Q. of the German 25th Army). The moral effect on the enemy, added to their casualties, is the Supreme Commander's reason for writing : " After enduring three days of unremitting hell from the air, the enemy was in no condition to meet the frontal assault." Only the German Paratroops were to show themselves as stubborn fighters as ever : there were three (incomplete) Divisions of them in the north, and they opposed the Highlanders' landing at Rees.

The climax of all the preparation came on Friday, 23rd March, another fine warm day, like early summer. All the Highland Division had moved into the assembly areas got ready for them by the 3rd Division. They had been given every detail of information the Division had been able to discover about the landing area, and General Tom Rennie came to visit Brigades to thank them personally. The evening was perfect for the operation. After tea, every man in the 3rd Division was told the Army Group plan in outline. At 5 p.m. the Gunners began their counter-battery programme. At 6 the almighty barrage began and slowly the rate of fire was increased. At 7 the *Pepperpot* was started. The din was deafening. It was like one prolonged peal of thunder, yet the sky was blue, turning gold : across it the thousands of rounds of tracer flashed. It was impossible to hear whether any shells were coming the wrong way, but in fact there was little retaliation. The Sappers blasted great holes in the bank to allow the *Buffaloes* to go through, and the Highland Division crossed at 9 p.m.

Elsewhere the crossings were made against slight opposition. Bob Moberly of the Middlesex quotes an unconfirmed report that " there was so much *pepper* in the area that the noise of battle was drowned in sneezing." As the last bomb from 200 Lancasters fell on the key town of Wesel, to the right of the Highland Division's bridgehead, the 1st British Commando stepped in and took the whole town for the loss of thirty-six casualties. The Highlanders had an altogether different experience. Their fighting was hard on the morning of the 24th, while on the right in the area of Hamminkeln, beyond Wesel, the 6th Airborne Division dropped. Later, about midday, the Highlanders lost their Commander. As he was visiting one of his Brigades in the narrow bridgehead a mortar bomb fell beside his jeep and he was killed. The obituary notice of Tom Rennie that appeared in *The Times* confined itself to his activities with the Black Watch and the 51st Division, ignoring his command of the 3rd Division for the landing in Normandy, which was the greatest achievement of his life. The many members of the Division who remembered him heard the news with sorrow. That afternoon the Prime Minister and C.I.G.S. visited Divisional H.Q., stayed about an hour, and later toured the Divisional area. Next day, the 25th, the town of Rees was finally reduced. General Whistler received a letter on the 25th from the D.D.M.S. of XXX Corps which, it is fair to say, typifies the deep appreciation of the assaulting formations. The D.D.M.S. wrote :

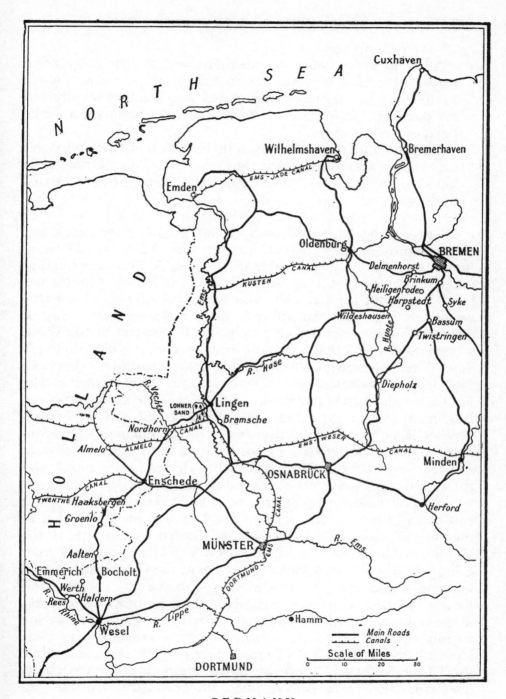

GERMANY

" My dear General,

" I want to send this note to thank you for the magnificent help that 3 Div. is giving me in this party in caring for the wounded. Not only have you placed your medical resources at my disposal, but in addition 8 Brigade have furnished a burial party—never a cheerful job.

" I know that they take this in their stride and that they don't expect any acknowledgment, but now that Tom Rennie is no longer with us to say ' thank you ' I'm taking it upon myself to do so . . ."

Between the 23rd and 28th, 1,298 wounded, 304 sick and 153 exhaustion cases passed through the Advanced Dressing Stations of 8 and 223 Field Ambulances, 8 Field Ambulance being reinforced by a Transfusion Team from 9 Field Ambulance.

On the 27th the Division, who were now following the battle across the river with something of the complacency that may be discerned in the crowd (but rarely in the players) at the Oval, were suddenly told that 9 Brigade would cross the Rhine that very day. Already there were four bridges across near Rees—London, Blackfriars, Waterloo and Westminster. That evening the K.O.S.B.s and Ulster Rifles and 45 Battery of the 20th Anti-Tank Regiment crossed the Rhine at Hönnopel and passed through derelict Rees to take over from units of the Highland Division. Here, fighting eastwards and northwards, the Highlanders were still meeting strong resistance from the German paratroops, and it was the shallowest part of the entire bridgehead.

Early next morning 9 Brigade were told to be ready to advance east to capture the little town of Haldern if it had not fallen to the 15th (Scottish) Division, who had landed on the right of the Highland Division. At midday XXX Corps confirmed that 9 Brigade would attack Haldern, and that the Guards Armoured Division would then charge through, with the 3rd Division and the 43rd Division mopping up and clearing the ground respectively to the right and left of the Guards. Early that evening 9 Brigade's patrols came in with the information that Haldern was clear after all, so the K.O.S.B.s immediately entered the town while the Ulster Rifles advanced to occupy the high ground north of the town, where an *autobahn* had been under construction. Pushing on, the K.O.S.B.s reached Werth to find the bridge blown and mines everywhere. Roads without bridges were no good to the Guards Division, and the Lincolns were at once ordered to pass the K.O.S.B.s to examine the next water obstacle—the River Aa, which had bridges at Lensing and Doing. B Company, under Major Shaw, set off at 5.30 that morning, and soon reported contact with the enemy.

From B Company Gosling went out with a patrol, found the bridge at Lensing blown, took four prisoners, and kept in touch with the enemy until nightfall. In a much-quoted Order of the Day, Field-Marshal Montgomery had just given men to anticipate " cracking about in the plains of Northern Germany . . ." So far there had not been much cracking about in this part of the front, so it was decided to loose a quick full-scale Brigade attack. H-hour was fixed at 1 a.m. In this and other respects, 9 Brigade were reminded of their assault over the Escaut Canal six months earlier. Forty assault-boats arrived, and at 1 o'clock the Lincolns crossed on the right, the Ulster Rifles on the left. Once they were across the Aa and clear of the bank resistance diminished. The Ulster Rifles took some extraordinary prisoners. " Perhaps the most distinguished was a tall fair-haired youth who claimed to have lunched with the Führer in Bocholt on the previous day ! " Major Bird, going round his platoons, ventured to criticise one of the slit-trenches dug into the Aa bank. Upon being informed that it was a German slit-trench, he examined it more closely and found that its occupants were also German ! By 4 a.m. all objectives were taken, and both Battalions were up to the next stream, the Holtwicker Bach. At 5 o'clock the Sappers had built a Class 40 bridge over the Aa : this was H-hour for the K.O.S.B.s, who crossed the *bach* and consolidated on the main east-west road without opposition. At half-past six leading tanks of the Guards Armoured Division appeared at 9 Brigade's front. There was a slight delay at a road-block, but this was by-passed, and not long afterwards the Armour was reported to be well on the way to Aalten.

At 6.45 that morning the Commander of XXX Corps spoke with the G.1 on the telephone, congratulating 9 Brigade on their operation, and giving out orders. The rest of the Division were now across the Rhine. The Division would function as three

separate Brigade Groups, prepared to move at short notice any-
where behind the Guards Division. In theory 8 Brigade had
three, and 185 Brigade six, hours' notice to move. Meanwhile
admin. orders were being issued and final preparations made for
the great jaunt into Germany : the last break-through had begun.

It was March 30th, Good Friday, and later that morning
General Whistler went round Brigades and addressed all the
officers. From one Brigade the officers were assembled in Haldern
Church—a strange Good Friday congregation ! It was noticed
that the General declined the pulpit, despite the obvious advantage
of addressing a large audience from beneath a sounding-board.
He briefly reviewed the recent battles, then turned to the
task ahead, outlining the plan for the XXX Corps advance,
north into the eastern borderlands of the Dutch provinces of
Gelderland and Overijssel, and east again into the North
German plain.

He then electrified his audience with a remark about the
latest progress of the 3rd Recce Regiment. They had not moved
to the Rhine bank at the end of Op *Heather*, but had remained
with 6th Guards Tank Brigade. The rest of the Division had
heard that they were up to something. Apparently they were.
All they themselves knew to begin with was that they would
provide the reconnaissance for the 6th Guards Tank Brigade
Group (including a Field and a Medium Regiment of Artillery),
which was to pass through the Commando Brigade Bridgehead
at Wesel and link up beyond with the Airborne Force. This
task itself sounded exciting enough. The C-in-C reckoned
" the key to the Rhine crossing was the important communicating centre of Wesel."[1] On the morning of the 24th they
watched in the warm haze the approach of the great air force
with feelings akin to those with which the Division had witnessed
the arrival of the Air Landing Brigade on the evening of 6th
June. This was an overwhelming force. The troops came in
1,572 planes and 1,326 gliders, with 889 fighters escorting and
another 900 providing cover over the target area, while 1,253
more put up a screen east of the river. The dropping began
before ten that morning and went on till one o'clock. Positions

[1] C-in-C's Despatch, Supplement to the *London Gazette* for 3rd September, 1946,
p. 4447.

were soon consolidated, and 6th Airborne Division under General Bols began a swift advance eastwards with 15th (Scottish) Division. The 17th U.S. Airborne Division, after linking with the main force of Ninth Army and being joined by the 6th Guards Tank Brigade Group, followed suit. It was at the head of this force that the 3rd Recce Regiment found themselves.

Through Wesel, which was damaged beyond any hope of repair, they concentrated with the tanks and airborne troops near Peddenberg at 3 a.m. on 27th March. There they heard that their objective was now Münster, fifty miles to the east. After much furious map-folding they led off at two that afternoon. Münster was a vital road-centre, and had been visited two days before by the Allied Air Force.[1] The main Wesel-Münster road, running just north of the River Lippe, was contested all the way, but they had covered thirty-five miles of it by the 30th, the day General Whistler was addressing the officers of the Division back at Haldern in the Bocholt area. They were working closely with the Americans of 17th U.S. Airborne Division, who were " moving down the road in a varied collection of jeeps, saloon cars, captured 3-tonners, horses and carts, with one original soul in a mechanical invalid chair. Others were travelling on the Guards' tanks, and, denied variety in transport, had satisfied their egos with top-hats, umbrellas and other tasteful items of civilian dress. They were all in high spirits, following their successful air-landing . . . As they passed through our harbour to attack we had the first of many opportunities to watch them in action. Top-hats or no top-hats, their fighting ability was of a very high standard."

At Buldern on the 30th they were slowed up, and therefore cut across country to the north-east, so as to come at Münster from the north on the Greven road. The Guards continued the attack from the west along the Wesel road. A Squadron of the Recce Regiment reached some high ground at Nottuln and got involved in a battle at Schapdetten. B Squadron therefore did another detour of fifteen miles to the north, getting round behind this hill, and entering a village where " the civilians were so

---

[1] The nature of this visit may be gathered from the Report compiled by the Monuments, Fine Arts and Archives Branch of the Control Commission, which remarks that : " the aerial bombardment of 25 March, '45, has destroyed the whole ancient character of this once fine city."

surprised to see us that they hadn't got their white flags ready
when we arrived." They passed through Roxel, and at nightfall
on the 31st were only six miles from Münster. At 11 p.m. B
Squadron at last got down to some sleep. " At 1 we were woken
for an *O* Group at half-past, ready to move at 2. We were to
take two light cars to Nienberg, trusting to their speed and silence
to take the Boche by surprise. There we should be sitting astride
a main escape-route for the troops still in the city. We were
then to move on to the far side of Münster to recce the Bridges
over the Dortmund-Ems Canal. . . . By 4.30 the patrols had
reached the beginning of the village, and found nothing to report.
One light car drove through the village and saw nothing. Within
ten minutes two carrier troops had rushed up the road into the
village, and within half an hour the whole squadron was in
position. We started taking prisoners then, and went on doing
so for two days. It was getting light and we settled down to
some breakfast. It was Easter Sunday. As the inhabitants got
up to go to church they were surprised to find English soldiers
in their streets."

But the final approach to the city was guarded by the Flak
guns. They were no further use as anti-aircraft defence : there
was nothing left to invite an air attack. They were fired as Field
guns with some effect. American paratroops came up to deal
with these guns, and on April 2nd simultaneous attacks went in
from north and west. The tanks followed the paratroops into
the city. " Prisoners came in at a rate phenomenal even for us ;
prisoners of all types. A small boy of eleven told us proudly
that he had given a false age to get into the army : he had said
he was fourteen. There were old men of the *Volksturm*, parachutists far from their natural home, flak gunners, all sorts. We
didn't stay about to watch them : we went to bed. It was the
best twelve hours of the whole week." They had carried the
triangular sign fifty miles beyond the Rhine to Münster, helping
to open up a new set of roads to the east, and to strengthen the
northern pincer that on April 1st met the 12th Army Group
pincer at Lippstadt, completing the envelopment of the Ruhr,
the caging of one and a half German Army Groups. They made
up some of their lost sleep, and then drove north to rejoin the
3rd Division.

The three Brigade Groups had set off in the wake of the Guards, with 8 Brigade Group leading. They had moved off late on the day after General Whistler had visited and addressed them. First they headed north into Holland, through Aalten to Groenlo. The Dutch reception was delightful after five weeks among the sullen or obsequious Germans. The moment a vehicle pulled up, its occupants were positively embarrassed by the offers of accommodation. In the early hours of that Easter Sunday morning, 8 Brigade Group was established in Groenlo, whose townsfolk had produced the usual glad festoons of orange and their national tricolour flags. Bob Moberly noted : " Some of the houses flew white flags ; they were the houses of collaborators, some of whom were being marched away when we arrived. Easter Sunday was April 1st, All Fools' Day."

But it was only a brief stay in Holland.[1] Ahead, the Guards were through Haaksbergen and Enschede, a spacious Dutch town at one end of the Twenthe Canal. The bridge was blown behind the first few tanks of the Guards, and so 8 Brigade was sent forward to clear Enschede on the 2nd. A few shots were audible, but otherwise it was a repetition of the Groenlo welcome. The Guards galloped on, and 8 Brigade, hard after, dashed through Oldenzaal and recrossed the German frontier to enter the town of Nordhorn on the 3rd. The fine weather had broken, and it was raining as they crossed the marshes and low woodlands of the frontier zone into the first undamaged German town they had seen. Nordhorn was a small modern textile manufacturing town at the junction of the River Vechte and the Almelo Canal. At first the streets seemed innocent of inhabitants, but later looting got under way. It was not a simple matter of soldiers, pistols and cameras, which would have been at least understandable : it was a furtive stream of *Hausfraus* with new buckets and brooms, sneaked from an unguarded hardware store in the South Lancs area. 8 Brigade immediately imposed a curfew that was only lifted for the purchase of food between certain hours. Houses were then searched for Gestapo ruffians

[1] The Div Club remained in Holland, at Bad Boekelo, near Groenlo. During these last stages of the campaign there was no short leave on the Continent, although the Div Club received those who were badly in need of rest. U.K. leave continued, men travelling by rail from Gennep to Calais.

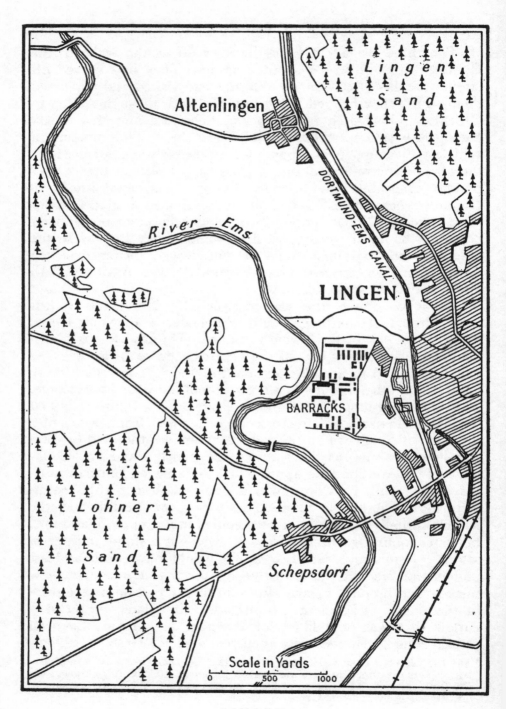

LINGEN

and the like. Civilian houses yielded a surprisingly large number of firearms.

While 8 Brigade were establishing themselves on Nordhorn, 185 Brigade passed through on April 3rd and 9 Brigade followed. It looked as if 8 Brigade were going to spend the rest of the war in Nordhorn, and Brigadier Goulburn was looking rather blue at this time : it was not his idea of winning the war. But he need not have worried. That night 185 Brigade were heading straight for battle, one that quickly involved the whole Division.

" On 28th March the advance to the Elbe began . . . The enemy tried desperately to assemble his remaining forces in opposition to our advance. The core of his resistance formed on the Ems-Dortmund Canal, facing the left and centre of Second Army. Bitter fighting ensued. . . ." Thus the C-in-C outlines the situation in his despatch. 185 Brigade, passing through Nordhorn, were only fifteen miles from Lingen, a fair-sized town standing upon the farther bank of the Dortmund-Ems Canal. To gain Lingen they had to get across both the River Ems and the canal, which in that area ran roughly parallel and between a half-mile and a mile apart. The double water-obstacle sounded formidable. Although this great north-south waterway had been crossed at various points in the south where it lay much nearer to the Rhine (indeed, April 3rd was the date on which the Ruhr envelope was sealed), it was fully expected that the Germans would try to hold it and prevent the XXX Corps drive to the north-east to the North Sea ports.

The K.S.L.I. had arrived at their dispersal point, Lieutenant-Colonel Pat Daly, their Commander, had issued his orders for the assault across the river and the canal just south of Lingen, and the complex details of boat-loads had been worked out, when at 8 p.m. came the cheering news that the Guards had seized a bridge intact across the river into Altenlingen two or three miles to the north.[1] The plan was immediately altered. The Battalion was ordered to march north to cross the captured bridge, pass through Altenlingen, and assault over the canal. The Warwicks and Norfolks, hastening to join the K.S.L.I., were held up from 10.30 p.m. till after midnight when a damaged

[1] It was for this exploit that Captain Liddell of the Guards was awarded the V.C.

bridge collapsed back down the road on the other side of Nordhorn.

At 11 p.m. the K.S.L.I. were ordered to cross and attack at 2.30, and once across the Dortmund-Ems Canal to turn south, securing Lingen and extending the bridgehead to allow bridges to be built on the main road leading into the town from the west. If this had not been achieved the Warwicks were to pass through them at 7 a.m. The K.S.L.I. were marching north to the bridge along difficult tracks across the *Lohner-Sand*. Here was a barren region of dunes[1] similar to the approach to Weert seven months before. " These tracks seemed to go on for ever," wrote Ian Rae, the Battery Commander with the K.S.L.I., " and as time dragged on it was becoming touch-and-go whether the first stage of the attack would take place in darkness at all." The following-up units found the axis even more difficult than the marching troops. It was slow going in a jeep by day ; the drivers of troop-carrying 3-ton lorries that crossed to the bridge by night performed a tremendous feat.

It was 4.30 a.m. when the leading companies of the K.S.L.I. reached the bridge. Silently they crossed the river and formed up for the advance through Altenlingen to the canal, which was slightly more than a mile from the river at this point. By 5.30 they had reached the Canal with scarcely any opposition. The boats were brought forward at once, and at 6.35 the Companies began to cross. So far there was no sign of life from the enemy on the other side, and according to Major Rae, " the scene resembled a regatta more than anything else." But then, as Guy Radcliffe records, two early-rising German soldiers were seen " to come out of their house to inspect the weather. Everyone at once started to fire, at which the Germans started to run out of all their houses to their positions." The fire of the K.S.L.I. forced them to take cover before they could reach the multiple ack-ack guns covering the crossing-place, though one or two

---

[1] This is the Geestland of the geography books. Owing to a cement of iron oxide under the surface, much of the central German lowland, as of Holland and Jutland, is heath, or marsh, or peat-moss. The typical example is the *Lüneburge Heide* where the C-in-C had his Tactical Headquarters at the time of the German surrender. Before the war it was observed that there was much to be done before the German's Geestland was as far reclaimed and tilled as that of Denmark and Holland, and a result of their policy of exploiting the occupied countries has been their failure to make up their own agricultural defects.

" made the crossing unpleasant." Corporal Coles, who was commanding one of the sections at this moment, at once directed his boat away from the landing-place, drawing the enemy's fire. In full view of the enemy he landed his section, set his Bren into action, and then led his section in a charge on the farm held by the enemy, all of whom were either killed or wounded." He won the M.M.

It is clear that the enemy had been deluded into thinking that the attack would come from the south. To that purpose the Divisional Artillery had been deceitfully firing on targets to the south of Lingen. The enemy's artillery and mortars meanwhile had been directed on to the bridge, following the appearance of two Messerschmidts over the scene of activities. But by 10.30 a.m. Sappers of 17 Field Company had built a Class 9 Bridge, to take the infantry close-support weapons. The Warwicks crossed into the bridgehead of the K.S.L.I. (who now had about fifty prisoners), and turned south. They had been pushing slowly forward in the lorries since 3 o'clock the previous afternoon. It had been impossible to prepare an evening meal, and now they were going into attack before they had had time to eat a proper breakfast. " The Troops were quite magnificent, as cheerful as could be." The attack went in with two Companies up and two following a bound behind to do the mopping-up. " I think we must have caught the enemy by surprise ; we came in right on his Battalion Headquarters . . . amongst the first bunch of prisoners were the Commanding Officer, Adjutant, I.O. and M.O. of III Battalion, Grossdeutschland Brandenburg Training Regiment . . . We were well up behind the artillery fire, and soon reached our final objective . . . the Battalion captured 170 prisoners in the day's fighting."

With a quarter of the town in the hands of the Warwicks, the Norfolks passed through at midday to deal with the rest. It was in the south that the attack had been expected : Lingen was a garrison town, and there were still some hundreds of troops to account for, mainly paratroops of II Para Corps. The Norfolks started their street fighting with two Companies up and made good progress, but soon they perceived that the Germans were infiltrating between them, and filled the gap with the other two Companies. The stiffest opposition came just beyond the main square, but by 6 p.m. " things were fairly well under control and a number of houses were burning merrily : the Battalion was just about exhausted. There had been no sleep for the majority for two nights past, and it is a very tiring thing to keep searching houses with Boche almost everywhere—and the type that is not prepared to give in. If the momentum of the attack could be kept up by passing a battalion through us the fate of Lingen would be sealed." This is what happened. The Lincolns came under command of 185 Brigade, and passed through the Norfolks at 8 p.m. They found that street fighting in the dark with no previous daylight reconnaissance was not a good proposition, and that as they edged their way forward they more than once came under fire from houses they had already searched. But when dawn came they could see what they were about, and at 9 o'clock they were joined by a Squadron of the Staffs Yeomanry—" old friends from the earliest days of the campaign " —and by a Troop of *Crocodile* flame-throwers, machines that the Norfolks had so much desired the afternoon before. The Lincolns said : " We soon learnt that the Boches have no great liking for flame, and it was a heartening sight to see them tumbling out of the houses ' in bundles of ten '—to use Quartermasters' parlance." The effect of the *Crocodiles* must have been rather like that of the Pied Piper five hundred and seventy years ago in not-far-distant Hamelin :

> " And ere three shrill notes the pipe uttered,
>   You heard as if an army muttered ;
>   And the muttering grew to a grumbling ;
>   And the grumbling grew to a mighty rumbling ;
>   And out of the houses the rats came tumbling . . ."

In ten minutes there were ninety prisoners, and the rest were making off. The co-operation between the infantry and the tank crews was very enthusiastic, and by early afternoon the Lincolns were not only on all their objectives, but C Company, under Major Gilbert, had taken the road-junction, south-west of the town, which the K.O.S.B.s were to have taken in the next phase !

That day the enemy launched a counter-attack in the Warwicks area, with about two companies of infantry supported by seven or eight S-P guns. This was the occasion of many brave actions by men of the Warwicks. Typical was the courage of Private W. Gibbon, who stalked a German S-P gun supported by German infantry and succeeded in putting it out of action with his PIAT. He remained to snipe with his rifle at the crew who tried to start up the S-P, killing one and wounding at least one other. Corporal T. Rowell found that the house he was occupying had become the target for an S-P which had been brought up to very close range. Several of his Section were buried under fallen masonry. He managed to release these men, reorganise his position, and hold it until the attack was beaten off. He was killed later, before he could receive the award of the M.M. It is difficult to see how the whole affair came about, but the fact remains that four of the S-Ps got into the town and " started milling about in the back gardens of houses." The counter-attack was broken up with considerable loss to the enemy, and all four S-Ps were taken.

9 Brigade were completely established in the southern part of the town. 8 Brigade arrived somewhat out of breath from some serious skirmishing in the neighbourhood of Nordhorn which had chiefly concerned the South Lancs. They took up positions covering the northern and north-eastern approaches to Lingen, leaving 185 Brigade to look after the sector between them and 9 Brigade. Colonel Pat Weston of the Middlesex took personal command of his A (MG) Company and 12 (Mortar) Platoon, some anti-tank guns and a Gunner F.O.O., and " Westonforce " was responsible for the left flank between the river and the canal. Bob Moberly remarked that " Westonforce " H.Q. " spread itself in a *Schloss* belonging to the brother of the most famous anti-Nazi in Germany, Bishop von Galen of Münster."

The nodal point, Lingen, was secure, and the advance was resumed. The Guards and 43 Div. led out to the north-east and east. The weather was warm again, and the countryside radiant in spring sunshine. The Ems looked peaceful enough, not unlike a placid East Anglian river, the Suffolk Stour, or the Gipping. But the bridges were broken and the roads were dusty with brick-dust. On April 7th the 3rd Recce Regiment, now back from their excursion to the Dortmund-Ems Canal farther south

at Münster, sent a patrol south to meet the Recce Regiment of
the Highland Division approaching Lingen from Elberge. 9 and
185 Brigades were pushing out south-east from Lingen.   In 9
Brigade the Lincolns had the first phase, and C Company on
Kangaroos were on the Battalion objective within 30 minutes of
starting. The Ulster Rifles advanced next, and then the K.O.S.B.s
passed through the Ulster Rifles, just after midday, directed on
to Bramsche. A thousand yards short of the objective the advance
guard under Major F. Holden was held up by very intense fire
from the little village of Polle Estringen Rottum. The following
account is given by a subaltern who joined the K.O.S.B.s just
before the Rhine crossing, and who was at first commanding a
platoon with Holden's advance guard. It is a vivid illustration
of the sudden swiftness of events in an action of this sort, and of
the decisions that confront a junior Infantry Officer at every
turn. He says :

"Reports did not seem to suggest anything much in our
way. We all felt that nothing much would happen. We were
wrong !
     As we moved slowly down the road there was a sudden
burst of fire ahead and then a long silence. We jumped off
the tanks and ran to cover at the side of the road, and as we did
so we heard the crack of enemy guns (it sounded like the usual
Flak gun in ground role), and the sound of our own tanks
opening up. We advanced as quickly as possible up the road,
half crawling, to reach *O* Group. Plans were swiftly formulated,
and M. was to send his platoon in to attack while the tanks
gave covering fire. Enemy position only roughly located . . .
I ran off to bring up the men of my platoon ; we were to be
in reserve. I lined the other side of the road, for some fire
was suspected from that side too. A few streaks of red tracer
whistled past and something seemed to burst in the trees overhead. Two of the men were hit. I went forward with F.
(Company Commander) to have another look at the enemy
position. The tanks, having given support, withdrew back
down the road, leaving us.
     I saw F. coming down the road again and he seemed to
be bent slightly . . . He spoke in a hoarse voice and I knew he

had been wounded. He was worried about some tank firing too late. He swayed forward into the open and I went after him to try to get him back. He proved very persistent and wanted to make sure that there was no tank left out in front. After frantic argument I persuaded him that there were no tanks near us which could possibly fire and endanger M.'s attack, and he left us on his way back to the R.A.P. I had to take over the remainder of the Company.

F. had given me a pretty good picture before he left but it was difficult to decide what to do, as M. was off into the blue and could not be seen. I decided to remove the remainder across the road into a hedge roughly facing the enemy position, try to locate M. and help him by fire. In order to do this I crawled forward with Sergeant G. to get a better view, leaving the two Platoons in the shelter of a ditch. Immediately we got out in front fire came down on to us, and the dust flicked up in front of my face. No doubt now about the enemy location ! The most imperative thing, however, was to get back, for we had been spotted. " Let's get back," I said. We crawled carefully and at every undue movement we heard the ping of a rifle bullet. G. got back all right, but as soon as I tried to go over the same little mound a bullet rushed just past my right ear. Stupid ! Even the text-books taught that sort of elementary mistake !

Back in the ditch again I decided on a plan, for by then a runner from M. had reached us. He told us that the opposition was big. There were four or more enemy AA guns supported by small-arms fire. I passed information back and decided to join M. to shoot him out or in as the case might be. However, as we were moving off another message reached me from the Battalion H.Q. telling me to withdraw and put in an attack on some houses on another flank. Another Coy. would attack the present enemy position under an R.A. barrage. I sent the runner back to M. telling him to get out.

We moved back across the road and formed up behind a small copse for the new attack. This time it would probably be all right, for there did not seem any possibility that there would be enemy in the group of farm-houses in the fields. I hurriedly put down a fire platoon and advanced across a field

to the nearest house. There was only one anxious moment
when a gun opened up at us in the middle of the field. We
kept going.

The usual routine of fire and movement on a Company
basis and we cleared the houses. The following Company
passed through us on their way in to the attack on the main
enemy position. By this time the Artillery barrage was coming
down. M. joined us later, with only a few minor casualties.
His information on the enemy had helped to pin-point the
Artillery fire.

We dug in and rounded up some prisoners. Practically a
whole Company of them ! They had been badly shaken by
the barrage and the German Company Commander was
weeping slightly over the disgrace, and the condition of his
men . . . One of the officers—a typical young Nazi—had been
badly wounded. His hand was smashed, and he had been hit
in the leg. He looked green, and kept yelling for morphia.

I entered a house full of terrified civilians (one girl was
hysterical), and had great difficulty in pacifying them. In the
cellars lay a small baby with its foot blown off. . . ."

D and C Companies and a troop of tanks attacked the main
position at 4.30 p.m. They held the village by 5.15, also 6 officers
and 118 other-rank prisoners and 12 Flak guns. They were preparing to move on Bramsche when startling orders were received
for the switch of the Division from the XXX to the XII Corps
" front."

The same evening, while the K.O.S.B.s were fighting for
Polle Estringen Rottum, the Warwicks put in a model attack on
the village of Mundersum. They, too, may best give their own
very graphic account.

" When the assault went in we were not at all sure what we
were up against. A civilian had come in shortly before, and
said the town was held by twenty *Volksturm*. However, we had
heard stories like that before and were taking no chances.
Now the tanks were drawing some return fire from what
sounded like 20-mm. A-A guns.

On Zero Hour our fire switched off to the flank and the

attacking Companies went in. There is no doubt the enemy were completely " foxed." The fire of the tanks and MMGs had all their attention. Our wide flanking movement brought us in from almost behind them. In a very short space of time we had close on a hundred prisoners plus some fifteen dead on the ground. Our own casualties were one killed and six wounded. Our only trouble came from the 20-mm. AA guns. of which there were no less than eleven, six of them being 4-barrelled affairs. These were sited farther forward of the village, and when they saw what had happened they swung them round on to our troops in the village. A troop of *Crocodiles* was just being sent to deal with them when Major F. Bell, M.C., M.M., commanding D Company, managed to get his 6-pr anti-tank gun into action against them at short range. This was enough for them and the crews started to bolt. Carriers rushed after them and rounded most of them up. During the course of this we had only one fatal casualty, Sergeant W. Groves : he was shot by a German who remained in a trench from which three others had already surrendered. After more " mopping-up," the Battalion settled down for the night in the charred remains of its captured village."

During the night they received the surprising orders for the Division's transfer to XII Corps, who had broken clean away on the right and were speeding eastwards. It was in the north that resistance was gathering. The Division therefore left the Guards and XXX Corps on the 8th, travelled fast and far, and by the end of that second week in April they were near the deep, wide lower Weser. Astride of the river stood Bremen, Germany's second biggest port. As they began to close in from the south, the 3rd Division met the most bitter opposition from units of Hitler's crack (and now cracked) troops—poor, desperate, frenzied men, bestial, with no decency left in them.

From Lingen 9 Brigade had gone first, thinking to harbour north of Osnabrück, " but once we were on the move, the wheels did not stop rolling till we had passed some 50 miles beyond." 185 Brigade followed to take up temporary positions covering the northern approaches to Osnabrück and a long stretch of XII Corps northern flank along the Bremen road. Then, on the

night of the 10th, 8 Brigade leap-frogged across the whole
Division.   An all-night move, a total journey of as much as 180
miles, over strange country roads often crowded with refugees,
was a tiring job for drivers of the long lines of lorries and gun-
tractors and carriers, of tanks and S-Ps.   Daylight revealed
thousands of tramping folk, the slave-workers from occupied
countries about whom most people had read without grasping
the meaning, streaming westwards along the roads, their total
belongings on their backs or in the assorted hand-carts and
perambulators they had acquired.

8 Brigade found themselves established across the main line
of escape for the German First Para Army, as the remains of
that force was driven back from Lingen by XXX Corps.   They
took over from a Brigade of the 7th Armoured Division, who had
been leading the XII Corps advance.   On April 11th the Suffolks
held Bassum, the East Yorks Harpstedt, and the South Lancs
Wildeshausen.   Each of these three little towns controlled a road
leading north-east into Bremen—between fifteen and twenty-five
miles away.   The possession of Wildeshausen was the most significant : it controlled the passage of the main Lingen-Bremen
road at the crossing of the River Hunte.   There the South Lancs
arrived at hot midday : and despite the rude interruption of
some enemy S-Ps and a small body of Infantry who managed to
penetrate the *south-west* corner of the town, " all Companies were
in close contact round the town perimeter " by early evening.
Shortly before nightfall the Germans cut the lateral Harpstedt-
Wildeshausen road just where the South Lancs' only supply road
led in from Twistringen in the south-east, and one of a troop of
S-P anti-tank guns that were sent down the road was knocked
out by a bazooka.

Later that night 185 Brigade came up on the east of 8 Brigade
to take over from a Brigade of the 52nd (Lowland) Division that
had been temporarily under command of the 7th Armoured
Division.   The Norfolks took over Barrien, the Warwicks went
into Syke, and two days later the K.S.L.I. relieved the third
Lowland battalion in the twin villages of Kirchweyhe and
Sudweyhe.   8 Brigade touched in to the right on the 12th, the
South Lancs not being sorry to be relieved in Wildeshausen by
the K.O.S.B.s of 9 Brigade and taking up a position in rear of

the Suffolks at Bassum. The K.O.S.B.s passed forty-eight unquiet hours and beat off several local counter-attacks before the excitement died down and they were relieved by a battalion of the 51st (Highland) Division which now came up on the left. Bob Moberly, writing of one of the counter-attacks directed by a company of parachutists against Wildeshausen station, which was defended by a Middlesex M.G. section as well as K.O.S.B.s, describes how " the German officer leading the attack was wounded and fell six yards in front of the guns. He was brought in, and stated that he had been ordered to capture the station and to hoist a Nazi flag on the roof as a success signal, for the rest of his battalion to come in and mop up Wildeshausen. 8 Platoon collected the flag that night, and the C.O. sent it to the Mayoress of Finchley as one of the Battalion's trophies of war."

At Sudweyhe, 185 Brigade were only two miles from the River Weser, and only six from Bremen. On 13th April, 9 Brigade occupied the positions of 8 Brigade, who set off up the main road from Bassum to Brinkum, the last small town before the marshes and floods that protected Bremen from the south. The 3rd Division were set to capture all of the great city west of the Weser.

Chapter Ten

BREMEN AND GERMAN SURRENDER

" April is the cruellest month, breeding
Lilacs out of the dead land . . ."
T. S. Eliot.

The Germans defended Bremen with the blind heroism of despair. The British 3rd Division displayed another sort of bravery : they fought and defeated the Germans knowing that the campaign was likely to be over in a few days, that if they avoided taking risks they might hope to survive the war. The trouble was that the battle of Bremen never looked at all like being a " walk-over." 18 SS Training Battalion fought grimly at the approach to Brinkum. By far the heaviest casualties of the month fell there between April 13th and 20th, but their effect was not to discourage the rest so much as to increase their determination to take their objective, and the Infantry proceeded to fight some of their best actions. They were given every support that could be got in the way of guns and tanks and aircraft. Nevertheless, the loss of life was hard to accept in view of the imminence of German surrender.

The eleventh month of the campaign was one of gain as well as loss : the Division advanced from the Rhine at Rees to the Weser at Bremen. The third week of April was spent in driving the enemy back from the general line Kirchweyhe-Barrien-Bassum (where they had confronted 7th Armoured Division), back over the flooded land at Brinkum, right back into the city. This was all part of the Bremen battle, because here the enemy were induced to squander their reserves in an attempt to keep the fighting away from the city. It was the mistake they had made in Normandy and in the Rhineland. Had they withdrawn their forces intact to the far side of the floods they would have been in a much better position to repulse the attack : but they clung to nearly every village and farm just *in front of* the water obstacle.

8 Brigade had already set off up the road from Bassum on Friday, the 13th. The Suffolks led and the South Lancs covered the open left flank. The Suffolks knew the first village, Nord-wohlde, to be undefended. Thence the road led four miles north to Fahrenhorst and turned north-east for a further four miles to Brinkum. A mile and a half short of Brinkum was a cross-roads, the Suffolks' final objective. They made good speed towards it, with Major Hugh Merriam's A Company ahead in three groups, moving in Bren-gun carriers and 15-cwt. trucks. A solid road-block was by-passed, and an enemy machine-gunner who opened fire on the farther edge of Fahrenhorst did not stay but disappeared into the woods. The country was very low-lying, with occasional woods and undulations. The road ran straight through a maze of side-lanes. Most of the names on the map referred broadly to collections of farms[1] and labourers' cottages rather than to villages. As in most country where stock-raising is predominant, houses were scattered all over the place, and fairly thickly along the main road. The leading carrier section with A Company was within a mile of the cross-roads when a German soldier was spotted near a house some fifty yards from the road. He managed to send up a red Verey light before they shot him. Continuing along the road, A Company ran into heavy fire from another road-block half a mile short of the cross-roads. The Company Commander sent a platoon round the backs of the houses on either side of the road. Nebelwerfer fire fell around them as they cleared a way forward. When they reached the last houses before the cross-roads, Hugh Merriam, who was with one platoon, shouted orders across the road to Meredith, who commanded the other, for the final assault.

Both platoons got across the cross-roads, though on the left the Company Commander had been wounded and that platoon was now led by Captain Rogers. They dug in as it grew dark. A section of the enemy approached from the right and were driven off, to be succeeded by " a considerable body " of rein-

[1] Here, as in the Rhineland and in Limburg, farmhouses were found to conform with the pattern devised in the Middle Ages, if not before, so that the people lived in one half and the cattle in the other ; and in some of the timberwork was carved a very early date. This is only to name one aspect of the Middle Ages that survived here-abouts, but it is curious to reflect that the Division was entering the region whence the first English had come to settle in Britain in the fifth century A.D.

forcements. The other platoon was keeping very quiet, and Meredith, not realising that it was still close-by, withdrew to the last house south of the cross-roads, now in flames. Meanwhile B Company had advanced to reach the lateral road well to the left of the cross-roads, and their Commander, Major A. H. Claxton, M.C., was killed when they came under heavy fire from the flank. Rogers' platoon were still in the house beyond the cross-roads, where they had lain low since the arrival of the German reinforcements, who were now dug in all round them. They were about to attempt their withdrawal when a German came up to the house and rang the bell. Someone inside moved his foot, and a grenade was thrown in. " There was a little more noise and the enemy came from all directions and began to throw grenades in through the windows." Rogers and Sergeant Foreman rallied the platoon as best they could and fought their way out. With the remnant of the platoon they got back to their Company area. The following morning several enemy posts were silenced, while a patrol from the Carrier Platoon encountered no enemy along the lateral road. But that night an A Company patrol established that the cross-roads were still strongly held, so at noon next day, the 15th, a two-Brigade attack was directed on Brinkum.

It was a lovely warm day : scarcely a breeze was wafted across the marshes to the villages and farmsteads amongst which 8 and 185 Brigades fought. To support their attacks they were allotted tanks of 4th/7th Dragoon Guards (the rest of 8th Armoured Brigade—the Stafford Yeomanry and 12th K.R.R.C. —came under command of the Division next day), and they also had the terrific aid of the flame-throwing *Crocodiles* of B Squadron, 7th R.T.R. Two Medium Regiments were added to the normal artillery support of the Middlesex mortars, the 20th Anti-Tank Regiment, and the three Field Regiments. While the Warwicks and Norfolks of 185 Brigade drove on Brinkum from the right, the Suffolks of 8 Brigade would drive forward from the unfortunate cross-roads. The main defences were held by 18 SS Training Battalion, with four companies, each of between 150 and 200 promising young SS maniacs, the most unreasonable and unreliable type of opponents : one company held the cross-roads, one held the rambling village of Leeste, another held the equally scattered hamlet of Erichshof, and the fourth remained with Battalion H.Q. back in Brinkum. The Warwicks would take Leeste and Erichshof, the Suffolks would clear their cross-roads, and then the Norfolks would pass through the Warwicks to capture Brinkum.

First of all, soon after dawn, a platoon of the Norfolks under Lieutenant Loynes was sent forward to cover the left flank of the Warwicks' start line. They brushed an enemy outpost and, after a fierce skirmish, the enemy withdrew. This was what the War-wicks afterwards recognised as " a real service to us." Lieutenant-Colonel D. L. A. Gibbs, the Warwick Commander since the Caen days, who had won a bar to his D.S.O. in the Venraij battles, had left them just before the Rhine was crossed. His successor, Lieutenant-Colonel R. C. Macdonald, who com-manded the K.O.S.B.s in the Rhineland, then came back to his old Battalion. The Battalion was now in its Assembly Area, and a drink of tea was issued all round. By 11.45 they were ready to start. The barrage began at 11.50, to drown the noise of the tanks and S-Ps as they got into position. At midday they moved into the attack.

Now the K.S.L.I. had been demonstrating away on the east flank that morning : the Warwicks attacked from the south. The SS troops were very surprised at this, as they expected an attack from the east. The Warwicks moved fast and the prisoners were soon " rolling in." B Company roped in seventy without very much trouble. A Company, under Major H. C. Illing, M.C., had most of the fighting to do, and Illing won a bar to his M.C. Having fought their way on to their objectives in Leeste, they " at once started exploiting forward to some farms which lay to the north, and which obviously had to be cleared before the Norfolks could really get going." Before they reached the first objective, Sergeant W. Frost, commanding a platoon, was blown into the air by a close shell-burst. Although his right arm and side were incapacitated and he was in great pain, he fought his platoon on to their position, killing 12 Germans and capturing 15 more. Then the fighting patrol under Lieutenant Genever went off to deal with the outlying farms, and at one moment, when they were pinned down by Spandau fire, Private Hathaway (shades of Shakespeare !) got up, under heavy fire at about 20 yards' range, ran to a flank, and got himself into a position from which he could engage the enemy. " Thanks to him the remainder of the patrol were able to assault and overcome the position." As C Company were getting a 6-pounder through mines and demolitions for use in Erichshof, the Suffolks over on the left moved against the cross-roads.

They moved against stubborn troops, who knew which way they were coming. They came under dense fire from enemy artillery and small arms, especially from snipers in most of the houses. Though the supporting tanks engaged these places unceasingly, they were unable to silence the fire from them, and the advance was painfully slow ; in some places it was held. At 5.30 the tanks were relieved to replenish ammunition by four S-Ps, and shortly afterwards a platoon of D Company reached the lateral road away to the right of the cross-roads, becoming involved in a confused hand-to-hand fight. Then two troops of *Crocodiles* arrived. They were sent up, with C Company following, to this right section of the lateral road ; to come at the cross-roads from the right, up the road from Leeste instead of the main Bassum-Brinkum road. " At about 8.15, as it grew dark, the *Crocodiles* went into action, squirting flame into every house and trench they approached. They went straight across the cross-roads. The enemy left their trenches and ran. The Battalion was wild with elation at the sudden change from deadlock to victory. But the cost had been high. . . ." Later a single enemy aircraft dropped three bombs into the blazing cross-roads, causing no casualties. At 1.30 in the morning A Company sent a patrol forward to within 100 yards of the level-crossing at Brinkum. " At first light the Company moved up to the edge of Brinkum. Light opposition was encountered, but the Company was ordered not to move any farther forward as 185 Brigade were by now in Brinkum, advancing from the east. The position was held all day while 185 Brigade fought through Brinkum, and at 9 p.m. A Company were relieved by a company of the Warwicks."

After the Warwicks had taken Leeste and Erichshof, the Norfolks began to go through them at 6 o'clock in the evening on their way to Brinkum. Once they had cleared a bridge of two enormous bombs they bounded forward easily, except that there were some unlucky casualties from snipers. But when the outskirts of the compact little town—about 1000 yards square— were reached, it became obvious that the Germans intended to make a last stand. Certainly there was no escape for them : the only road from Brinkum back into Bremen was a causeway across the floods and an admirable target. By 8 o'clock the Norfolks had penetrated about 300 yards into the built-up area, and two farms and several houses were ablaze. But, like the Lincolns in Lingen, they found that " you can infiltrate but not fight in a town in the dark : and this was going to be a fight." The advance continued at 4 next morning, April 16th, and " the *Crocodiles* with A Company under Major Atkinson went really well, frizzling a lot of Boches." By 2 p.m. A and C Companies were on their objectives and now prisoners were coming in. " The Artillery now softened up the last bit of the town before B and D Companies went through, and by 5 o'clock all that remained was a small housing estate to the north-west of the town. All companies were fully extended, so a Company of the Warwicks came under command and helped us to finish the job. In all we counted some 60 dead, and took 5 officers and 203 other ranks prisoner. Our own losses were 3 killed and 12 wounded. Brinkum had been a model battle for co-operation of all arms." It had, indeed, and the losses were astonishingly light in view of the fanaticism of the Germans, particularly of the SS N.C.O.s. Cases were reported of their deliberately blowing themselves up with a grenade in order to wound their captors. The Warwicks mention one German who did this, although he was so badly wounded that he hardly had strength to draw the pin from the grenade.

That day, the 16th, while the Suffolks were at the approach to Brinkum, the rest of 8 Brigade were opening out the left flank towards Delmenhorst. The South Lancs sent out some very aggressive patrols, while the East Yorks attacked and captured the villages of Heiligenrode and Mackenstedt. Preliminary artillery concentrations were fired on to Heiligenrode bridge, then on to Gross Mackenstedt and the road leading east. During the morning General Whistler called in at the East Yorks' H.Q. to wish them good luck.

" Soon after midday," Colonel Renison has written, " D

Company made their first bound, and after a decent interval, as we thought, I went up with the Brigade Commander and David Willison, the Sapper, to see how things were going. We were a little surprised, when we got there, to find the Company in a ditch only just across the road, and a tank in the middle of the cross-roads firing at a house fifty yards away. Shots were coming out of several houses and singing in the trees overhead. . . . When things got moving, the Company Commander, Bob Laird, came over to my trench and flopped down beside me, only to draw himself up to one of his shattering salutes as he realised the Brig. was there too. It was also somewhat comical, with a platoon fighting a few yards away, to see civilians come out of a blazing house and start busily salvaging their possessions."

Meanwhile A Company made excellent progress on the left flank. One platoon was soon established on the bridge—a weak wooden structure over the stream—in Heiligenrode, and the village occupied. Now C and B Companies moved through, A and D made for Mackenstedt. It was a difficult attack, involving a complete left wheel with an exposed right flank. The stream that had filled the fishpond for the monks in Heiligenrode also ran north through Mackenstedt. Gross Mackenstedt lay on the far western side of the stream, and here the blown bridges deprived the East Yorks of close tank support. But both Companies quickly established themselves.

Bill Renison continues : " Banger was already up to see by what routes he could get the evening meal up. I had lent him my own jeep while I was using the mobile Tac H.Q. . . . David Willison was concerned with the mines[1] and the number of trees that had been felled across the road, though the latter could be bulldozed out of the way in no time. . . . It was necessary, of course, for the two forward companies to carry their food across the wreck of the bridge. Banger had from somewhere produced a magnum of champagne, which he left with Tac H.Q."

At about midnight, while the Colonel was " getting worried about A Company, whose wireless had broken down," Ron Brown (the Adjutant) came through on the air from Main H.Q., which had remained for the night back in the pub on the Bassum-

[1] Lieutenant-Colonel " Swazi " Waller of the South Lancs had been blown up in his jeep that afternoon.

Brinkum road. " At the wheel of my jeep, while returning from bringing up the rations, Banger had been blown up on a mine at the cross-roads close by Heiligenrode where the Brigade Commander and I had spent our time in a ditch during the afternoon. Transport, including tanks, had been milling round there all evening . . . Ron had been back to the Field Ambulance and been told that Banger must certainly lose a leg, but that with his iron will it was hoped he would pull through. This was a tragedy that somehow I had never envisaged and I think that all of us had come to regard Banger as invulnerable . . . The night passed quietly as far as the enemy was concerned . . . Early in the morning I got the news I had been dreading : Banger had collapsed and died during the night. No words can really express what this meant to the morale of the Battalion, and as the hours and days passed by I realised more and more how much I had depended on him in so many things . . . He was buried during the afternoon."

But his spirit was never buried, nor could it be. *The Times* published one tribute to Banger : The *Snapper*, the paper of his Regiment, published many, from men who had followed him in a Rugby pack, or in a black Sudanese Company chasing a whole Battalion of Italians over 200 miles across Abyssinian mountains, or in A Company that morning on the Norman shore after he had talked to them in the spirit of the Elizabethans and gone into action in the same spirit :

> " This story shall the good man teach his son
> And Crispin Crispian shall ne'er go by
> But we in it shall be remembered,
> We few, we happy few, we band of brothers."

" That a regimental officer should become a legend almost throughout an army was no more than his due," wrote Bill Renison. His deeds had certainly become legend in the Division. " He was human to a most lovable degree, and he believed that the good in most men far exceeded the evil, and he knew how to call forth the good." He loved and championed his men, and they him. The whole Division was proud of him and saw in him a representative of all that was best in themselves.

On the 18th, 19th and 20th of April, 8 and 9 Brigades com-

pleted the approach to Bremen by clearing right up to the floods
to the north-east of Mackenstedt—at Moordeich and Stuhr—
and advanced north right up to the main east-west Bremen-
Delmenhorst railway at Mittelshuchting and Kirchhuchting.
Here there were hardly any floods.   At Kirchhuchting the
Division was practically in Bremen.   This was the obvious line
of attack—from the west along the Delmenhorst road.   After all,
it was the only dry approach ! So the Germans thought.   Anyway, that approach had to be secured in order to mislead the
enemy.

The account of the Lincolns' part in this fighting shows
clearly the mood of the Division now that the end was literally
in sight across the flooded fields.   This, as we anticipated on
page 24 at the beginning of our story, is how we fought when
given strength to match the might of Germany.   " The Lincolns
led," says Harrod, " supported by a Squadron of the Sherwood
Rangers, who did us proud throughout the action.   It was the
best day's hunting the Battalion ever had.   There was long, hard,
gruelling fighting, but the enemy was deficient in artillery, while
we had everything we needed, including *Crocodiles*.   Each Company in turn went into action with such dash and determination
that units of the Horst Wessel Division, the remnant of 18 SS
Training Battalion, U-boat crews, R-boat crews, and all the
ragged *Volksturm* could do nothing but retreat . . . Though at
nightfall on the 18th a small area of Stuhr north of the branch
line was still in enemy hands, the Battalion had come a long way
and taken over 100 prisoners.

" Early next morning B Company put in so fierce an attack
that the enemy broke in disorder, and those who were not mown
down in the open ground by our artillery or machine-gun fire—
or by the C.O. (Lieutenant-Colonel Cecil Firbank, D.S.O.)
excitedly firing fifty rounds rapid from an attic window in
B Company H.Q.—disappeared over the horizon like something
from Walt Disney.   It is doubtful if they noticed Bremen as they
passed, or Hamburg ! "

At 10 o'clock on the third morning the Battalion was put in
again and captured Kirchhuchting twenty-four hours in advance
of the Division's schedule.   In their day's " bag " were the C.O.,
Adjutant, two Company Commanders and the remaining 250

other ranks of 18 SS Training Battalion, withdrawn there from Brinkum. They brought 9 Brigade's total of prisoners " caged " in April past the 1,000 mark.

The previous evening the K.O.S.B.s had passed through the Lincolns to attack Mittelshuchting. They fought hard and were still going forward after dark. At dawn B Company went on to secure the railway embankment, but only after a warm struggle. The South Lancs of 8 Brigade had previously carried out what they called " a text-book operation in the approved four phases " on the 18th. This had given 9 Brigade a solid base for their attacks, as well as yielding seventy German prisoners and immobilising twenty more. At midday that day the following message was received at Divisional H.Q. :

" Personal from XXX Corps Commander. Commander-in-Chief has asked me to congratulate Commander 2nd Battalion the Royal Warwickshire Regiment on very fine performance put up by that Battalion during the last three days' fighting. His exact words were ' Please congratulate my Regiment.' I would like to add my congratulations. I have watched that Battalion take on an SS Training Battalion and fight them to a standstill."

On the 19th, Field-Marshal Montgomery visited the Warwicks, inspected and addressed them. They had captured a fine Nazi standard in Leeste and this had been presented to the Field Marshal. He expressed great pleasure at the gift and told them that it was now flying outside his caravan.

Now the Division was ready for Bremen. The whole assault on the city was co-ordinated by XXX Corps Headquarters. XII Corps had resumed the advance eastwards. Under XXX Corps, the 3rd Division would go into the attack as soon as the 43rd and 52nd Divisions came abreast on the far side of the Weser. The 3rd Division's task was roughly equivalent in scale to taking the Gateshead district, that lies across the Tyne from Newcastle. The flooded meadows served it as a moat. No sign, scarcely a movement, was observed in the great mass of buildings. On the 21st, as 9 Brigade were relieved in Huchting by the 51st Division and regrouped with 185 Brigade, the Corps Artillery was firing propaganda leaflets into the city, giving the burgers twenty-four hours in which to make up their minds to surrender, or take the alternative consequences. Still no sign came from the city, and on Sunday evening, the 22nd, the bombers arrived to do their work. It was a spectacle quite different from that earlier one on a Friday evening in July, just outside Caen. The sight of these great shafts and fountains of dust and masonry springing up all over the distant town, while the earth shuddered under their feet, stirred little compassion amongst the men of the Division. The French understood : not so the Germans.

Next morning the Division enjoyed the story of how the 52nd (Lowland) Division had just reached Achim (half-way from Verden to Bremen) the previous evening about the time of the expiry of the surrender ultimatum, when the bombers could be seen approaching ; and how they found the railway telephone there still open to Bremen, and got the Bremen stationmaster on the phone. He must have been able to hear the bombers coming, and offered to act as intermediary with the German garrison commander, the uncompromising General Becker, when down came the first bombs and dislocated the line. " Alas for his pacifist zeal ! " comments one of the battalion writers. The German civilians in the Divisional area watched the final preparations for the assault with every appearance of complete indifference to the fate of Bremen. At Div. H.Q. Victor Blundell (A.D.O.S.) told the fantastic story of a German farmer who actually approached him for the loan of troops to work in his fields : he complained that with the coming of the British Division all his foreign labour had left him, and was much aggrieved about it !

The 23rd was a great day of regrouping and briefing. The following additional troops came under command of the Division for Operation *Bremen* : 31st Armoured Brigade (from 79th Armoured Division, to look after the menagerie !) ; 4th/7th Dragoon Guards (with 185 Brigade) ; 22nd Dragoons (with 9 Brigade); 4th Royal Tanks (*Buffaloes*, to lift one battalion of 9 and 185 Brigades respectively) ; A Squadron of 7th Royal Tanks (*Crocodiles*, half a Squadron each to 9 and 185 Brigades) ; 12 K.R.R.C., 86th Field Regiment, R.A. ; 198 Anti-Tank Battery and B troop of 582 Searchlight Battery, R.A.; and 222 Squadron of 16 Assault Regiment, R.E. General Whistler himself briefed all the officers, a Brigade at a time, again making use of the local Lutheran Church. He began cheerfully with the remark that this might well be the Division's last battle. As divulged above, the plan was to assault from the south across the floods, while the 51st Division feinted from the west. And from the long recipe at the beginning of the paragraph, the allocation of the tanks, it will have been guessed that 9 and 185 Brigades were to lead, 8 Brigade to pass through later.

From the south two roads led into Bremen : the one on the right ran fairly parallel with the river from Sudweyhe over a soft marsh to Dreye, past the floods and through the outlying villages of Arsten and Habenhausen, into the suburbs and the Stadtwerder Vorst : the one on the left led across the floods from Brinkum to the village of Kattenturm and on into the suburbs, the Neuenlander Vorst, past the Airport away on the left, and into the Süder Vorst. 185 Brigade would attack along the general line of the right road, 9 Brigade along the left. The left road itself was badly cratered just north of Brinkum, and in Kattenturm it was expected that the bridge would be broken over the Ochtum, a wide stream that ran along the northern edge of the floods. The Division had somehow to get these two roads open.

The 24th was the last day of preparation for the assault troops : they would advance that night. The weather was unsettled, with showers and sunshine. Dozens of boats, yards of bridging, miles of white tape for marking routes, and hundreds of unit and divisional signs for the same purpose, appeared all over the assembly and marshalling areas, just as they had before the Rhine crossing. And the same complicated loading tables had to be worked out for those troops who were going to splash into action on the backs of *Buffaloes*. During the afternoon Typhoons disported themselves in the sky above Bremen, diving down to shatter Arsten and Kattenturm with their rockets whenever a bright interval, a patch of clear sky, gave them the opportunity. The medium bombers came over again to add the finishing touches to their earlier work of destruction : the weather was still too uncertain for the Heavies. The guns roared all day in harmony with the rest of the Corps Artillery over the river as the other Divisions advanced on the doomed city.

It looked like being a fine night : in the western sky the sun
set red and splendid to delight proverbial shepherds and sailors :
our soldiers were no less elated, waiting with the usual excitement
and anxiety, making last-minute adjustments, rehearsing their
own parts in their own minds, whistling, singing, perhaps more
confident than ever before, but impatient to begin.

The K.S.L.I. were to lead 185 Brigade, attacking at 11
o'clock : on the left the 9 Brigade attack would be led by the
Ulster Rifles at midnight.   The K.S.L.I. knew a good deal
about the village of Dreye, their objective, which was heavily
defended, and which they had to take swiftly, preventing the
enemy from falling back to re-form.   The main Osnabrück-
Bremen railway line ran north through their positions : it was
raised above the swamped land, and passed to the west of Dreye,
crossing a bridge over the road that led *back* from Dreye to
Arsten and Bremen.   Already Z Company of the K.S.L.I. had
done some valuable patrolling down this railway embankment.
Ian Rae, the Battery Commander with the Battalion, relates
how on one occasion Major Read, the Company Commander,
with two men, went down towards an enemy signal-box strong-
point, after an artillery bombardment but in full daylight, " and
snatched an SS corporal out of the bottom of his slit-trench,
returning to their own lines without incident and with a very
angry prisoner."   A deserter gave the K.S.L.I. evidence that the
German Company H.Q. had been hit by shell-fire and the Company Commander killed.   He gave away the position of the new
H.Q., and confirmed platoon positions.   That night Y Company
were to go straight for the main position, a factory, while W
Company on the right cleared up to the Weser, and Z Company,
to their relish, had the job of advancing along their railway bank
and flanking Dreye and cutting off German retreat from the
village.

At ten minutes to eleven the artillery fire plan began, drenching the German positions with heavy concentrations.   At eleven
Y and W Companies moved off close to the road and Z Company
worked their way along the embankment.   Tanks of the 4th/7th
Dragoons and A.V.R.E.s set off along the road.   As usual, the
din was terrific.   Y Company found the factory an ugly proposition and lost their Commander, Captain Heatley, in the

first few minutes. Their Adjutant writes : " Captain Clapham, from the reserve company, at once reorganised them in the most gallant manner under intense fire, and succeeded in capturing the factory. Both companies quickly cleared the village." The *Crocodile* flame-throwers were putting up a terrifying performance, and were invaluable at the factory. Just beyond it, A.V.R.E.s came to the rescue by lobbing their Petards at a road-block. " Two or three of these missiles were sufficient."

Major Read was now leading Z Company in a bayonet charge along the railway embankment, firing from the hip and clearing the first platoon position and an Ack-Ack gun-post. Charging one weapon-post, his ammunition spent, he used his machine carbine as a club. At that point he was wounded in the leg, having both bones broken. " He refused to be evacuated, cheering on his men, shouting to the Germans to come out and fight." This officer was awarded a bar to his M.C. " The success of the company was due in no small extent to Private Wood of the Intelligence Section, who went ahead of the charge in the most dauntless manner, yelling at the Germans in their own language to come out and surrender."

By now the K.S.L.I. had carried out their plan with complete success, and taken more than two hundred prisoners. The rest of the Brigade attack was a " walk-over." At least they had first to plod across the floods in *Buffaloes*, but then both Warwicks and Norfolks walked straight into their respective objectives— Arsten and Habenhausen. The Warwicks dismiss their own skilful, complex operation with a paragraph : " One could go on writing for a long time about the detail of this operation, but it is enough to say that the whole thing went exactly as planned. Our objectives were captured, and at 4 a.m. the Battalion was completely firm, with its guns in position, over a hundred prisoners, and no casualties." The enemy are stigmatised as " a spineless lot : the barrage drove them all into their shelters, and the *Buffaloes* took them completely by surprise. I do not think we fired a single shot. Great credit must go to the *Buffalo* Regiment, who successfully completed the ferry-service just as it was getting light, in spite of the difficult landing."

The Norfolks passed through the Warwicks at 1.30 p.m., and their great array of tanks and SP's moved steadily forward.

" The softening-up of Habenhausen had been complete, and those of the enemy who had not made off were only too glad to give up without a fight . . . By 6 that evening it was all over, and a few locals, headed by the village policeman, were filling in bomb-craters and working under the supervision of the Pioneer Officer." The Germans who did not stay for the Norfolks' barrage made for the great modern barracks that stood farther back in the town amongst 9 Brigade's objectives. They intrude unpleasantly in the story of 9 Brigade, of the K.O.S.B.s in particular.

9 Brigade's attack was in some respects similar to 185's. The leading battalion, the Ulster Rifles, had most of the fighting. The subsequent advance into the city in daylight on the 25th was brisk and not seriously opposed, although that day and the 26th brought one or two nasty situations. But, altogether, the fighting bore out the general appreciation that the main battle of Bremen would be fought outside the city.

Like the K.S.L.I., the Ulster Rifles went first : like the Warwicks, they had to go in *Buffaloes* over 2,000 yards of water into the attack. They would move at midnight, capture Katten-turm, and seize the road bridge that they knew to be already prepared for demolition. The 4th Royal Tanks, who had helped to drive the Highland Division across the Rhine and the Canadians across the Ijssel, reckoned that this was technically their most difficult task, as it was the longest. One of the obstacles they had to navigate was a dummy airfield that had been bombed by the R.A.F. and was cratered accordingly. Another snag was likely to be the cattle-fencing : in normal times this was pasture land and there was abundant wire to get caught up in the *Buffaloes'* driving sprockets. But amongst all the " pepper " that was being scattered across the sky from the now quite regular Middlesex and Ack-Ack *pepperpot*, a single Bofors of 92nd Light Ack-Ack Regiment might be seen to be firing a three-round burst of tracer every minute, an invaluable navigational aid !

" At last the word was passed down the line," Ken Bradshaw writes. " Everybody clambered aboard, and a great roar rose up as forty-seven *Buffaloes* sprang into life. Just as the convoy was moving, off the Brigade Commander, with a clutch of press reporters, arrived and wished the Battalion good luck." The barrage played *crescendo* to muffle the *Buffalo* bellow. The three mysterious tracers sailed by periodically, and " seemed so evidently fired for a purpose that we thought the Boches might tumble to it, until we realised that the trace was in the base of the round . . . The moonlight was so vivid, so luminous, that the silhouettes of these monstrous amphibians could be seen at seven hundred yards distance . . . One could not help thinking of H. G. Wells . . ." The Ulster Rifles were full of admiration for the 4th Royal Tanks. Not a *Buffalo* was either lost or permanently bogged. And after a 2,000 yards night-crossing they touched down exactly at the assigned " crook in the *bund* "—the bend in the bank of the Ochtum which the leading company (C) were to take and consolidate.

This was done promptly, though the company came under small-arms and bazooka fire when they were still fifty yards from the shore. They rushed from their *Buffaloes* as soon as they ·landed, and found German gunners just bringing into action two Flak guns. The gunners were dealt with and the guns turned and fired into Arsten, the Warwicks' objective, until the ammunition ran out. The bank was defended stubbornly against A Company, who cleared the rest of it. Opposition was based principally on a large house set about twenty yards back from the bank. Lieutenant Songest's platoon settled this, though he and several N.C.O.s and men were hit. The position was eventually carried by a very gallant rush by a section under Corporal Lambourn, who was awarded the M.M. for his great courage. There were other manifestations of this spirit before Major Tighe-Wood's company were done, and when D Company passed through, their advance was not opposed. Through them B Company dashed for the great prize : the Kattenturm bridge.

The leading section, under Corporal Holt, rushed the first position and eliminated it. McCrainor, the leading platoon commander, had been ordered by Major Cummins to by-pass any opposition that was not serious enough to detain him. This he was able to do when resisted at the cross-roads near the bridge : they " slipped round the enemy and seized the bridge before it could be blown." Then " the enemy at the cross-roads and along the *bund* were liquidated at leisure. Altogether, four officers, twenty or thirty other ranks and one camp follower were found in the Company locality : so that had the position been assaulted frontally serious opposition would have been met."

Five officers and 128 other ranks was the Ulster Rifles' final haul of prisoners : they boggled at the *Schwimm-Panzer* in astonishment. One of their fatuous officers solemnly complimented the Ulster Rifles on " the finest tactical manœuvre he had seen performed by British troops in the whole campaign ! " Notwithstanding this, it was an extremely fine and successful action, and the Commanding Officer, Lieutenant-Colonel Drummond, was most fittingly awarded the D.S.O.

The K.O.S.B.s followed through the Ulster Rifles, and by 11.30 that morning they had consolidated in the area of the important road junction in the Neuenlander suburbs, over a mile beyond the Kattenturm bridge. Their forward company was A Company, who were disposed near another cross-roads, where the main road from Habenhausen led in from the right. Here a strange and, at one time, dangerous situation arose, largely out of the coincidence of the Norfolk attack on Habenhausen, which, in the early afternoon, drove back a body of German troops into this area. Very fortunately, Lloyd, the Platoon Commander, who was most intimately involved in it all, has written up a personal account of the episode, from which he has allowed me to quote the following, beginning with the arrival of the company in position soon after 11.30 that morning :

" Within a short time we had reached our objective. Very easy going, and not at all as I had imagined ! Here we were to sit, until the Lincolns passed through us and took the barracks that lay somewhere ahead.

" While the platoon was digging in, I took a section forward to examine a large building which looked down on top of us. I also wanted to improve, if possible, my given position, as it was very near a cross-roads and had a very poor field of view in front. We reached this building and cleared the first room. As we moved through a series of rooms I became aware that it was part of a block of buildings which stretched out for some way and surrounded a square. It was obviously the barracks ! As quickly as we could we cleared the first series of rooms and then lay and observed. The barracks had been badly damaged by shelling, and probably by our low-flying aircraft. It was possible that it did not contain any enemy. I could not observe anything in the square. We pushed through the first part of the block fairly quickly, and I then decided to move into the open. It was an unwise risk to take, I suppose, and it was not really our job at all. The whole place seemed empty! There was only one small incident, which occurred when one of the men observed some movement outside in the square. We investigated and found two German soldiers hiding in a shelter together with a girl. They were dirty and unshaven and very willing to give themselves up. They said the SS Troops had withdrawn from the area. I sent them back to Company H.Q. with a message to the effect that we had reached the Lincolns' objective and found it devoid of enemy, as far as we could judge. We all felt rather pleased with the success of our ' recce,' and felt that we might save a Battalion attack on a worthless objective. Apparently this is exactly what it did.

" I was not very satisfied with the situation, however. I felt that I would like to move farther forward, or at least have some sort of O.P. out in front. The presence of a large building dominating the platoon position did not seem to me at all the ideal ; particularly when we were so blinded out in front owing to the peculiar nature of the ground. Yet for some tactical consideration or other we were not allowed to move. I hoped no stray sniper would sneak back into that building.

" I sent Sergeant H. out to see if there was a place suitable for an O.P., and he came back leading a prisoner. This man said that he had some friends who were ready to give themselves up, so H. set off again to see if he could bring them in. He had not been gone long before I heard firing out in front and H. came back fairly hurriedly with his patrol. Apparently the enemy, who were supposed to be ready to surrender, had opened fire and proved to be in greater numbers than we were led to believe. H. had returned fire and got away.

" He was all for taking a larger body of men out to ' get ' this small pocket, and, as he was obviously in the right mood, I let him go. I did not think that there was much possibility of any large body of enemy. I was wrong. The patrol came back, having shot up some enemy, but they had also seen more movement at one end of the barracks. I sent back a message to state the position. Could it be possible that some enemy had infiltrated back into the barracks? It later turned out that this *was* what had happened. Having been driven out of another position by a neighbouring attack, they had moved across our front and had gone into the barracks. At the time, of course, we were not to know this.

" Then suddenly we were sniped at from our right flank. We were completely exposed on this flank ! I could hear the bullets whining very close and hugged the ground frantically. The terrifying thing was that we could not locate this solitary sniper. A man who was lying close to me was hit in the head and died shortly afterwards. Each of us tried to crawl as best we could to safety. Then another man was hit in the arm. Try as I could I was not able to locate the fire, and the platoon behind us could not pin it down. By now I was afraid to raise myself an inch off the ground. M.'s Piat man had been hit too. I wriggled as best I could to a small wall in order to get some protection from this enemy who was picking us off one by one. I could hear the ping of bullets all the time, and they seemed very close indeed. However, I managed to reach the wall all right. Then a cry from H : ' They've hit me,' and he went lunging past, clasping his arm and making a run for it. I then began my tortuous crawl back, hugging the ground desperately until I came out into the open again. I got to my feet and ran, ran as hard as I could. Once back, I yelled for the mortar, hoping that I could put some smoke down to cover the rest in. However, as I got the mortar up, I saw that M. and the other man had got through. We sent the casualties back and redistributed ourselves in the trenches. The enemy then counter-attacked our position.

" By a stroke of ill luck the main direction of the attack was on the side where we could see least, but we had good covering fire from the other platoon on our right, who saw the enemy advance more clearly. It was indeed their fire support that kept the enemy from over-running our position, for they attacked in strength. We returned fire as best we could under the circumstances, but we were not in a very happy situation.

Then, thank God, the tanks came up : they had been sent by Company H.Q.

" I heard the tank on my right firing at the enemy, but it had not come far enough up and most of the fire went over our heads. This meant that we had to keep our heads down and prevented us firing. The air seemed to be filled with the whine of bullets, and the dust kept kicking up around us. I sent a runner over to the tank to tell it to move farther up, but the tank commander did not seem to understand. This runner had to cross ground under fire about three times before he could get his message understood, and on one occasion he was blown off the top of the turret by the blast of a near-by explosion. I heard Corporal H. calling and went over to his trench. He had lost three of his men and poor B. had been killed by a shell. He was still cheerful but had only a few men left. I called for reinforcements and some men from the rear platoon came up. We were now being shelled, for the enemy had spotted the tanks—they were using Panzerfausts and possibly 88's, but it was difficult to tell what was coming down. I remember something burst very close and temporarily deafened me ; the acrid smell of powder went deep down into my lungs, making me retch. Earth tumbled down on top of me, but I was all right.

" The volume of fire from the tanks and the neighbouring platoon, together with our own, eventually drove the enemy off. It was too much for them. The noise of shelling died away mysteriously, and the tanks started moving about in front of us. When this happened the enemy withdrew. Fire suddenly ceased.

" We waited till another unit came up to relieve us, and then moved off on tanks to another part of Bremen to put in a final attack. This attack went in smoothly, and by the time our tired (and proud) remnant arrived to take up position, it was more or less all over."

The Lincolns, as Lloyd supposes, were diverted from the attack on the barracks, and at two that afternoon they attacked instead the Bremen airport and Focke-Wulf works, whence fire was still being directed upon the Divisional axis. The airfield was in full view from Brinkum,[1] where 8 Brigade troops were able to watch the Lincolns' battle as they might have watched the Tattoo at Aldershot. The Lincolns' only comment on their battle is that " it was heavy enough fighting in parts, for we were in no mood to be stopped by anything, and by now the Boche had, on the whole, little heart for the job. By 5.30 p.m. all objectives were secured, and long patrols were out searching hide-outs and trench-systems, and prisoners were pouring in." At the end of that full day's fighting the Division had taken 22 officers and 900 other ranks prisoner. The battle was definitely won.

The next day, April 26th, was the Division's last day in action proper. 8 Brigade passed through 9 Brigade at dawn. The South Lancs cleared up to and across the main Bremen-Delmenhorst-Oldenburg railway line in the area of the gasworks. Their Battalion H.Q. in the gasworks offices dominated the rest of the Brigade's objectives to the north-west of the town. The Suffolks went on from there to clear the whole of the Woltmershauser Vorst. That left the Rablinghauser Vorst for the East Yorks, the north-west corner of the city, where it tapered into a bungalow housing-estate and into the hamlets of Seehausen and Hasen-büren farther down the Weser bank. For this final military operation of the campaign I must quote Bill Renison, their Commanding Officer : his narrative shows exactly the mood of the Division in those last days.

" There was no opposition of any kind," he says, " till we reached the limit of our objectives. There D Company came up against two young Nazi fanatics dug into the side of a dyke." (The threat of the flame-thrower got them out.) " I went round in the scout-car to see what was happening and met an extremely irate young member of D Company doubling his two prisoners down the road as fast as he could go, urging them on with a stream of abuse. As he was practically dead-beat himself, I put him on the front of the car, while the Boches continued to run . . .

" I was recalled to thoughts of battle when the Tank L.O. asked me if I could understand a message from C Company

[1] From Brinkum, a few evenings earlier, the Suffolks had observed the landing of a small German plane, which took off early next morning. Then the German radio had announced that Himmler had paid a brief visit to Bremen !

saying they had 9 officers and 150 other rank P.O.W. I couldn't, and went off to investigate. They had come upon the control centre of the local Ack-Ack defences facing the expected attack from Delmenhorst ! Hallam had caught most of the staff underground. They weren't combat troops in any case, and surrendered without much argument, although the officers were rather indignant.

" C Company, tails up, moved steadily forward with the stream of prisoners swelling behind them—a mixed bunch of Luftwaffe, sailors and all sorts. Proceedings became pure farce when those already in the bag started to shake hands with or congratulate the late-comers as they arrived at the double. . . . The Brigadier was in great form, and was to be seen, armed with a 12-bore, standing in the middle of the road behind the leading troops, with his gun at the ready."

Bremen was reduced to a wreck. There were areas where high, terraced houses and blocks of modern flats were undamaged, but there were vast gaps and open spaces amongst huge heaps of rubble. In a few front gardens the lilacs were alive. The whole region of the railway was a tangle of twisted wreckage, with the girder bridge hanging into the Weser. (A Liverpudlian says : " I thought of the Lord Street area of Liverpool.") The dockyards, the harbours and submarine bases were all in the same state, and, as far as could be seen, so was the city across the river where fighting was still fierce in the great City Park. From an Air O.P. it was observed that " in the centre of the town, only the green leaden roofs of the Cathedral and the *Rathaus* stood, and in one part there was nothing to be seen above ground at all for a mile in any direction." It is an ironical reflection that the Cathedral should have survived : it was founded in the year 789 by the Englishman Willehad, and that Englishman is still the patron saint of Bremen. Like two other Englishmen in the eighth century, Willebald and the great Boniface, he devoted his life to Christianising the heathen of north-west Europe, a process that has never been completed.

Before the Division's task was completed, the East Yorks were ordered to continue, on the 27th, north and west along the river bank to enable a 17-pounder troop to cover the Weser River approach. Again they met with slight, desperate, hopeless opposition. Here, as late as the early hours of Thursday, May 3rd, the guns of a troop of the 92nd Light Ack-Ack Regiment engaged and destroyed two boats on the river and silenced a persistent signal station on the far bank.

But by the evening of April 26th a change had begun to take place in Bremen. The German civilians had begun to emerge, and regard, with cow-like expressions, their conquerors. And the liberated slave-workers—Poles, Russians, Czechs, Dutch, French, even Italians—had begun to " make merry at anybody's expense." Staff cars appeared, representatives of the Navy, of an American Task Force (Bremen was to be their occupation port), engineers and military policemen had all arrived. That day 9 Brigade were ordered out to relieve a Brigade of the 51st Division in the neighbouring town of Delmenhorst. A disaster dulled the Ulster Rifles' triumph of the previous day, when, setting off in a carrier towards Huchting, Major Bird, Lieutenant Tony Hancock and a section, drove over a magnetic sea-mine concealed under the road. There were no survivors. After a day of pouring rain, 185 Brigade were also ordered out : they settled in the country west of Delmenhorst on the 28th " to protect the open right flank of the Canadian Army." But though the Gunners had some excellent shooting at odd bands of soldiers fleeing from the Canadians across the coastal plain, there was no further fighting.

Thus the Division waited for the German High Command to recognise the inevitable. It was not the way they had imagined the end : they had expected it to come as it came, for example, to the United States 3rd Division,[1] who on May 4th cleared Berchtesgaden ! On that day all the German armed forces in North-West Germany, Holland, Schleswig-Holstein and Denmark surrendered unconditionally through Admiral Friedeburg, and the Division received the order :

RESTRICTED (.) Cancel ALL offensive ops forthwith and CEASE FIRE 0800 hrs 5 May 45 (.) further details later.

[1] This famous American Division, under General Truscott, distinguished itself on the extreme left of the Sicily landings, took Palermo, and fought all the way up Italy. It may be remembered how near the British 3rd Division came, in 1943, to fighting a parallel campaign.

In a few days the Division was moved south into the middle of Germany in accordance with the regrouping for the Occupation. They were then ordered to prepare to move to Berlin as the British element of the garrison for the German capital. This was cancelled, and the Division was withdrawn to Belgium and prepared to be flown to America, to take part in the seaborne assault on the mainland of Japan. This, too, was cancelled as the Japs surrendered. Early in October the Division left Europe for duty in Egypt and Palestine.

General Eisenhower, in his summing-up of the campaign, stresses the importance of " three episodes as being the most decisive in ensuring victory. The first of these," he goes on to say, " was the battle of the Normandy beaches. We sailed for France, possessed of all the tactical information that an efficient intelligence service could provide, but we had yet to take the measure of the foe we were to meet . . . The second vital battle was that of the Falaise pocket, where the enemy showed that fatal tendency to stand and fight when all the logic of war demanded a strategic withdrawal . . . The third decisive phase in the campaign consisted of the battles west of the Rhine during February and March, where once again the enemy played into our hands by his insistence upon fighting the battle where he stood. . . ."

While the 3rd Division was on the mainland of Europe it fought in all three of these decisive battles, which led swiftly to Germany's defeat : no other British Division had the distinction of fighting in all three of them. In the eleven months from the invasion of Normandy to the surrender of the enemy, fifteen hundred and seventy-nine members of the Division were killed in action. They are mourned by the survivors, whose minds had turned away from the war some days before the instrument of surrender was signed, and who instinctively looked forward into the days of peace. But sometimes they will still feel inclined to glance back along the road they helped to open up from La Brèche, in Calvados, to Bremen.

THE END

APPENDIX A

CASUALTIES, HONOURS AND AWARDS

Summary of Battle Casualties to the Division between 6 June, 1944, and 30 April, 1945

MONTH	KILLED	WOUN-DED	MISSING	TOTAL	WOUN-DED AND RETURN-ED TO UNIT	TOTAL LOST TO DIV.
June, '44	417	2280	811	3508	—	3508
July, '44	379	1810	315	2504	—	2504
Aug., '44	108	848	132	1088	—	1088
Sept., '44	53	278	36	367	10	357
Oct., '44	223	1048	117	1388	87	1301
Nov., '44	69	327	32	428	17	411
Dec., '44	17	66	17	100	15	85
Jan., '45	18	122	31	171	14	157
Feb., '45	71	345	55	471	—	471
Mar., '45	113	389	25	527	12	515
April, '45	111	526	65	702	15	687
	1,579	8,039	1,636	11,254	170	11,084

When the number of Non-Battle Casualties to the Division is added, the total number of men lost to the Division over the period stands at 16,241. The great majority of Battle Casualties are suffered by the 4,500 men of the Rifle Companies.

Summary of Decorations Awarded

Unit	VC	CB	CBE	DSO	Bar	OBE	MC	Bar	MBE	DCM	MM	Bar	BEM	U.S. Decoration	French Decoration	Belgian Decoration	Dutch Decoration
H.Q. 3 Br. Inf. Div.	·	1	·	·	·	7	·	·	3	·	·	·	1	·	·	1	5
H.Q. 8 Br. Inf. Bde.	·	·	·	1	·	1	·	·	1	·	·	·	1	·	·	1	2
1 Suffolk	·	·	·	1	·	·	9	·	·	2	9	·	·	·	1	1	1
2 E. Yorks	·	·	·	4	1	·	11	·	1	2	10	·	1	·	2	1	1
1 S. Lan. R.	·	·	·	·	·	·	10	1	2	1	12	·	1	·	2	1	·
H.Q. 9 Br. Inf. Bde	·	·	·	1	·	·	1	·	·	·	·	·	·	·	·	·	·
2 Lincolns	·	·	·	1	1	·	9	·	·	2	20	·	·	·	2	1	1
1 K.O.S.B.	·	·	·	1	·	·	8	·	·	3	9	·	1	·	2	1	1
2 R.U.R.	·	·	·	2	·	·	11	·	·	2	15	·	·	·	2	1	·
H.Q. 185 Inf. Bde	·	·	·	2	·	·	·	·	1	·	·	·	1	·	·	·	·
2 Warwick	·	·	·	2	2	·	11	1	1	·	21	·	·	·	2	1	1
1 Norfolk	1	·	·	1	·	·	11	·	1	2	11	·	·	·	2	·	1
2 K.S.L.I.	1	·	·	1	·	·	10	1	·	·	16	·	·	·	2	1	1
2 Mx.	·	·	·	1	·	·	6	·	·	2	8	1	1	·	2	1	1
3 Recce.	·	·	·	1	·	·	9	·	·	1	5	·	·	·	2	1	1
H.Q.R.A.	·	·	1	1	1	·	·	·	1	·	·	·	1	·	·	·	·
7 Fd. Regt.	·	·	·	1	·	·	7	·	1	·	5	·	·	·	2	1	1
33 Fd. Regt.	·	·	·	1	·	·	5	·	·	·	3	·	·	·	2	·	·
76 Fd. Regt.	·	·	·	1	·	·	9	·	·	2	5	·	·	·	2	1	·
20 A.-Tk. Regt.	·	·	·	1	·	·	3	·	·	·	3	·	·	·	2	1	·
92 L.A.-A. Regt.	·	·	·	·	·	·	2	·	·	·	·	·	·	·	2	·	·
R.E.	·	·	2	·	·	8	·	·	·	·	26	·	1	1	2	2	1
R. Sigs.	·	·	·	·	·	·	1	·	·	·	4	·	·	·	2	3	·
R.A.S.C.	·	·	·	·	·	1	3	·	3	·	1	·	·	·	2	·	·
R.A.M.C.	·	·	2	·	·	3	·	·	1	·	9	·	1	·	2	1	·
R.A.O.C.	·	·	·	·	·	·	·	·	1	·	·	·	·	·	·	·	·
R.E.M.E.	·	·	·	·	·	·	2	·	1	·	1	·	·	·	2	3	·
C.M.P.	·	·	·	·	·	·	·	·	1	·	4	·	·	·	·	·	·

APPENDIX B

An Address read to the 3rd Recce Regiment at an official Reception by the Mayor and Parish Priest of St. Paul, near Flers, Normandy, 21 August, 1944.

Officers and Men of the British Army,

I have been asked by the Civil Authorities, by the Parish Priest, a Chevalier of the Legion of Honour, and by the whole population to welcome you to this small village. Our first feeling is one of gratitude and happiness. You can be sure it has been a rare joy for us all to see the British troops arrive and drive the Germans away before them. This minute is a very stirring one, chiefly for those, and I think they are many, who, in spite of everybody and everything, have remained the faithful friends of England and her allies. This gathering seems to be like the meeting of old friends in the open air and sunshine, on going out of a dark and damp dungeon.

For this ceremony no place could be fitter than this one. Here we stand near the grave of the valiant sons of this village who laid down their lives for their fatherland and the freedom of the world, side by side with the gallant British and American soldiers. How happy they must be to see that their own children, brothers and sisters, can breathe freely again.

For the last four years there have been many misunderstandings between our two nations. Of course the whole responsibility does not rest with you alone ; we have had our own share of it, and it is a large one. But your sacrifices for the common cause, your present victories and the return of your armies on the French soil, open a new era of comradeship and good understanding. Though you are a peace-loving people, you wage a war to liberate France and Europe, and to secure the freedom of the whole world. We feel sure that before long the sons of Normandy and Brittany, as well as those of the rest of France, will be proud to join in this crusade, and, when they have been

equipped with modern weapons, to fight with you for the final
crushing of tyranny and the restoration of peace and freedom all
over the world.

> Welcome to you all ! !
> Long Live England ! ! !
> Long Live France ! ! !

APPENDIX C

Two critics of the 3rd Division's performance in the battle for Caen

Justice and truth seem not to have been near the forefront of David Belchem's mind in 1980 when his book *Victory in Normandy* appeared. While the late Eric Lummis was at work on an account of the 1st Suffolk's undaunted D-Day assault on *Hillman*, I was able to show him the correspondence I had had with Carlo D'Este when he was writing *Decision in Normandy*, the first serious description of the whole Normandy campaign which revealed a true understanding of the 3rd Divisions's actions on that day. We agreed that none of the neighbouring assault divisions was confronted by a headquarters bunker so formidably strong and well-sited as *Hillman*, which the Suffolks had overcome by the end of that day. Nor did the other assault divisions meet a Panzer attack as threatening as 21 Panzer Division's, which Bill Eadie's Staffordshire Yeomanry and the other 3 Div support units so decisively drove off. Then, when we examined the speed of advance on the 3 Canadian Div and 50 Div fronts, we found their performance closely comparable with ours. So Lord Lovat's sneer at 8 Brigade's achievement in his complacent account of his own (with its revealing title, *March Past*, 1978, p311) was ill-informed and ill-judged. The official verdict (*Victory in the West*, I, 1962, p213) was properly appreciative of the two British and one Canadian seaborne assaults on that stormy sea-shore: 'to have swept away all but a few isolated fragments of Hitler's Atlantic Wall and to have fought their way inland for an average depth of four to six miles on most of a twenty-four miles front was surely a notable feat of arms'.

Michael Howard has persuasively suggested that 3 Div's D-Day plan to capture Caen, nine miles inland and with vital river-crossings, was in the nature of things 'aspirational'. This was demonstrated about an hour after midday, when 9 Brigade, our Reserve Brigade, lost its commander, intelligence officer and other staff, soon after coming ashore; all seriously injured, and one killed, by one mortar bomb. At once, the Corps Commander, Lieut-General Crocker, changed 9 Brigade's plan, and with it the whole division's. Instead of heading boldly for Carpiquet airfield alongside 3 Canadian Div, 9 Brigade was switched to shield our left flank along the Orne and Caen Canal. That was the end of any hope of taking Caen on D-Day. It had nothing whatever to do with slow advances that afternoon alleged by Wilmot, Belchem, *et al.*

Clearly, the Corps Commander was not determined to take Caen at all costs on D-Day, and was anxious about the active presence of 21 Panzer Division. As the days passed, there was a curious silence in the national press about the presence of 3 Div in Normandy. Divisions that had led the assault were not pleased to see those that had made their name in N Africa and put up understandably stale performances in Normandy continuing to get 'star' treatment in the newspapers. Our men naturally felt indignant and wondered what their families would be thinking. Ill-informed journalists followed Wilmot's lead and hinted at our infantry's slowness on D-Day, and at their Brigadier's and their Div Commander's lack of driving-power, for not being in Caen that night. If this book has done nothing else, it will I hope have nailed that journalism as unpardonable calumny.

GLOSSARY

A.A. (or Ack-Ack)—Anti-Aircraft

A.D.O.S.—Assistant Director of Ordnance Supply

A.G.R.A.—Army Group, Royal Artillery

Air O.P.—Spotting plane flown by Royal Artillery observation officer. See also O.P.

A.R.E.—Assault Royal Engineers

A.R.V.—Armoured Recovery Vehicle

A T E A—Amphibious Tank Escape Apparatus

A.V.s R.E. (or Avres)—Assault Vehicles, Royal Engineers

Bangalore Torpedo—Explosive charge used against concrete emplacements, etc.

Bazooka (properly *Panzerfaust*)—German infantry anti-tank weapon

Beehive—Explosive charge used against concrete emplacements, etc.

Box girder bridge—Bridge carried and laid by Churchill tanks of A.R.E.s

Brigade group—Fighting formation composed of normal units of Brigade plus Gunners, Sappers, Medical units and, if an Infantry Brigade, supporting tanks

Buffalo—Armoured Amphibious troop-carrier

Bulldozer—Tracked path-clearing vehicle

Class 9 Bridge—R.E. classification for bridge that will support 9 tons

C.M.P.—Corps of Military Police

C.O.—Commanding Officer

COSSAC—Chief of Staff to Supreme Allied Commander

C.R.A.—Commander, Royal Artillery

Crab—Flail mounted on Sherman gun-tank

C.R.A.S.C.—Commander, Royal Army Service Corps

C.R.E.—Commander, Royal Engineers

C.R.E.M.E.—Commander, Royal Electrical & Mechanical Engineers

Crocodile—Flame-throwing tank

C.T.C.—Combined Training Centre

C.V.—Command Vehicle (lorry or caravan fitted up as mobile H.Q.)

D-D—Dual-Drive (amphibious)

D-day—Code for day on which an operation is to begin

D.D.M.S.—Deputy Director of Medical Supply

D.R.—Despatch Rider

Driver i/c—Driver, internal combustion (engine)

DUKW—Amphibian load carrier

Echelons—base establishments "laddered" back from forward units

Fascine—Bundle of palings, carried on A.V.R.E. and dropped into anti-tank ditch to enable tank to cross.

Flail—Device for clearing path through minefield

F.O.B.—Forward Officer, Bombardment

F.O.O.—Forward Observation Officer

G—General, e.g. G III (General Staff Officer, grade III)

G.A.F.—German Air Force

GOC—General Officer Commanding

Half-tracks—Vehicles with front wheels and rear tracks

Hards—Stretches of beach specially prepared for embarking vehicles on to Landing Craft

H-hr—Code for hour on which an operation is to begin

I—Intelligence

Kangaroo—Armoured troop-carrier

Kapok—Light pontoon bridge. Material for such

K.R.R.C.—King's Royal Rifle Corps

LCA—Landing Craft, Assault

LCOCU—Landing Craft Obstruction Clearance Unit

LCP—Landing Craft, Personnel

LCT (R)—Landing Craft, Tank (Rocket)

LCV—Landing Craft, Vehicle

LMG—Light Machine Gun

L of C—Lines of Communication

L.P.—Lowering Position

LSI—Landing Ship, Infantry

Lt. A.A.—Light Anti-Aircraft

M 7—Model 7, 105 mm. howitzer mounted on Sherman tank chassis

M 10—Anti-Tank gun mounted on Ram chassis

MMG—Medium Machine Gun
NAAFI—Navy, Army, Air Force Institute
N.F.—Northumberland Fusiliers
O Group—Group of men gathered to receive orders
O.P.—Observation Post
P.G.R.—Panzer Grenadier Regiment
PIAT—Projector, Infantry, Anti-Tank (cf. Bazooka)
Porpoise—Watertight ammunition "sledge" towed ashore
  behind tanks and S-P guns
Provost—Military Police
Q—Quartermaster's branch, Administration
R.A.—See C.R.A.
R.A.C.—Royal Armoured Corps
R.A.M.C.—Royal Army Medical Corps
R.A.S.C.—See C.R.A.S.C.
R.A.P.—Regimental Aid Post (R.A.M.C.)
R.E.—See C.R.E.
Recce—Reconnaissance
R.E.M.E.—See C.R.E.M.E.
R.H.R.—Royal Highland Regiment
R.M.—Royal Marines
R.T.R.—Royal Tank Regiment.
S.C.R.A.—Staff Captain, R.A.
S.D.—Service Dress
S-P—Self-propelled
SS—Special Service
SS (German)—Schutz-Staffel, élite corps
Staghound—U.S. light armoured reconnaissance car
Stonk—Technical gunnery term that came to be applied to
  artillery fire generally
Tellermine—(lit. Plate mine) German Anti-tank mine
Weasel—Amphibious light tracked carrier
X Craft—British "midget" submarines

INDEX